PITT
LATIN
AMERICAN
SERIES

Gaitán of Colombia

by Richard E. Sharpless

UNIVERSITY OF PITTSBURGH PRESS

GAITAN

of Colombia

A POLITICAL BIOGRAPHY

for Mercedes, Marisol, and Eduardo

and

for Raymond Franke

Published by the University of Pittsburgh Press, Pittsburgh, Pa. 15260

Copyright © 1978, University of Pittsburgh Press

Feffer and Simons, Inc., London

Manufactured in the United States of America

Library of Congress Cataloging in Publication Data

Sharpless, Richard.
    Gaitán of Colombia.

    (Pitt Latin American series)
    Bibliography: p. 217
    Includes index.
    1. Gaitán, Jorge Eliécer, 1898–1948.   2. Populism—Colombia—Biography.
3. Populism—Colombia.   I. Title.
F2277.G24S48/778   986.1'062'0924 [B]   77-74552
ISBN 0-8229-3354-3

Excerpts from "Populism and Reform in Latin America" by Torcuato Di Tella, in *Obstacles to Change in Latin America*, ed. Claudio Veliz, are reprinted by permission of the Oxford University Press. Excerpts from *The Development of the Colombian Labor Movement* by Miguel Urrutia and from *Colombia: The Political Dimensions of Change* by Robert H. Dix are reprinted by permission of Yale University Press.

Photo on title page courtesy of Lunga, Grafico de Prensa, Calle 17 no. 5-26, Bogotá, D.E., Colombia.

Contents

Acknowledgments ... vii

1 Introduction ... 3

Part I. The Formative Years, 1898–1928

2 The Populist Seedbed ... 11
3 The Background of a Populist ... 29
4 The University and *Socialist Ideas* ... 42

Part II. Testing the System, 1928–1944

5 Early Politics ... 55
6 The Revolutionary Leftist National Union ... 71
7 The Professional ... 85

Part III. Gathering Momentum, 1944–1946

8 Building the Populist Movement ... 103
9 Followers, Foes, and the Campaign of 1946 ... 120
10 The Gaitanista Program ... 130

Part IV. The Drive for Power, 1946–1948

11 Gaitán and the Liberals ... 139
12 Gaitán and the Gaitanistas ... 148
13 Gaitán and the Ospina Government ... 158

Part V. Epitaph and Epilogue

14 The Aftermath ... 177
15 The Legacy ... 183

Notes ... 193
Bibliography ... 217
Index ... 227

Acknowledgments

The author gives special thanks to the following Colombians: to Gaitán's widow, Amparo Jaramillo de Gaitán, and his daughter, Gloria, who opened their homes and memories and provided much of the material used in this book, including access to the collection in the Casa Museo Gaitán; to Luis Emiro Valencia, Guillermo Hernández Rodríguez, Leopoldo Borda Roldán, and Alfonso Garcés Valencia, for much background information and often brilliant analyses of Colombian history; to Alberto Miramón, former director of the Biblioteca Nacional, and Jaime Duarte French, director of the Biblioteca Luis Angel Arango, and their staffs, for the privileged use of their facilities.

Grateful acknowledgment is made to Professor Samuel L. Baily, Rutgers University, who guided this work through its difficult dissertation stage, and to Professor Robert J. Alexander, also of Rutgers, who provided inspiration, hard criticism, and a fine example. The author also is indebted to Professor Robert H. Dix, Rice University, and Professors John Pollock and Gwen Hall of Rutgers University for useful suggestions and criticism. Rutgers University is thanked for providing a University Fellowship that materially aided in the research for this book.

A close friend, teacher, and comrade, Raymond Franke, contributed more than he knows and has my deepest appreciation. My wife, Mercedes, who bore it all for too long, is owed *un millón de gracias!* Finally, thanks are given to Mrs. Hilda Cooper of Lafayette College, who contributed her skills and patience.

Gaitán of Colombia

1
Introduction

Shortly after one o'clock in the afternoon of April 9, 1948, Jorge Eliécer Gaitán left the building where his law office was located in the central commercial district of Bogotá. He was accompanied by several friends and political associates who had gathered in his office to congratulate him on his successful legal defense, the evening before, of an army officer accused of homicide. Gaitán expected to have lunch with his friends at a nearby restaurant before returning to his office for a mid-afternoon appointment with a visiting Cuban student leader who wanted to secure Gaitán's help in renting a hall for a political meeting. As Gaitán's group began to walk in the street, filled with midday crowds, it was approached by a heavy, poorly dressed, unkempt man brandishing a pistol. The man pointed the pistol at Gaitán. The latter turned to walk away, but before he went more than a few steps the man fired several shots. Gaitán fell to the sidewalk mortally wounded.

Despite frenzied efforts to save his life, Gaitán died shortly afterward in a hospital. His death brought the collapse of the hopes of millions of his countrymen for a better life. His assassination ignited a massive uprising by his followers in the capital and throughout the country. Colombia, already wracked by widespread terror and unrest, was plunged even deeper into *la violencia*—civil war, repression, and death.

This is a political biography of Jorge Eliécer Gaitán (1898–1948), a Colombian populist politician who emerged from an obscure background to stamp a deep imprint upon his country. In the process he not only made himself one of the most controversial and popular figures in modern Colombia, but influenced the very substance and direction of its politics. He did this by identifying with the hopes and aspirations of millions of poor people and by convincing them that his interests were their interests. In the plazas and meeting

3

halls of Colombia he shouted: "I am not a man! I am a people!" Astonishingly, many believed him. And because they believed him they followed him in a movement without precedent in Colombian history—a movement which brought the country to the verge of transformation and left repercussions that are still felt today.

In less than fifty years of life Gaitán did many things. He was a political agitator, educator, parliamentarian, jurist, party leader, and organizer of a vast political movement. To all of them he brought unbounded energy, magnetic enthusiasm, limitless confidence, a vivid imagination, and a penetrating intellect. Yet he was more than the sum of the things that he did in a spectacular career. Gaitán was a man of immense compassion and genuine concern for the exploited and oppressed. He also was an opportunistic politician seeking social acceptance and self-aggrandizement. He was a preacher of social democracy and a fighter for justice. He spoke a revolutionary rhetoric and practiced a bourgeois reformer's politics. He was a rare kind of man: a modern caudillo who combined a personalist, paternalistic, educative political style with the manipulative, sophisticated techniques of the twentieth century.

This study focuses on the political role of Gaitán and the related phenomenon of Gaitanismo. The man is studied as the outstanding representative, and his movement as the primary expression, of the populist sentiment that emerged in Colombia during the late 1930s and 1940s. Gaitán is viewed as an articulator, a manifestation of the force of the mobilizing urban middle and lower classes and a segment of the rural population. He is examined as a response to the modernization crisis of a transitional society, appealing through a combination of traditional personalism, modern political methods, and an anti–status quo ideology to groups seeking identity, protection, and community.

Gaitán practiced a type of politics that appeared in Latin America during the decades following the First World War and that is generally described by students of Latin America as "populist." Though practitioners of populist politics have differed remarkably, depending upon country and historical circumstances, they have many essential elements in common. They all, for example, constructed their brand of politics as a result of the particular nature of Latin American economic development. In order to understand the wider context within which Gaitán and Gaitanismo—and populist politics generally —emerged, it is useful to summarize briefly that economic development.

Until the twentieth century the Latin American economies were primarily commercial and export oriented. The prosperity of these economies depended upon the demand exhibited by the more developed nations of Europe and North America for Latin American raw materials and agricultural exports. This type of economic development displayed certain distinctive features: a commercial, export agriculture based upon extensive land-use methods and dominated by large landowners; mining enclaves largely controlled by foreigners and dependent upon foreign capital and technology; an infrastructure developed to support the export sector and mostly financed from abroad; and an urbanization process dependent upon and supportive of the export economy. At the upper levels of the social strata were groups who consumed products imported from the more advanced industrial nations but who showed little or no interest in developing national productive forces not related to the export sector.[1] The mass of the population, neither participating in the expanding export economy nor receiving any of the prosperity generated by it, remained marginal and largely unaffected by this type of development.

In the first decades of the present century, and especially after 1930, modern industrialization began in Latin America. This resulted, in part, from an expanding consumer market in the urban centers. The principal impetus, however, came from crises in the traditional export sector. During World War I, and later during the Great Depression, Latin American imports of manufactured products were gravely curtailed. In response, the major Latin American countries began adopting policies that encouraged and protected the growth of national industries. These industries, generally labor-intensive, were usually of the import-replacement type and geared to the production of light consumer goods. Only after World War II, and then primarily in the larger countries such as Argentina, Brazil, and Mexico, did heavy manufacturing appear in limited forms. In the recent period, and again generally limited to the larger countries, industrialization has continued but has become more capital-intensive, increasingly controlled by transnational corporations (usually headquartered in the United States) with access to capital and advanced technology.

Modernization in Latin America has been partial and distorted. It has not kept pace with increasing internal needs, represented by a rapidly growing population, nor has it overcome the basic dependence of the area. This situation results primarily from oligarchic control in league with foreign, principally North American, interests: economic development is shaped to satisfy foreigners, the domestic oligarchy, a small middle class, and a relatively small labor aristocracy. The majority of the people find no place in this scheme of things.

This general pattern of economic development has been accompanied by two interesting and significant phenomena. First, there has been a general tendency, accelerated in this century, toward extensive agriculture tied to the import-export trade. Staple crops intended for European and North American markets monopolize vast tracts of land which could be more rationally utilized to satisfy internal needs. The livestock industry of the Río de la Plata region exemplifies this type of agriculture. The debilitating logic inherent in this situation has been increasingly aggravated by the addition of the machine to the process of extensive agriculture.

Second, since the beginning of the century there has been a process of mass migration from the countryside to the urban centers, a process that has quickened in recent decades. The reasons for this migration are demographic growth, lack of economic opportunities in rural areas, and the expectation of securing a better life in the attractive urban centers—the so-called demonstration effect. Generally, these migrants, who now comprise the single largest urban social group, have not been incorporated into the white-collar sector nor the industrial work force, and at best maintain marginal status as subproletarians in cheap and nonproductive service functions.[2] They most often are semiliterate, underemployed, and carry over from the countryside, at least in part, some of the traditional values, including an orientation toward authoritarianism, hierarchy, paternalism, machismo, and the psychological syndrome of passivity-violence.[3] Additionally, their economic activities do not foster the class consciousness that results from the experience of employment in large enterprises and that is often manifest among white-collar employees, industrial workers, and others intimately linked to the modern economy.

The historical configuration described above is a seedbed for populist politics of the type practiced by Gaitán. Before proceeding, however, some words of explanation are in order. The term "populist," as used in general parlance, is imprecise and difficult to apply to a particular context, despite the fact that populists, as mentioned above, have many elements in common. But a formulation developed by a Latin American scholar of the subject is useful for our purposes.

Torcuato Di Tella has defined populism as a "political movement which enjoys the support of the mass of the urban working class and/or peasantry but which does not result from the autonomous organizational power of either of these two sectors. It is also supported by non-working class sectors upholding an anti-*status quo* ideology."[4] Di Tella points out that the sources of populist strength are: "(i) an elite placed at the middle or upper-middle levels of stratification, impregnated with an anti-*status quo* motivation; (ii) a mobilized mass formed as a result of the 'revolution of expectations'; and, (iii) an ideology or a widespread emotional state to help communication between leaders and followers and to create collective enthusiasm."[5]

It is important here to note the relation between the social and political characteristics of populism and the unbalanced economic structure of the Latin American continent. Partial modernization and development produce some middle-sector people who understand that the state of human knowledge makes further and rapid modernization possible. They also believe that increasing demographic pressure makes rapid modernization highly desirable. Many of these people want more power and prestige for themselves but find that they are blocked or retarded by the monopolization of power by domestic oligarchies.

This causes considerable tension and discontent. Many of these middle-sector people also understand the nature of the alliance between the domestic oligarchies and foreign interests and wish to break the hold of this alliance on their own countries.

Thus the distortions caused by the unequal development of world capitalism give rise to radical and leftist ideologies among middle-sector, Latin American groups. These ideologies, which usually are indigenous—and often ambiguous—stress nationalist goals such as development through industrialization, integrative mass political mobilization, and the redistribution of wealth and benefits.

The clientele of the middle-sector groups are (1) subproletarian masses drifting in from the countryside; (2) urban labor groups, either organized or unorganized; and (3) rural workers, usually on plantations, and small independent farmers. All of these people long for a higher standard of living and a more meaningful citizenship. The contrast between their condition and what they see around them is enormous. Furthermore, the disaffected elites help them realize that this contrast is irrational and unnecessary. Many of the clientele, especially in the first group, are disoriented and demoralized. It is not surprising, therefore, that populists find their primary support among the unorganized in the urban centers.

Populist leaders attempt to organize, educate, and raise the level of political consciousness of this clientele. The basis of the political appeal is personalism, the trusted charismatic leader who, they hope, will lead them to a better life. Personalism grows out of the traditional Latin American value system. It appeals to organized labor groups as well as to those less susceptible to organization around ordinary trade union issues—the subproletariat.[6] A concentric relationship develops between the popular caudillo and his mobilizing, lower-class followers. The "Great One" coming out of and surrounded by the disaffected middle-sector elite promises to spur development and to provide his followers with employment, housing, education, and a better life generally.

A continuing question in Latin America, then, is, Can the politics of populism provide a solution to the problem of change? Pertinent to this question is the further one: In what ways can personalism provide the "ideology or a widespread emotional state to help communication between leaders and followers and to create collective enthusiasm"? Juan Perón in Argentina and Getulio Vargas of Brazil have given their answers to these questions.

The following work is offered as a study of how Jorge Eliécer Gaitán answered these questions in Colombia. It seeks answers to the specific questions: Under what circumstances—economic, social, and political—did Gaitán operate? What kind of family and class background did he have? What education, personality, and character produced this populist leader in twentieth-century Colombia? How was Gaitán's movement organized? Who comprised its membership? What kind of programs did he offer? What were the limitations of his movement and why did they arise? And, finally, how successful was he?

I
The Formative Years, 1898–1928

2

The Populist Seedbed

Jorge Eliécer Gaitán's birth in Bogotá on January 23, 1898, coincided with Colombia's transition between two historical eras. Within a year the so-called War of the Thousand Days (1899–1902) broke out. This most destructive of civil wars between the Liberal and Conservative parties brought to a close a forty-year period of almost continuous political conflict.[1] The end of the war came about through a negotiated peace that left the Conservatives the dominant political force and the Liberals provided with a guaranteed, if subordinate, role. The more important result, however, was the establishment of relative political peace that endured for more than four decades. During those years important changes occurred that transformed Colombia in fundamental ways. The process of modernization began and accelerated.[2]

The development of the export trade in coffee, oil, bananas, and other products in the first decades of the twentieth century necessitated the building of an infrastructure—roads, ports, railroads, and communication systems. Capital, labor, and resources began to be used in new ways. This development in turn gave rise to the first modern industries, such as textiles, food processing, cement, etc. Ancillary enterprises, such as banks, insurance institutions, commercial houses, and service industries accompanied this growth.

Economic development resulted in the appearance of new social groups: educated middle sectors that found new opportunities in commerce, industry, and government; an industrial and nonindustrial urban working class; rural laborers on commercial plantations; and small coffee farmers with direct ties to national and international markets. In the atmosphere of economic modernization, the feudal ethos of the hacienda and the passive outlook of its inhabitants, inherited from the colonial past, began to corrode. The paternalistic *patrón-peón* relationship began to be increasingly affected by a more spacious outlook,

11

a greater dynamism and sense of innovation and change, and a more impersonal social style.

A deeper and more pervasive political consciousness also arose. People began to think more in national terms and less in regional and local ways. They began to demand a greater influence over, and response from, political institutions and to conceive of the state as an instrument of modernization and power.

The rapid economic and social changes that Colombia experienced, especially after 1925, engendered tensions and conflicts that set the stage for Gaitán and the particular politics he practiced. The disequilibrium caused by rapid industrialization and urbanization was magnified by international capitalist economic crisis and world war. The demands placed upon the system by the new social groups for greater political participation and a larger share of wealth and benefits were met with resistance by the dominant class, which itself was divided over how best to respond. When, by the 1940s, an impasse had resulted amid rising social tension, political polarization, and economic disruption, conditions were ripe for Gaitán to forge his populist coalition.

Economic Development

In the last quarter of the nineteenth century it was discovered that much of Colombia's mountainous terrain was admirably suited for the cultivation of *café suave*. A rapid expansion of coffee production and export began in the late 1870s and continued into the 1940s. Starting with an output of 114,000 sixty-kilo sacks in 1874, production reached more than 1 million sacks in 1913, 3.4 million in 1932, and 5.1 million in 1943.[3] Much of this coffee was grown on family-sized farms in newly colonized lands in western Colombia. As a result, thousands of subsistence farmers were drawn into the market economy. William McGreevey estimated that in the half century from the 1870s to the 1930s a fifth to a quarter of the rural population (900,000 farm family members in the 1930s) was brought into the market economy by coffee.[4]

The growth of the coffee sector had important consequences. It provided a substantial internal market of independent growers for textiles and other mass-consumption products. Textile mills—the first modern industrial plants —were established in the western department of Antioquia in the first decade of the twentieth century. By 1918 the textile industry centered in Medellín, Antioquia's capital, employed an estimated six thousand workers.[5] Other industrial enterprises, notably beer, food processing, and cement, began in other regions, especially in the national capital, Bogotá.[6] Concomitant with the increase of coffee exports was the development of railroads and the transportation industry, which carried coffee to ports and also facilitated the growth of local industry. In 1904, 565 kilometers of railways were operating in Colombia. During the next decade the number of kilometers in use doubled, and between 1922 and 1934 doubled again.[7] The opening of the Panama Canal further encouraged the construction of transport systems and ports in western Colombia.

Several factors combined to stimulate rapid economic growth in the 1920s. The first was the payment of a $25 million indemnity by the United States as compensation for the separation of Panama. A second was the general world prosperity, which enabled Colombia to obtain foreign loans and attract investment from abroad. Almost $200 million in foreign loans and indemnity payments entered the country between 1923 and 1928; U.S. investment during the decade rose from $30 million to $280 million.[8] A third factor was the sharp rise in demand for Colombian products abroad and high world coffee prices. Exports rose from a total value of 52.7 million pesos in 1922 to 132.5 million pesos in 1928.[9]

Much of the foreign capital entering the country during the decade was invested in infrastructure development: the construction of ports, highways, railroads, utilities, and other public services. In the period 1925–1929 an average of 26 percent of the gross national product was invested in this manner, which facilitated economic integration, urbanization, and industrialization. Per capita gross product for the five-year period attained the high growth level of 5.2 percent annually.[10]

Private-sector capital, often associated with coffee interests, invested heavily in manufacturing during the decade. Additional plant was constructed by the food-processing industries, and several raw-materials-processing companies were established. The combined public and private investment generated a high level of economic activity. One good indicator of this was the amount of freight moved by railroad and on barges on the Magdalena River. In 1923, 583,000 tons moved on the river while the railroads carried over 1.5 million tons. By 1928 these had increased to 1.5 million tons and 3.1 million tons respectively.[11] At the same time, the expansion of telegraph and telephone services and the introduction of radio and air travel facilitated communication and supported the integration of the country.

After 1930 there was a sharp drop in the influx of foreign capital, combined with a severe deterioration in the terms of trade. Imports also decreased, a phenomenon that continued during the war years of the 1940s. The resulting restrictions in the inflow of capital goods limited economic growth to levels well below those of the previous decade. However, an import substitution process, combined with astute expenditure policies by the public sector, helped raise the level of economic activity.

During the period 1930–1944 the internal investment rate averaged 16 percent, and per capita gross product increased at an annual rate of 2 percent until 1938, and somewhat less thereafter.[12] But by mobilizing internal resources, industrial expansion continued. Between 1930 and 1933, for example, over eight hundred new industrial establishments were organized.[13] After 1930, and especially after 1934, governmental policies that utilized new methods of expenditure and investment, taxation, tariff, mobilization of savings and channeling of credit, monetary stability, and expansion of the internal debt supported continued public investment in transport services, municipal public works, energy, agriculture, and industry. Investments in public works and services, principally financed with internal resources, facilitated continued rapid urbanization and integration. Import substitution, in turn, shifted capital and active population to industries and services where productivity was higher. Industrial output accelerated and the utilization of installed capacity intensified.[14]

The growth rates shown in table 1 indicate that significant changes occurred in the structure of the Colombian economy within a relatively short time. Although in 1953 agriculture was still the most important sector of the economy, its share of the gross national product dropped to little more than a

TABLE 1: PRODUCTION OF GOODS AND SERVICES

Activity	Share of Total Production			Average Rate of Growth	
	1925	1945	1953	1925–1953	1945–1953
Agriculture and livestock	58.8%	47.0%	36.9%	2.9%	2.7%
Artisan industry	2.9	3.1	3.8	5.6	8.4
Construction	2.6	6.1	4.8	7.0	7.7
Energy, communications, public utilities	0.4	0.7	1.2	8.7	12.7
Government	5.7	5.5	6.9	5.4	8.9
Manufacturing	7.6	13.4	17.2	7.7	9.2
Mining	1.5	3.7	3.7	8.1	5.7
Personal income from rentals	9.5	6.1	5.2	2.3	3.8
Trade, finance, services	8.7	10.2	12.9	6.1	9.0
Transport	2.3	4.2	7.4	9.1	13.7
All sectors	100.0	100.0	100.0	4.6	5.9

Source: United Nations, Department of Economic and Social Affairs, Economic Commission for Latin America, *Analyses and Projections of Economic Development. III. The Economic Development of Colombia* (Geneva: United Nations Department of Economic and Social Affairs, 1957), p. 16, table 3.

third from almost 60 percent in 1925, while the manufacturing sector had risen to second place, with 17.2 percent of the share (21 percent with artisan industries included). Considerable growth also occurred in the transportation, communication, and public utilities sectors, all of which were of vital importance in supporting not only economic activities, but integration, urbanization, the diffusion of ideas and cultural modes, and the internal movement and migration of population. High growth rates in the government, trade, finance, and services sectors also indicate shifting employment patterns to urban-based occupations usually engaged in by the middle sectors and the working class. By 1953 the percentage of the economically active population not engaged in agriculture had grown to 46.2, up from 31.5 in 1925.[15] Most of these persons were concentrated in urban centers.

Rapid urbanization was an accompanying fact of economic development, as indicated in table 2. What is significant is that of the 42.8 percent of the population described as urban (living in communities of 1,500 or more persons), 39.1 percent was concentrated in cities of 100,000 or more persons, that were, of course, the principal centers of economic activity.[16] It should be noted here that Colombia is exceptional in Latin America because its urbanization (and economic development) has not been centered in one major city, but in four regional urban centers (Bogotá, Medellín, Cali, Barranquilla) and several sub-regional, medium-sized cities.

The active urban population was engaged in activities fostered by economic growth. The percentage of those employed in the industrial sector increased during the period 1925–1953 from 3.4 percent to 6.4 percent. Those engaged in transport, communications, energy, public utilities, trade, public health, education, government, and personal services increased from 17 percent of the total labor force in 1940 to an estimated 26 percent in 1953.[17]

TABLE 2: POPULATION GROWTH AND DISTRIBUTION

	Distribution			Average Rate of Growth	
	1925	1945	1953	1925–1953	1945–1953
Active population	37.2%	35.9%	34.0%	1.6%	1.5%
Inactive population	62.8	64.1	66.0	2.3	2.6
Urban population	23.2	34.0	42.7	4.4	5.2
Rural population	76.8	66.0	57.3	1.1	0.4
Total population	100.0	100.0	100.0	2.1	2.2

Source: ECLA, p. 17.

Internal migration contributed to the urbanization process. The expansion of the coffee sector in the 1920s lured many peasants from other regions into the western departments, especially Caldas, and to the slopes of the eastern cordillera of the Andes beyond the east bank of the Magdalena River. Towns in these areas, notably Girardot, in Cundinamarca, Ibagué, in Tolima, and Armenia, Pereira, and Manizales in Caldas, grew into medium-sized cities as a result of their connections with the coffee business. The rapid expansion of the petroleum industry during the same period, centered on the city of Barrancabermeja, Santander del Sur, also attracted immigration. By 1924 there were almost three thousand workers employed by the U.S.-owned Tropical Oil Company, a number that continued to increase as the oil industry expanded over the next decade.[18] The construction of highways, railroads, ports, and communication facilities enticed peasants from their lands in the early decades of the century. Generally, when their work was terminated, they moved with their families into the cities seeking employment in municipal construction and the new industries.[19]

Mobilization and Social Conflict

Though substantial growth rates were registered by the Colombian economy during the period 1925–1949 (see table 3), living standards for the majority of the population remained low. The urban groups generated by modernization suffered from high levels of inflation, unemployment, and underemployment. As early as the mid-1920s, as a result of foreign capital inflow and intensified economic activity, salary and wage groups began to experience a severe price inflation. Between 1923 and 1929 a group of income-elastic products such as

TABLE 3: RATE OF GROWTH OF GROSS DOMESTIC PRODUCT (GDP)

	Average Annual Rate of Growth
1925–29	7.3%
1930–38	4.1%
1939–44	2.2%
1945–49	6.2%

Sources: Colombia, Consejo Nacional de Política Económica y Planeación, Departamento Administrativo de Planeación y Servicios Técnicos, *Colombia: Plan General de Desarrollo Económico y Social*, 2 vols. (Bogotá, 1961–62), part 1, p. 7; Robert H. Dix, *Colombia: The Political Dimensions of Change* (New Haven: Yale University Press, 1967), p. 32.

meat and dairy products increased in price by 90 percent in Bogotá.[20] For most of the years between 1942 and 1964 the cost-of-living index for blue-collar workers seldom increased by less than 5 percent annually and at times rose to well over 10 percent.[21] Wages seldom kept pace with the cost of living. Urrutia estimated that the basic real wage in the manufacturing industry did not increase between 1938 and 1954,[22] and it can be assumed that other wage and salary groups—less well organized than the industrial workers—experienced the same phenomenon.

Gaitán organized his populist movement in the 1940s, a time of severe economic stress. During the disruptive war years unemployment and inflation rose precipitously. Though the domestic economy expanded rapidly in the immediate postwar period, the rate of inflation continued high and had a devastating effect on the lower classes.[23] Further, in the postwar period migration to the cities accelerated (see table 2). The ranks of the urban subproletariat began to swell as employment opportunities failed to keep pace with demand. Increasing numbers of urban workers were forced into marginal service activities.

National income was distributed unequally. As late as 1953, 58 percent of the active population received 31.5 percent of the national income, while 5 percent received 41 percent.[24] The unequal wealth distribution was perhaps best exemplified by income tax returns for 1947. In that year 75,000 persons reported incomes of more than two thousand pesos (the value of the peso was approximately $0.57 U.S.), of which 350 persons had incomes in excess of 100,000 pesos. This group, consisting of managers and owners, accounted for 30 percent of aggregate personal income reported, while seven-eighths of those reporting incomes earned under 1,000 pesos.[25] The latter contributed 60 percent of total receipts. These figures, however, do not include large amounts of income that simply went unreported, a practice not unusual at the time.

Housing standards also remained poor for the majority of the population. Housing censuses taken in 1938 and 1951 indicate that the annual rate of increase in total dwellings was 1.1 percent, which was lower than the 2.2 percent rate of population increase. Most important for the urban groups was the fact that urban dwellings increased at an annual rate of 3.6 percent while the urban population grew by 5 percent annually (in the twenty-six largest cities the ratio of housing construction to population growth was 6 percent to 5.6 percent annually). These figures support other findings concerning increasing crowding of lower-class housing and the spread of urban slums.[26]

The harsh conditions engendered by Colombian capitalism, the exclusion of the overwhelming majority of the population from the benefits accrued by economic growth, and the continued monopoly of the government by landowning and capitalist groups resulted in growing social unrest. The entrance of peasants into the market economy and the conversion of many of them into proletarians provided them with new perspectives. The traditional influences of political caciques, landowners, and priests waned in the new impersonal atmospheres of commercial plantations, factories, and towns. As their hopes for better lives were frustrated and their feelings (and experiences) of exploitation increased, they slowly began to develop class consciousness and an awareness of their potential strength. As a result they contributed to what Antonio García has called the "crisis of the traditional order."[27]

The first stirrings of class conflict occurred in 1918 when dock and transportation workers, probably influenced by socialist and anarchist ideas brought by foreign ship crews, launched strikes for better wages and working conditions. In that year modern trade unions began to form, and in January 1919 a workers' congress met in Bogotá. Out of that meeting emerged a Socialist party dominated by the working class. The Socialists, who counted their greatest strength among dock and railway workers, succeeded in gaining substantial numbers of votes in the congressional elections of 1921 in cities where they had organizations. In the cradle of Colombian industrialism, Medellín, they actually polled 23 percent of the vote.[28]

The Conservative governments responded with hostility to the growing labor movement. In 1927 antilabor legislation was passed that allowed a company to fire any employees engaged in union activity. The government also deported and jailed strike leaders, transported strikers to other regions, and generally persecuted organized labor. Nevertheless, labor agitation continued. In 1924 and 1927 strikes broke out against the Tropical Oil Company because of low wages and unhealthy working conditions.[29] And in 1928 a massive strike occurred against the United Fruit Company in the banana zone that resulted in an army massacre of workers.[30] In these and numerous other strikes, protests, and agitation during the 1920s, communists were actively involved.

The growth of working-class organizations, the appearance of socialist and communist groups, and the agitation of young intellectuals who wanted to convert the traditional Liberal party to "progressive" ideas, all served as indicators of social tensions and desires for fundamental changes in the twenties. The sectors that supported these developments, themselves largely the products of economic growth, demanded the transformation of existing institutions and the recognition of new ones, such as trade unions. Their pressures, combined with the ineptness of Conservative governments in dealing with the new realities, and the onset of the world economic crisis, contributed to the rise of a reformist Liberalism.

In 1930, following almost a half-century out of power, the Liberals gained the presidency when Enrique Olaya Herrera was elected by a coalition of moderate Conservatives and Liberals. But the election of another Liberal,

Alfonso López, in 1934, under the slogan *"Revolución en Marcha"* ("Revolution on the March"), signaled a change in attitude toward the new masses within a part of the Colombian ruling class. López's constitutional reforms, his recognition of organized labor, social and labor legislation, and the first significant attempts at agrarian reform, were a response to the stirrings of the previous decade. Seeking to incorporate the new social classes and groups into a forward-looking Liberalism, he brought them into a coalition with traditional Liberals and the most progressive elements of the Colombian bourgeoisie that created a counterweight to the Conservatives and their allies in the church, armed forces, and traditional peasantry. He also demonstrated that government could be a force for change, representing interests other than those of the ruling class. Indeed, López prepared the way for a genuinely popular, national and mass politics.

One indicator of social mobilization during the period under discussion was the growth of the organized labor movement. In 1929 there were only 8 legally recognized working-class associations in the country. By 1937, during the first López government, there were 159. Following a decline during the "pause" of the Eduardo Santos administration (1938–1942), the number recognized by the government climbed to 453 in 1945 during López's second term. In 1935, the year of the founding of the first labor federation, the Colombian Confederation of Workers (CTC), there were 42,600 union members. By 1947 union membership had risen to 165,600 workers. In 1945, of the 135,000 manufacturing workers in the country, 23.6 percent were unionized.[31] Of course, the percentage of the total labor force in the country that was unionized remained relatively low (4.7 percent in 1947), but organized labor was a strong supporter of Liberal governments during the thirties and forties. The CTC, combined with the Communists who were powerful within it, was a major ally of López and rallied mass support for his programs.

The rural areas of Colombia, long the scene of land struggles, also experienced shocks brought about by changing conditions. In 1917–1918 the first rural worker organizations appeared as agrarian agitation occurred in agricultural centers connected with the international market. Rural unions with anarcho-syndicalist tendencies were organized in the United Fruit Company's banana zone on the Caribbean coast near Santa Marta, and violent strikes broke out over working and living conditions on the large coffee haciendas located in the lower valley of the Bogotá River.[32] By the mid-1920s agrarian unrest was rampant in widespread areas of Colombia. Rural workers continued to agitate for improved conditions and the right to plant coffee trees on their subsistence plots in the coffee zone rising from the east bank of the Magdalena River; large-scale land invasions occurred in the Sumapaz region near Bogotá and on haciendas located in the fertile Cauca Valley of western Colombia. This rural violence culminated in 1928 in the strike against United Fruit. Army repression of the strikers, resulting in hundreds of fatalities and injuries, aroused national indignation and contributed to the fall of the Conservative party from power.

Several factors in the first half of the 1930s contributed to continued and even intensified unrest in the countryside: demographic pressure; the fall in world coffee prices; the return of some urban workers to the countryside after 1929; a more sympathetic attitude on the part of certain officials in the ruling Liberal party; and the organizational efforts of the Communist party and Gaitán's Revolutionary Leftist National Union (Unión Nacional Izquierdista Revolucionaria—UNIR), both of which concentrated their activities in the countryside. As a result, rural worker and peasant organizations continued to grow and expand in an atmosphere of acute agitation and sometimes violence.

The specific issues included working conditions on haciendas populated by tenants; disputes over the ownership of land; the questioning of titles held by absentee owners; and defensive activities, including uprisings, in regions of indigenous populations.[33] The outcomes of these struggles were mixed. In some areas peasants remained on lands they had occupied or had titles recognized by the government. In many instances, however, local—and sometimes national—authorities used force to repress agitation. Not until after the passage of Colombia's first agrarian reform legislation (Law 200 of 1936) and the promise of improved conditions through additional reform measures by the López administration did rural discontent subside significantly. Even so, the agrarian problem remained dormant, only to erupt again in more violent form in the 1940s.

In addition to organized labor, small and medium-sized farmers linked to the international market, and rural workers mobilized by socialist ideas, a "new" middle class began to emerge during the 1930s and 1940s. Its members consisted of the upwardly mobile, usually rural emigrants to the cities, who found employment in occupations associated with the new economic activities.[34] Generally less attached to the upper class and its values than the traditional middle-sector groups, this new element was darker-skinned, more ambitious and money-oriented, less socially rigid, and more inclined toward political innovation. Its economic condition also was, on the whole, more precarious. It, like the groups previously mentioned, found its way into the Liberal party and later provided substantial support for politicians like Gaitán.

On the whole, economic development and the social changes it engendered created conditions that increasingly conflicted with the structures and institutions of a traditional agrarian society. For the first time the dark-skinned mestizo and mulatto masses began to threaten the economic and racial domination of the white, land-owning elite. As these masses began to respond to the opportunities, compulsions, and threats of development and change, they eroded the old relationships and molds, and exerted intense pressure upon the new. Nowhere did tensions inherent in the modernization process become more apparent than in the political arena.

Political Ferment

The political pact agreed upon by the exhausted adversaries of the War of the Thousand Days did not mark the beginning of mass democracy in Colombia. It was an understanding between contending elements of the political elite. The vast majority of the people were excluded, as they always had been, from participation in the important affairs of the nation. The Colombian ruling elite, which Gaitán called the "oligarchy," remained in control of economic, political, social, and cultural life and the important decision-making processes. This domination was taken for granted by the white or near-white elite, based upon the assumption that it was inherently superior to the largely ignorant, poverty-ridden and dark-skinned majority whom it had a natural right to control. If the elite after the turn of the century developed a republican system that allowed a modicum of opposition, civil rights, and "free" elections, this by no means meant that the majority was allowed significant participation. Within the Colombian "Athenian" democracy the majority was held in check by its dependence upon powerful landowning families and interests and by such means as literacy and property requirements for voting.[35]

Politics and political parties generally were reflections of ruling-class interests. Nineteenth-century conflicts over family and regional interests, church-state relations, centralism and federalism, corporatism versus laissez-faire economic policies, and access to the spoils of office were of concern primarily to the country's rulers. They enlisted the people whom they controlled or influenced under either the Conservative or Liberal banners. For those used as cannon fodder in the violent conflicts, the ideologies or issues over which the parties fought were abstractions. But they were controlled by the intricate relationships inherent in the near-feudal *patrón-peón* relationship and the obligations it imposed. They gave their lives in war and their votes in peacetime, all the while reinforcing the hereditary hatreds for those of the opposite party, of whatever social rank, that were indelibly stamped upon them from birth.[36] For them to resist the will of the *patrón* was tantamount to treason. It was to lose respect, endanger livelihood, and possibly life itself. Thus, a relatively small number of powerful landowning families and associated commercial groups—often comprised of members of the same families—were capable of mobilizing a dependent, largely rural population into partisan bands known as Liberals or Conservatives to fight in their internecine struggles. As Robert Dix has observed, the political parties, "a mirror of the hierarchical social pattern," utilized hereditary loyalties to galvanize support in interelite conflicts.[37] As such the parties became as much instruments of control from above as vehicles for elite interests.

Politics, however, did not involve merely a series of maneuverings between contending factions for power and control of the national treasury. There were differences in philosophy and programs, as the nineteenth-century conflicts suggest. The Conservatives were usually large landowners set in their feudal-like ways and outside the mainstream of nineteenth-century economic development. They were allied with the clergy who were opposed to the secular and individualistic ideas of liberalism. Also allied with the Conservatives were commercial interests who benefited from the imperial, pre-Independence custom of allocating state monopolies to favored groups. The Conservatives supported a culture of dogmatic authority, rigid hierarchy, and a strong role for the Roman Catholic church.[38]

The Liberals, on the other hand, were motivated by a secular, commercial spirit. They often were large landowners, too, but with links to the international market. Associated with them were intellectuals who were interested in objectifying the ideas of political and economic liberty elaborated by European and North American thinkers of the eighteenth and nineteenth centuries. Also in the Liberal groups were artisans and small landowners interested in expanding their economic opportunities. Liberal slogans revolved around free trade, secular education, circumscribing the power of the Catholic church, and individualism generally.[39]

Nineteenth-century Conservatives and Liberals, proud of their family ancestry and European descent, thus battled over a multiplicity of interests and policies, at root economic, shouting their respective slogans of "Tradition" and "Liberty." What is important is that neither of the two was interested in subverting the system of oligarchic domination. Political conflicts were not between "ins" and "outs," but among "ins" fighting for a greater share for themselves. When conflicts threatened the system, or when changing circumstances altered the Colombian reality, the oligarchy rediscovered its common interests. Internal differences were put aside and adjustments made so that power remained with those who historically had possessed it. The arrangement made after the War of the Thousand Days was an example of this.

Political stability achieved in the first decades of the twentieth century provided, as noted earlier, an atmosphere for economic development. The issues that had divided Conservatives and Liberals in the previous century became less important as groups from both parties sought to take advantage of new economic opportunities. The integration of Colombia into the world market and its increasing attractiveness for foreign capitalists had, in effect, nullified many of the reasons for the old quarrels. Conservatives and Liberals adjusted their thinking accordingly. They found common ground in the tenets of a laissez-faire capitalism that offered unrestricted potential and profits for those with access to capital, political influence, and the capability to control labor. In certain respects, the Liberals who had advocated economic freedom and a minimum of state interference had won in the marketplace what they had been unable to achieve on the battlefield. The Conservatives, apparently in permanent control of the government, found nothing distasteful when confronted with the new prosperity. The values of the seignorial and bourgeois systems might after all prove compatible. The social costs or the political consequences of what the new order might engender were, of course, ignored. The interests of the majority did not figure in the oligarchy's calculations.

Nevertheless, events began to undermine what Fluharty described as "this rich social narcissism."[40] Economic development and the resulting emergence of new social groups posed a dilemma for the traditional parties, especially the Liberals. Commercial agricultural laborers, independent small coffee farmers, factory workers, clerks, and the myriad of others in occupations created by commerce, industry, and the urbanization process seemed less susceptible to control or influence in the old ways. The Liberals, who long had attracted similar groups, were the most affected. The slogans that had energized party adherents in the previous century began to lose their appeal. Recognizing this, one of the great Liberal chieftains of the War of the Thousand Days, Rafael Uribe Uribe, as early as 1904 called for a "socialized" Liberal party in order to save it from extinction. His intention was the transformation of the party into a vehicle for championing such aims as the redistribution of wealth, limitation of the rights of inheritance, state intervention in economic and social areas, and state protection of the working classes.[41] Uribe was, as the historian of the Liberal party, Milton Puentes, wrote, "perhaps the first of the great continental politicians who recognized that liberal, Manchesterian individualism had died with the romantic nineteenth century."[42] Uribe's advice went unheeded in Liberal circles until after the First World War.

Historically the Liberal party's major strength was in the cities, although it could marshal strong support in the coffee zones and certain rural areas. As Urrutia pointed out, its principal problem "has always been that of reconciling the liberalism of the urban and rural bourgeoisie with the political attitudes and demands of the organized and unorganized urban proletariat."[43] With the rise of an organized, militant, and sometimes violent labor movement, the party's problem was compounded. By and large the upper-class leadership rejected the extremist tactics utilized by the still weak organized workers. In response the more radical sectors of the labor movement turned away from the Liberals and organized the Socialist party. When the Socialists attracted substantial numbers of votes in 1921 in cities where Liberals might have been expected to do well, elements in the Liberal party grew alarmed. Led by another old hero of the 1899–1902 civil war, Benjamín Herrera, and supported by young intellectuals like the journalist José Mar, the Liberals appealed to the Socialists by shifting away from their devotion to laissez-faire individualism and free enterprise. In their March 1922 convention held in Ibagué, Tolima, the Liberals adopted a moderate reform platform that expressed a concern for social justice and called for such measures as "defense and protection of workers . . . effective betterment of their conditions . . . guarantees of their rights under the law."[44] The ideological shift was sufficient to attract Socialist support for the presidential bid of Herrera in 1922. The candidate was unsuccessful, but he won in the major urban centers, thus reestablishing the Liberal hold on growing areas that provided the base for the party's electoral victories in the next decade. In time many of the Socialists found their way back into the party that their threat had helped modernize. By the late twenties there was evidence that elements in the Liberal party were attempting to adjust to the challenges of the twentieth century.

Some of the credit for the redirection of Colombian liberalism must be granted to a new generation that came of age in the years following the First World War. Collectively known as Los Nuevos (the "New Ones"), these mostly upper-class young men vehemently rejected the values of their predecessors, the Generation of the *Centenario*, who earlier had established the basis for political peace.[45] Stung by the loss of Panama and concerned with the role of foreign capital, they demanded protection of the national territory and its resources. They urged the restructuring of the state and activist policies to meet the necessities of an emerging industrial-urban society. They met in places like Bogotá's Café Windsor to discuss heatedly the Mexican and Bolshevik revolutions, or debate the new ideas on art, literature, and politics sweeping in from postwar Europe. Intensely idealistic, strongly nationalist, those Nuevos attracted by socialism contributed to the ferment that gradually edged the Liberal party leftward. Some of them, like Gaitán, remained within the ranks of Liberalism throughout the decade. Others, like Gabriel Turbay, Luis Tejada, José Mar, Moisés Prieto, Alejandro Vallejo, and Roberto García Peña, temporarily abandoned Liberalism to form the Marxist group that laid the foundations for Colombia's Communist party.[46] Toward the end of the decade the intellectual Germán Arciniegas and others founded the magazine *Universidad*. It was a forum for Los Nuevos, who in its pages discussed many of the ideas that were to underlie the Liberal programs of the following decade.[47] Eventually, most of the socialist youth were incorporated into the Liberal party after its triumph and went on to become prominent spokesmen, idealogues, and politicians. But their early activities and agitation had prepared the ground for the emergence of a Liberalism concerned with defending the nation's patrimony, encouraging progressive social and economic policies, and defending the rights of the people.

Not all of Los Nuevos were attracted by socialism, communism, or a reformist Liberalism. Several of them (Silvio Villegas, August Ramírez Moreno, Eliseo Arango, and José Camacho Carreño are the most prominent[48]) formed as a nationalist faction within the Conservative party. Collectively known as the Leopards, influenced by Charles Maurras, leader of Action Française, and later by the Spanish Falange, they espoused a doctrine that not only defended the material interests of Colombia, but its spiritual integrity as well.[49] In 1924 they issued an antirepublican manifesto that stated, in part: "Before the misguided adventures of the urban proletariat, which represent the systematic rebellion of the individual against the species, we invoke the traditional sentiments of the *campesino* classes, who represent the spirit of the land."[50] As the rightist counterparts within their party of the socialist Liberals and Communists, the Leopards prepared the way for the emergence of a reactionary conservatism in the 1930s.

Economic development, social change and conflict, and political ferment provided substantial challenges to Colombia's traditional order by the end of the 1920s. When a series of events, including the banana zone troubles, revelations of financial malfeasance and ineptitude in the government, and the onset of the world depression, shattered the confidence of Conservatives and Liberals alike by 1930, the oligarchy, many of whose members were now convinced of the need for some reform, turned in a new direction. Moderate Conservatives and Liberals joined forces to elect Enrique Olaya Herrera, a Liberal aristocrat and former ambassador to the United States, as president in 1930. Olaya's coalition Government of National Concentration was intended to carry the country through a period of economic crisis and social tension. Its purpose was not innovation or disturbance of the status quo, but it did give some attention to the most urgent problems confronting the country. Higher tariffs were adopted to benefit industry and agriculture, a moratorium on debts was imposed, and land foreclosures were forbidden. Limited legislation granting land titles was passed, as well as some laws beneficial to urban labor. The government sponsored some worker housing construction and provided funds for public education and health.[51] These limited measures hardly were sufficient. Rural agitation and labor conflicts intensified during the early thirties. Many Liberals, disenchanted with the new government, turned to Gaitán and UNIR. Perhaps luckily for the Olaya government, a brief conflict with Peru over territory in the Amazon region erupted in 1932–1933 and diverted attention temporarily from domestic problems. Yet by the end of the Olaya administration the groups clamoring for change had, if anything, increased their volume.

In 1934 Alfonso López Pumarejo, a Liberal, was elected president. His ascendency was not so much the result of consensus within the oligarchy as it was of division. Conservatives who normally would have violently opposed López still were weak and divided. They lacked firm leadership and defined policies to deal with the new conditions of Liberal supremacy and rapid socioeconomic change. The Liberals also were split between those with nostalgia for traditional politics and the ardent young reformers. Fortunately for the latter the groups benefiting from and seeking change were sufficiently strong within Liberalism to force a López candidacy. As a result this privileged son of an aristocratic family, a talented journalist, banker, politician, and agent of foreign capitalists, forged a progressive electoral coalition and developed a reformist program with broad appeal. Rallying behind López were the urban middle sectors and similar upwardly mobile groups, the urban working class, rural residents from areas of agrarian unrest, and some of the new industrialists. Leadership of the coalition was provided by the younger intellectuals and politicians, members of upper-class Liberal families involved in modern commercial and agricultural enterprises.[52] The impetus provided by this coalition proved to be irresistible; even the moderate Liberals who would have preferred a more conservative president went along temporarily.

The first López administration was called the Revolution on the March. If it was not exactly a revolution, it was a significant march away from the usual substance of governing. It was a departure from the traditional "occupation of the administration" toward the concept of the state as a director and administrator of socioeconomic change.[53] In effect, the most progressive elements within the oligarchy took upon themselves the task of reducing the country's backwardness and dependency through economic development while simultaneously meeting some of the most urgent demands of the masses caught up in the modernization process.[54] It was reform from above: the utilization of the state with its capacity to mobilize resources in order to overcome the structural defects and weaknesses of a still young capitalism.

López first dealt with an archaic constitutional system. He pushed through amendments ("codifications") to the constitution that gave the state the right to intervene in economic affairs "for the purpose of rationalizing production."[55] Property was defined as having a social function which implied obligations, and when individual property rights conflicted with the public or social interest, the former were required to give way. Property also could be expropriated with prior indemnification or, in certain cases, without it. Other amendments declared that labor was a social obligation that enjoyed the special protection of the state (which assured the rise of organized labor), guaranteed the right to strike, and established that public welfare was a responsibility of the state. In addition, López enacted amendments that met traditional property and literacy requirements for voting and set limitations on the power of the church.

Armed with these constitutional weapons, López and the Liberal majority in the 1936 congress passed a series of implementing laws. A direct, progressive taxation system was adopted, designed to shift more of the burden to the wealthier classes and generate more state revenues. Labor legislation was passed that set up a special labor tribunal, strengthened the unions in their negotiations and in the enforcement of contracts, and provided a minimum wage, eight-hour day, and welfare benefits for workers. An agrarian reform was adopted, based upon the principle that land belongs to those who worked it; it was designed to secure tenure for squatters and generally improve conditions in the countryside. Educational reforms gave the central government control over most areas of primary education, which was made mandatory; large funds were invested in education at all levels. Finally, legislation was passed that placed foreigners and foreign interests on an equal legal level with Colombians.

As is true so often with Latin American legislation, the results did not nearly match the intentions of the López reforms. Limited successes were recorded in all of the areas mentioned above, but basic structures, institutions, and relationships remained intact. Changes in the tax system did not greatly burden the wealthy or result in a redistribution of wealth; taxes were passed on in the form of higher prices. The labor legislation covered a minority of the labor force, while wages and productivity remained low and working conditions generally stayed poor. The agrarian law that granted squatters tenure was in effect the recognition of a de facto condition in certain areas of the countryside; the provisions for reversion of uncultivated land to the state and for redistribution never really were invoked. The education expenditures made little impact upon the growing population; church influence remained strong, and traditional educational methods continued to dominate the system. In terms of Colombia's economic development, the country was still dependent on foreign markets, capital, and technology. Internally, it remained crippled by its limited regional integration, limited capacity to mobilize resources efficiently, and dependency upon an archaic and generally technically unqualified bureaucratic structure.[56]

Despite the limitations of the Revolution on the March, it did mark the beginning of an attempt to come to terms with rapidly changing conditions. As Dix wrote, "the leaders of the state had injected into Colombia's traditional game of politics the adrenalin of conscious modernization."[57] The state had taken a new direction and assumed new responsibilities; the new social forces, including the labor movement, were recognized and some of their initial demands were met; a precedent had been established for future reforms. However reluctantly, at least part of the oligarchy had recognized the existence of the increasingly restive masses and had made some efforts to come to terms with them.

The short-term consequences of the López reforms were divisions and tensions that contributed to the tragedy of the late 1940s and 1950s. Expectations were aroused among the people that would not be fulfilled. For the overwhelming majority the revolution of rising expectations implicit in the López era was frustrated. The people did not receive a much greater share of the national wealth, nor did the political system open sufficiently to include them in a meaningful way. Class divisions remained deep. In short, the integration of the majority into the nation failed to occur. Frustration followed promise; bitterness and despair followed hope.

Opposition to the López reforms was vehement within both parties. By the end of the administration in 1938 the Liberals were seriously divided between the reformers and the traditionalists. The division continued and deepened during the administration of the moderate Eduardo Santos (1938–1942), friend of businessmen and initiator of the "pause" in the Revolution on the March. From the right the Conservatives, now led by a reactionary, Laureano Gómez, poured out a stream of vitriolic denunciations against the man and the policies they held responsible for subverting the social order.

By the early 1940s it was evident that a serious social crisis was approaching in Colombia. The forces for change were on a collision course with the champions of tradition. The reformist impulse represented by López was inadequate to meet the aspirations set loose by modernization. Nor was the oligarchy willing to give way before the new realities. The popular clamor for a place in the system was being ignored, frustrated, or repressed. The ruling class itself was divided over how best to proceed. Conditions in this half-modern, half-traditional society, economically unstable and politically polarized, peopled with newly awakening masses, were ripe for the populist politics of Jorge Eliécer Gaitán.

3

The Background of a Populist

In later political campaigns Gaitán made much of his humble background. One of his childhood friends, Leopoldo Borda Roldán, reported that Gaitán once told a crowd at a political rally that he had a very deprived childhood—a statement that infuriated the proud and sensitive senior Gaitán.[1] On other occasions Gaitán mentioned that he often was without shoes in his youth, despite the fact, according to Borda, that the children of those days seldom wore shoes when they were playing in good weather. Obviously, these exaggerated stories were Gaitán's way of identifying with the poverty-ridden people whose support he was seeking. They also reveal something else about the man: his pride in being able to refer to a past that he largely had overcome through his own efforts, as everyone knew. Gaitán grew up close enough to real poverty to understand its consequences. The circumstances of his youth help to explain his subsequent development into a champion of the poor. In those years the strong character, the aggressive ambition, and the combative personality were formed. But the love of books and learning, the fascination with ideas, and especially the compassion he always demonstrated for the unfortunate also came alive.

The occupations of Gaitán's parents provided an atmosphere that was unusual for lower-middle-class families of that era. His father, Eliécer Gaitán, was a sometime journalist, occasional political polemicist, history teacher, and, finally, seller of second-hand books.[2] He had collected a large personal library in order to write a history of Colombia. However, his inability to earn an adequate living for his family from his various enterprises forced him to fall back upon his one major asset: the book collection. The young Gaitán grew up surrounded by books, and, although his father was in many ways an impractical man, he nevertheless was alive with ideas, demonstrated an active interest in public affairs, and from an early age regaled his son with heroic stories about the nation's past.[3] The boy was exposed at an early age to the interests and attractions that remained throughout his life.

Of the parents, Gaitán's mother, Manuela Ayala de Gaitán, had the most profound influence upon him. She was described as a remarkable woman who possessed a deep humanity and strong character.[4] A graduate of Colombia's teacher-training institute, the Escuela Normal, she taught in various small towns around Bogotá where she was known for her progressive, somewhat feminist views. These cost her several jobs, excommunication, and, on one occasion, a threat on her life instigated by an outraged priest.[5] She later founded and directed a school for the children of Liberal families where she could teach unimpeded. Borda relates that in addition to being one of the best teachers of her time she was in the forefront of struggles for improving the conditions of schoolteachers. Manuela took a deep interest in Jorge's development, teaching him to read and write, providing him with his initial primary schooling, and urging him to seek a higher education, which she perhaps realized would provide him the means to escape the limits of his background. Gaitán remained close to his mother throughout her life. He remembered her with "deep gratitude." She was for him "an extraordinary woman . . . of forceful spirit, who cared lovingly for my destiny. The sanctity of her life was illuminated always by a studious intelligence and indomitable will."[6] It is noteworthy that these qualities also appeared in her son.

The intellectual and social environment provided by his family was one important influence on Gaitán's development. His personality and character, however, were forged in an atmosphere of conflict—within the family and with his teachers. Despite the independence and assertiveness that Manuela demonstrated in her work, she apparently accepted her unequal role within the hierarchical, authoritarian, Hispanic family. She usually did not question—except when the vital interests of her favorite Jorge were concerned—the authority of her husband.[7] Don Eliécer apparently took every opportunity to assert that authority, perhaps the more so inside the family because of his failures outside of it. He was that most anxious of men, the petit bourgeois who above all wants to appear prosperous and respectable, but who only succeeds in staying a few pesos away from actual poverty.

Gaitán, the eldest child, was expected to assert his responsibility for his six younger brothers and sisters yet submit to the discipline of his father. While there is evidence that Jorge carried out the first with zeal and energy, the second he fought with such acrimony that an open break eventually occurred between father and son. Jorge strenuously resisted the authority of his father, especially in regard to what the former considered his best interests. When his father insisted that he take up a practical career like accounting and assure himself a secure if mundane position, Jorge steadfastly refused; he insisted on obtaining a higher education at all costs, a position supported by his mother.

The unruliness and rebelliousness that Gaitán demonstrated toward his father were also manifest in his school experiences. He resisted the rigid educational discipline and rote methods that were standard for the time. He argued with the instructors, insisted on explaining the lessons, declaimed in a loud voice, led student disorders, and attempted to dominate everybody. When disciplined, he often reacted violently. He was expelled from one school for throwing an inkwell at a teaching Christian Brother.[8]

The one school that made a favorable impression on him was the Colegio Araújo, for which he received a scholarship in 1913.[9] It was founded by Simón Araújo, a well-known educator and proponent of Liberal views, for the sons of Liberals who disagreed with the conservative ideas dominant in most schools. Araújo was a man of formidable energy who obviously impressed the young Gaitán. In a 1916 address the latter praised his teacher highly for his dedication, patriotism, and educational standards.[10] However, this respect did not deter Gaitán from his usual behavior while attending the school. He continued to assert himself and express his opinions vigorously. Perhaps, as Osorio suggests, he was compensating for his poor appearance, dark skin, lack of money, and inferior social position in a school where most of the students came from upper-class backgrounds.[11] In any case, Gaitán's behavior obviously had some appeal, because he became a popular student leader. And although he was not a first-rate student academically, despite his intelligence, he developed a serious interest in literature and culture and began to practice the oratory for which he later became famous.[12] It was during these years that Gaitán began to develop a serious interest in politics and took the initial steps toward a political career. Here he also articulated his dreams of a glorious future that included European study, success as a lawyer, marriage into the upper class and, finally, triumph as a president of Colombia capable of dealing with the country's social and economic ills.[13]

However, Gaitán did not graduate from the Colegio Araújo. The school often had been subjected to persecution by Conservative and clerical officials and lacked official certification. The young Gaitán, his opportunistic eyes already wide open, transferred in the final year of secondary school to the Colegio of Martín Restrepo Mejía, where he settled down to work and, with top grades, received his diploma in 1919.[14]

A characteristic that appeared early in Gaitán's life was a driving ambition to succeed, to overcome all opposition, to make his dreams reality. This was encouraged by his mother, but it does not account for the intensity with which he pursued his goals. A more likely explanation is the social context in which Gaitán grew up. The family was lower middle class; that is, both parents were employed in white-collar occupations, but they seldom were far from poverty. In the early years of Jorge's life the family moved to the neighborhood called Egipto, a working-class area of narrow streets, single-story adobe and plaster houses, where poverty and suffering was a grim, constant presence.[15] In addition to the depressing effect of these dismal physical surroundings, Gaitán was subjected to humiliations of other sorts. He wore the hand-me-down clothes of his father that, despite the imaginative adaptations of his mother, never quite fit, and that especially contrasted with the finery of his more affluent classmates.[16] He was forced by his father to hawk used books and the cheap editions of the latter's political journalism at the railroad station, in the markets, and other places where crowds gathered—usually during vacations when other boys his age were enjoying themselves.

A factor that certainly played a role in Gaitán's development was his dark skin. Physically he was short, stocky, black-haired, and bore on his broad face the unmistakable traces of Indian ancestry. He grew up in a society that was sharply divided along race as well as class lines; very early in his career he earned the derogatory epithet "negro Gaitán." Wealth, power, and status in Colombia—especially in the Andean highlands—historically belonged to those with white or near-white skins. The dark-skinned majority essentially was excluded by a centuries-old, institutionalized racism that had become a social norm. Gaitán, because of his physical characteristics, undoubtedly became aware of his "difference" at an early age, certainly when he was enrolled in the Colegio Araújo.

It might be expected that in a society where the extremes of wealth and poverty always were openly evident, conditions like those of Gaitán's youth would be more easily supportable. But the boy was infected by the middle-class attitudes of his parents, especially his father, who made a great virtue of respectability and spoke often of success. Additionally, Gaitán grew up in a society that was beginning to show evidence of prosperity, where money was becoming more abundant and opportunities for advancement were opening to the talented and educated. The ideas advanced by his parents, the world exposed to him by education, the hunger for material possessions, all combined to encourage an ambition that seemingly was larger than circumstances warranted. But, characteristically, faced with obstacles, Gaitán looked upon them as challenges to be overcome.

In later years Gaitán remarked that his youth was like an old pair of shoes: he was happy to have had them after he was able to change them for a new pair. He said, "Our life of yesterday may have been arduous, severe, unjust; but if these limitations filled us with a combative fire or a tenacious will to conquer, it is clear that we appreciate them for being the cause of our little victories. But we cannot love them, because their lacerations were painful; and pain, while worthy of respect, is not attractive."[17]

Not only was Gaitán ambitious, he was determined to rely upon his own resources. An incident from his university days is typical. Knowing of her son's desire to study in Europe, and perhaps hoping to alleviate somewhat the hardships he was facing in obtaining his education, Manuela went to the president, Marcó Fidel Suárez, for help. Despite the political differences between the Conservative Suárez and the very Liberal Manuela, the president had respect and admiration for Gaitán's mother as a teacher and received her willingly. He offered her son a minor post in the Rome embassy that would have permitted him to study at a university in the city. However, Gaitán refused the offer. He informed the president that he preferred to make the trip through his own efforts. Years later, when discussing the affair, he expressed satisfaction with the decision. He said that he resisted accepting a bureaucratic solution to his problems because the idea repulsed him personally. He added that the final achievement of his goal to study abroad through his own efforts provided immense gratification.[18]

Knowledge of the circumstances surrounding Gaitán's youth provide some understanding for his rebelliousness, inordinate ambition, and desire to succeed. But what of the social conscience that also appeared in his early years? This is more difficult to explain adequately. Yet out of the anguish, insecurity, and "limitations" Gaitán spoke of there developed a desire to correct the abuses and injustices that he saw around him. When he finally entered the world of his youthful dreams—of wealth, power, prestige—he never forgot those people who lived around him in his youth. He always was moved by their suffering. A friend of his university days, Ricardo Jordán, wrote that Gaitán once wept when seeing homeless people sleeping on the street under newspapers on a stormy night. Gaitán cried, "There must be an end to such wretchedness, such infamy!"[19] These sentiments led him into the great struggles of his life, led him to forego an assured high place in society for the immense difficulties involved in the fight for social justice. Perhaps the only possible explanation for his compulsion to champion the cause of the poor and oppressed was an identification with them that went deeper than the politically expedient. Perhaps he really believed that "I am not a man! I am a people!" Perhaps he was aware that his own position, no matter how high, was not secure so long as the people remained downtrodden. In any case, Gaitán's intense ambition, his desire to rise above the limitations of his background, cannot be separated from his authentic concern for the welfare of the people. What Gaitán acquired in his youth, probably unconsciously, was the belief that ultimately his success and that of "the people" was joined.

He also must have sensed that the normal channels to political power were closed to him by his class status and dark skin, that to get ahead he had to challenge the system. He certainly was ambivalent about the upper class and the oligarchy—he admired it and its power, yet he resented it and wanted to replace it. Gaitán, like others with similar backgrounds and in similar circumstances, seemed to understand that his ambitions would be frustrated if he did not choose the one path open to him: to become a populist leader in order to become a national political leader. His concern for the welfare of the people and his personal ambition, instead of conflicting, coincided.

The University Center of Cultural Propaganda

Gaitán's first major effort on behalf of the working class was in the field of education. Like his early experiences in politics it provided a knowledge of conditions in the country and enabled him to test his ideas and develop his organizing skills. The attitudes he then expressed about education, the political methods he utilized, and the ideas formulated in those early days remained constant throughout his life. They are worth examining because they establish a base for the continuity in thought and action that is a characteristic of Gaitán.

Like most members of the middle class, Gaitán believed in the efficacy of education as a primary instrument for both individual and collective improvement. Throughout his career, educational reform played an important role in his social programs. For himself, the idea of obtaining a first-rate education became almost an obsession. When he succeeded it was not surprising that he would transfer his concern to others.

As early as 1918, when he was still in secondary school, Gaitán wrote a letter to the Bogotá daily *El Tiempo* supporting the establishment of Sunday schools to enable workers to "acquire the knowledge that can arm them with new methods for satisfying their needs."[20] Since education at the time was limited to an extremely small percentage of the population, and was concentrated in classical subjects far from the everyday needs of the majority of people, what Gaitán had in mind was a program of literacy training and instruction in subjects of practical use like hygiene.

The success of university students in Lima, Peru, in organizing a university extension program for workers provided Gaitán with the example he needed.[21] During his first year at the National University, he convinced other university students to help him and in May 1920 established the University Center of Cultural Propaganda.[22] Support was solicited and received from the minister of education; the first public lectures were delivered in the foyer of the state-owned Colón Theater. Several prominent men were persuaded to support the venture, including Dr. Simón Araújo, Dr. Diego Mendoza Pérez and Dr.

Francisco Arteaga. The first lecture was delivered by a well-known Bogotá physician, Dr. Julio Manrique, who spoke on the prevention of various diseases common in the city. The press, especially *El Tiempo*, provided coverage, and noted that during the first lecture distinguished *damas y caballeros* of local society were present.[23]

The workers were not forgotten, however, and throughout May student members of the center delivered lectures in plazas around the city.[24] This was followed in July by a fund-raising gala sponsored by young women of society. Gaitán, whose social ambitions were rapidly being realized along with his proletarian concerns, delivered an address as president of the center explaining the goals of the organization. He frankly stated that he wanted to involve young society women in the center's efforts in order to end their "ancient custom of boredom and indifference to social interests." How this was received was not reported; however, Gaitán went on to propose a characteristically ambitious extension of the center's work into instruction for prisoners, physical education for public-school children, lectures for *campesinos* in surrounding villages on market days, and the establishment of centers in other cities and departments. Gaitán ended by observing that education "was not the work of a day," and that the first job of the center was to expose the people to the potentialities of education.[25]

Following initial success in the capital, Gaitán and the students Ernesto González and Guillermo Hernández Rodríguez carried the cultural propaganda campaign to the cities of Girardot and Ibagué. According to press reports they were well received.[26] They delivered public lectures, solicited books door-to-door (which were then distributed in local hospitals), and attended various social functions organized to support their work. However, the group apparently did more than carry out good works. In an interview, Hernández recalled having delivered socialist speeches during the excursion as part of his effort to bring enlightenment to the workers.[27]

Gaitán was the organizer and driving force behind the center. Within a very short time he was practically the sole active member. The beginning of the university year interrupted activities; probably, too, the energies of the upper-class students whom Gaitán recruited flagged after their initial enthusiasm subsided and the enormity of the task became apparent.[28] But in late December 1920 he managed to gather another group of students for an organizing trip through the western departments of Tolima, Caldas, and Valle. In Cali, capital of Valle, he succeeded in establishing a center. However, the contents of the students' lectures had changed notably, or at least were reported differently. In Cali on December 31 Gaitán delivered a violent attack on what he called "our mutilated and prostituted politics." He added that it was the task of "renovating youth" to extend their hands to the fallen and humble and make fraternal cause with them. The editorial writer of the Cali daily *Correo del Cauca* described the address as a "valiant protest against the vortex of bestiality that surrounds us."[29] But others saw it differently. Predictably, newspapers began to report critically on the center's work, and in January Gaitán was accused of ir-regularities with funds raised by benefits for the center in Cali. Thus he rather abruptly learned the narrow limits within which Colombian public political discussions took place.

He reacted in a manner that was repeated again in the future when faced with a difficult situation that required some decisive response or action: he became ill. Perhaps the illness was authentic in this case, but it is interesting to note the appearance of illnesses at certain critical junctures of Gaitán's life. From the small town of Cachipay, where he was recovering from an illness induced, he said, by his labors, he wrote a letter to the presumably sympathetic, left-liberal Bogotá daily *El Espectador* in which he almost pleadingly denied the charges. He gave a long detailed account of the trip, including the number of days spent in each city, the work accomplished, and testimonials to the group's success. He added that he and his associates had "struggled and suffered" far from home in carrying on their work, that they had endangered their health and, in the light of this, the charges against them were unjust. More revealingly, Gaitán mentioned that he was attacked in Cali for furthering the Liberal cause, which cost him Conservative support.[30] The matter seems to have been dropped without further complications, thus absolving Gaitán, but it marked the effective end of the University Center of Cultural Propaganda.[31] As he was to do on other occasions when assailed, or when he judged that some project he was engaged in was encountering severe problems, he simply broke the connection. Such behavior was, in time, to earn him charges of opportunism.

First Political Campaigns

From his youngest days Gaitán had heard stories from his father about the great heroes of the Liberal party. Both of his parents had suffered at one time or another for their political views. The school that most impressed him was a repository of Liberal ideas. The city in which he grew up, although still immersed in many ways in the traditions of Spain and the colony, nevertheless was alive with an interest in politics. An astute observer remarked on what seemed to be a fixation: "The constant unwearied interest of *Bogotanos* is politics . . . politics as a national principle, as policy, and as a kind of superlative sport. All their historical sense, their gift for dialectics, their passionate patriotism and their facile acuteness of expression favor this fascinating avocation."[32] With this kind of atmosphere as well as the knowl-edge that the kind of success he wanted in life depended upon involvement in public affairs, it was not surprising that Gaitán very early became enmeshed in politics. He also was acting upon a basic truth of the time: unless one was born to family and wealth, politics was the principal avenue to the top. It was a natural career for an ambitious young man like Gaitán to follow. The monopolization of land, resources, and wealth by a privileged minority and by foreigners means limited opportunities for those without access to them. However, government, which in Latin America traditionally has served as intermediary between contending economic interests, and which, because of the demands of national sovereignty, requires national personnel, offers unique possibilities for those seeking wealth and power.[33] In the twentieth century especially, the aspiring, expanding middle class has understood this. Restricted by economic colonialism and limited industrialization, the middle class has sought an outlet for its ambitions through politics.

Gaitán's initial political experiences were important because they exposed him at an early age to the hard realities of local politics. He not only learned to face hostile, sometimes belligerent audiences, but began to master the techniques of political speaking and organizing. For the first time the inimitable Gaitán style emerged, and the aggressive behavior that previously was inflicted on family and teachers found a suitable outlet. His initiation occurred during the 1917 presidential campaign, when he was nineteen. He supported the candidacy of the Conservative poet Guillermo Valencia, leader of a coalition comprised of a Conservative nationalist faction headed by Laureano Gómez, Liberals led by the old caudillo and party chief, Benjamín Herrera, and moderates influenced by Eduardo Santos, publisher of *El Tiempo*, and the writer L. E. Nieto Caballero. The candidate ran on a moderately progressive program that supported guarantees for political rights, expanded education, protection for workers, and a limited social welfare program.[34]

The unknown Gaitán was not welcomed with open arms. He first had to make a reputation, which meant being recognized. This he accomplished with characteristic flair and enthusiasm. At school he vociferously spoke for Valencia, disrupted classes and routine, and made a general nuisance of himself. When the school authorities put an end to this, the intrepid youth went to the coalition's headquarters and offered his services. He was humorously refused; but, undaunted, he went to a Valencia rally in his neighborhood, waited until the main speakers were finished, then mounted the platform and delivered a heated address.[35] Then he went on an unsolicited speaking tour of the villages around the capital. The Valencia group apparently decided that it would be better to have him under some control: Gaitán was "discovered" by Benjamín Herrera who, after hearing one of his speeches, sent him on a speaking tour of western Cundinamarca and the department of Tolima, areas that later provided faithful support for his political adventures. However, there also were Conservative strongholds located there, a fact that Herrera may or may not have told the aspirant.

At this point it is reasonable to ask if Gaitán was motivated only by a desire to get into politics and build a reputation, or if there were ideological considerations as well. Clearly, both played a part. In early December 1917, although not yet a university student, Gaitán appeared as a secretary of the Coalition Directorate and the Centro Liberal Universitario, a student-affiliate of the Liberal party. In a resolution signed by him and printed in *El Tiempo,* some of his thinking on the issues appears. The resolution urged Liberal youth to support Valencia as a candidate of justice, democracy, and law against the enemies of territorial integrity, public liberties, and the national treasury.[36] In another article, printed in *El Motín*, Gaitán praised Valencia as the candidate of all the "youth hungering for modernization." He went on to urge support for Valencia as the candidate of the poor, the workers, and the humble closed out by the system of inequality.[37] These sentiments are the same as those expressed in later years.

The young campaigner's trip received favorable reviews in the procoalition newspapers. What was most often remarked upon was his ability to arouse audiences with passionate, vibrant oratory. He traveled with a group of young men like himself and often appeared on the same platform with Felipe Lleras Camargo, who also was experiencing his political initiation. A commentator compared the differences in style between the two: Lleras, the very essence of moderation, appeared somewhat timid but spoke with elegant and sober words about the platform of the coalition and the need for peace, work, and education; Gaitán harangued the crowds, clamoring in the name of the oppressed, denouncing the national catastrophe being perpetuated by those in power.[38] Here was the incipient populist, arousing crowds with his oratory, attacking, denouncing, turning words into weapons. The method developed in those dusty plazas was refined and elaborated, but it remained the same. At nineteen the future caudillo was already being formed.

The trip turned out to be more than a pleasant political excursion. It involved some real dangers that provided opportunities for the speakers to demonstrate their courage and coolheadedness in the face of provocations by both Conservative and regular Liberal opponents. In mid-January, Gaitán was received with enthusiasm in Girardot, a city on the Magdalena River. He then went on to several nearby towns: Tocaima, where a Conservative priest attempted to disrupt his speech; Ambalema, where dissident Liberals nearly lynched him; finally, to Honda, where he was greeted by an opposition-led demonstration. The Ambalema episode caused considerable comment. Gaitán was accused of over aggressive attacks on dissident Liberals, insulting respected politicians, and making threats that blood would flow if there was fraud in the upcoming election.[39] These were the reasons for the personal attack on him. According to another observer, however, Gaitán behaved laudably. He refused to leave the platform without protesting the behavior of the crowd and challenged anyone to come forward with arguments to counter his own.[40] He obviously was learning the ways of politicians, because the account claimed that his parting comment was in praise of the "civilized" behavior of the majority of the citizens of the town, who would oppose him word for word, but never stoop to murder. Gaitán's own account indicated that his group had advance word that several dissident Liberals, organized by the owner of a cigar factory and accompanied by some workers of an opposition newspaper—all well-fortified by drink— planned to disrupt the speechmaking. Despite the insistence of local coalitionists that the rally be postponed, Gaitán decided to go ahead because "youth fears nothing when struggling in the interests of the Republic." Of course, Gaitán also had high praise for the local friends who saved him from the attack. He wrote that for Ambalema he would preserve the most "fervent memories" and "deep affection."[41]

The campaigning earned Gaitán recognition among Liberal chiefs, especially Benjamín Herrera, and a reputation as a spirited and courageous speaker. At an early age he had found a place within the party that, with the exception of one brief interlude, he would remain loyal to for the rest of his life. He would disagree with many in the party and attempt to change it from within, but he would not abandon it.

During the four years following the Valencia campaign Gaitán remained active in student politics. He was a member of the Liberal University Directorate, which guided the youth branch of the party, and achieved enough of a reputation to receive votes in 1919 on a slate submitted by the group for inclusion on the Liberal candidate list for the Cundinamarca departmental assembly.[42] He participated in party debates over the question of abstention from electoral participation because of recurring fraud committed by the Conservative party. Writing as a member of the university directorate, Gaitán made a well-reasoned argument in favor of continued participation. He claimed that because the party had no continuing contact with the electorate between elections, no weekly conferences for workers, no schools or training institutes, the only time that the people could learn of Liberal platforms and doctrines was during elections when they could hear party orators.[43] When a faction of the Liberal party in the western Cundinamarca town of Facatativá decided upon abstention in the assembly elections of 1919, Gaitán was dispatched to the city where he succeeded in bringing the dissenters into line.[44]

This political work convinced Gaitán of the need for a permanent, extensive party organization. In later years as a party leader, and in his own movement, he stressed the need for strong, local organizations that would provide continuing political education for members, as well as a permanent organization that local people could identify with and be a part of. This was an expression of his view that political work was a permanent, on-going business and not simply the mobilization of voters for periodic elections. He apparently saw no contradiction between his position on the need for systematic, serious political work and his manipulative, personal style. The reports of his speeches indicate that he already had instinctively grasped the effects of demagoguery on simple country people. As an observer noted, "The *campesinos* listen to and admire Colombian politicians not because they understand them, but because they are fascinated by gestures, florid speech, and impressive words."[45] Or, as Gaitán in a cynical moment remarked to a friend when asked what he said to the people in his speeches: "Oh, what's most important is to speak to them. The word without content is the only thing that attracts the multitude."[46]

By the time of the presidential campaign of 1922, Gaitán already was an experienced campaigner and party worker. He was entrusted by Herrera with a difficult assignment: making a speaking tour through Conservative strongholds in Boyacá and northern Cundinamarca, a mountainous region notable for its harsh conditions, where feudal practices still were evident, and where the influence of the church was particularly strong. That he should receive such an assignment was an indication of the confidence Herrera had in him; there is no evidence that he was accompanied by any other Liberals. But he did have the advantage of working for a Liberal party united behind Herrera, its candidate. The old veteran of the civil wars had managed to bring together all Liberal factions for the first time in the twentieth century. He sought to make the Liberal party a forum for all progressive forces in the country, including socialists, republicans, and liberals.[47] He also opened places for young men like Gaitán. During the 1922 campaign, youthful Liberals like Eduardo Santos, Alfonso López, and others, who would lead the party to power after 1930, emerged and began to make their influence felt.

Gaitán delivered his first address in the town of Lenguazaque on January 1, 1922—the first time a Liberal ever spoke there, according to a message sent to the Liberal headquarters.[48] Throughout January and into early February he spoke in town after town. Reports of his activities published in Liberal Bogotá dailies indicate that, as usual, he was received with enthusiasm by Liberals.[49] But also every report mentioned attempts by Conservatives or local priests to disrupt his speeches. He ended the campaign in Ubaté on February 3 amid a scene of wild confusion. There, when Gaitán attempted to speak, a near riot ensued, instigated, it was reported, by the Conservative mayor. Gaitán had to leave the platform while respected local Liberals calmed the crowd. But the irrepressible Gaitán returned to finish his speech and was borne off afterward on the shoulders of his supporters, amid the "most grandiose delirium."[50]

Despite the discomforts involved, the trip proved to be politically profitable. It spread Gaitán's reputation and led to efforts to have him named a departmental assembly candidate from the districts visited. His candidacy was supported because he was a figure "with the most solid preparation in administrative and political questions and who counted heavily with the youth of the area."[51] Early in 1923 Gaitán was elected to the departmental assembly of Cundinamarca from the city of Girardot, thus successfully concluding the inaugural stage of his political career. As if to point to the direction of his future political efforts, he introduced a proposition asking assemblymen "to direct their congressional activities toward a vigorous, daring, and efficient fight to solve social problems." He admonished them not to adopt shallow reforms, but to achieve through cooperative institutions in production, distribution, and consumption a degree of equality among the social classes.[52]

Gaitán's childhood and youth gave evidence of several of his dominant traits—traits that later enabled him to become a populist leader. He demonstrated very early a strong character, ambition, self-reliance, a love of combat, respect for learning, and identification with the people. From his mother, who influenced him most, he inherited his practical zeal; and from his father, his speculative aspirations. A further driving force was his sense of humiliation in the face of poverty and racism. He also fit easily into the patriarchal psychology. An eldest son, he assumed his patriarchal mantle early in relation to his brothers and sisters. In these early years, he was already teaching his peers the uses of both rebellion and conformity.

4

The University and Socialist Ideas

In February 1920 Gaitán entered the Faculty of Law and Political Sciences of the National University in Bogotá. It must have been a moment of pride and satisfaction. He had overcome the obstacle of near poverty to achieve an opportunity that still was rather rare for someone from his social class. But he had successfully resisted perhaps an even greater obstacle—his father, who had put constant pressure on him to go to work and help support the family. The final decision to study law had caused a serious family crisis. Don Eliécer declared his son out of favor; Jorge was forced to move out of the house.[1] However, his mother took his side as usual and promised to do extra work in order to help him. The consequences of that decision in terms of family tranquillity can only be imagined.

There is little doubt that Jorge experienced rather severe economic hardships as a student. Osorio informs us that he subsisted largely on a diet of bread, cheese, and *agua de panela*, a drink consisting of brown sugar and warm water commonly used, especially by the lower classes.[2] Gaitán said that because of the lack of a proper place to study he read in the open patios of the Capitol and in city parks.[3] His financial condition often excluded him from the diversions of his more affluent classmates, and he would refuse invitations with the excuse that he had more lofty concerns.[4] However, he made an effort to keep up his appearance. One photograph of the time shows a young man lounging casually, attired with a stylish cap jauntily worn, light-colored suit, two-tone wing-tip shoes, pipe in hand—a portrait of any undergraduate of the 1920s.[5]

Despite his status as a university student, there is no evidence that Gaitán's behavior changed substantially. The public toughness, the assertive, aggressive personality was still manifest—if now somewhat tempered by an affected air of self-importance.[6] The anxieties, the compensating behavior remained.

Yet the enormous self-confidence also was present. A close student friend, Ricardo Jordán, reported that he always "spoke of the future as if it belonged to him," and one afternoon said that he (Gaitán) would be president one day.[7] According to Jordán, Gaitán was not a good student in the usual conformist sense, although he studied hard and read widely in many disciplines, a practice he continued throughout his life.[8] This may be explained by the fact that the instructors and the doctrines they taught were conservative and contradicted what Gaitán said was the "revolutionary temperament" of the students.[9] But despite financial hardships and conservative domination of the university, his enthusiasm never flagged. Nor did his idealism. Gaitán said that he and his friends were motivated not by the desire to "open the dirty doors of the politicking bureaucracy," but by the ambition to have a profession. He claimed that he and his fellow university students worked like thinkers and thought like active men.[10]

During the years Gaitán was a law student the intellectual life of the country was in ferment. University students and intellectuals were attracted by socialism and the Russian Revolution. The country was beginning to experience the first impact of industrialization and such words as "labor problems" and "proletariat" were heard. In literature new trends like "modernism" were widely discussed. There was an abundance of discussion groups, clubs, associations that questioned, argued, took positions.

Gaitán's interest in literature took him into a group called the Rubén Darío, after the Nicaraguan modernist poet.[11] During these years he also conducted interviews with visiting celebrities and wrote short articles on artistic and intellectual topics for the newspapers *El Espectador* and *Gaceta Republicana*.[12] This was common practice for an educated young man of the time making his way in a city that prided itself on being "the Athens of South America." By and large, his journalistic and literary output was undistinguished, but it is of interest that Gaitán was fascinated by strong men, by the heroes of the age of Homer, who lived intense lives with "all the frankness and sincerity of their temperaments."[13] This theme appears time and again. For example, in funeral orations delivered in 1919 as a student representative before the tombs of two national heroes, Generals Rafael Uribe Uribe and Guillermo Quintero Calderón, he had fulsome praise for those patriots who had overcome personal adversity in pursit of their visions.[14] These were obvious examples upon whom Gaitán was modeling himself. And the successes he had achieved, the obstacles overcome, reinforced his belief in the merits of strong will and tenacity.

Gaitán's major literary effort was his law school thesis, *Las Ideas Socialistas en Colombia*. Socialism was of vivid interest in student and intellectual circles. Since the end of World War I a modern labor movement had emerged and had adopted a socialist ideology. In 1921 the Liberal party, after several electoral defeats by socialist candidates, adopted the more moderate and viable socialist ideas, thus beginning a process that was called the "socialization of the Liberal party."[15] By 1924 a communist movement had gained strength among some intellectuals, journalists, and radical politicians. In this group were numerous classmates and contemporaries of Gaitán, including the *El Espectador* journalists José Mar and Luis Tejada, and Gabriel Turbay, Diego Mejía, and Roberto García Peña. For these enthusiastic young men the ideas of the various socialist schools and the experiences of the Russian Revolution were revelations that seemed to speak directly to them and that pointed the way for the revolutionary "redemption" of Colombia. They helped to organize workers, practiced radical journalism, and eventually formed the Communist party of Colombia.

While these young men vehemently championed radical ideas and causes in the 1920s, their theoretical knowledge and long-term commitment to Marxism were questionable. Antonio García claims that none of them had more than a superficial knowledge of the economic and philosophical works of Marx, Engels, or Lenin.[16] Indeed, when the Liberals came to power in the 1930s, many of them returned to the fold and eagerly accepted bureaucratic posts.

On the other hand, while most of his contemporaries were active outside the Liberal party, Gaitán remained within its ranks. He saw no future in any of the socialist or communist groups then existing. In the first pages of *Socialist Ideas* he recognized that while those groups performed useful work, they had not in fact understood the characteristics of Colombian political life, had misinterpreted events, and had followed incorrect tactics.[17] He pointed out that he supported the socialist ideas presented in his thesis but did not consider himself a member of a socialist party, because such a party did not exist.

Influenced, perhaps, by the traditional loyalty of Colombians to one of their two major parties, Gaitán placed his faith in the Liberal party as the instrument for carrying out the transformation of Colombian society. It was a position he maintained throughout his life except for a brief period in the 1930s. He claimed that the Liberal party represented the progressive forces that best could work for necessary reforms, and he urged that progressive groups strive to make over the party to carry out this task (p. 64). However, there were other developments that pointed to the transformative potential of the party. Ideologically, it was moving to the left as a result of Herrera's overtures to socialists and labor groups and their subsequent incorporation on the basis of new, progressive programs—the socialization of Liberalism. Electorally, the presidential campaign of 1922 had demonstrated that the party's growing numbers of supporters were located in the cities. Further, industrialization and urbanization were accelerating the growth of the groups that supported Liberalism.

This, coupled with the belief that their exposure to new social and economic conditions would lead them to demand reforms, provided Gaitán with substantial credibility in arguing for the Liberal party as the agent for change.

Socialist Ideas, however, was not a blueprint for transforming Liberalism. It was the first examination of the impact of capitalism on Colombia.[18] It argued that despite the country's agrarian economy and relative backwardness when compared with the industrialized nations, capitalism did indeed exist there and was responsible for the miserable conditions in which millions of Colombians found themselves. The author examined the country's legal orientation as a reflection of capitalism, discussed the problems of capital and land in Colombia, and concluded with a section devoted to "evolution and tendencies of the socialist schools" in which he elaborated his political philosophy.

Socialist Ideas was not a rigorous Marxist analysis of the Colombian reality. Despite his eclectic reading in socialism and political economy, Gaitán lacked, according to García, the theoretical knowledge required for such a task.[19] Nor was the work supported by thorough empirical data. It was "more intuitive than dialectical." What Gaitán brought to the thesis has been described as a "socialist sensibility": "Without completely understanding the economic phenomena, he understood their importance in modern life and proceeded to utilize them in the interpretation of the national reality. It cannot be said of him that he was an orthodox Marxist and even less a theoretician of the class struggle. But he was profoundly attracted by the establishment of a revolutionary order based upon a more just distribution of wealth."[20] However, Gaitán accepted two fundamental theses of Marxism: first, that socialism was a stage in the evolution toward communism; second, that a communist society was inevitable.[21] He was profoundly convinced of the evolutionary process operating in history and of the necessity for passing through stages of development. This provides important insight into understanding his political action.

In the opening chapter of *Socialist Ideas*, "Systems, Laws and the Medium," Gaitán discussed his concepts of law and their relationships to society. They were in profound disagreement with ideas then current. He stated that the basis for all individual rights was society and denied that men were born with natural or preexisting rights (p. 68). Following from this, when there was a conflict between the rights of an individual and the rights of society, the former had to cede. The mission of the state was then to arbitrate the relationships of individuals within society (p. 69). This set the stage for the interventionist state.

Gaitán further believed that the state was obliged to protect those within society and to provide equal justice for all. Since material relationships were fundamental to every society, one function of the state was to ensure just distribution of material means to the individual. Without satisfaction of the material conditions of existence, justice, equality, and the development of the individual were impossible (pp. 72–73).

He claimed that "the noble and just life is impossible within the existing rigidly individualist society of free enterprise, where the state represents the wealthy class, where capital has been granted absurd privileges in the economic development of the country, and where labor is assigned a secondary role" (pp. 73–74). For Gaitán the state had the right and obligation to change the legal structure that governed society in order to correct these injustices: "Laws should not simply spring from the mind of the legislator but should conform with nature, which is essentially dynamic and mutable. When the medium [the means of production] changes, the law must change . . . and if nature, in its perfection, shows us the injustices of the present individualist system, acknowledging a greater amount of equity and happiness under the socialist concept, not only is it impossible not to claim it, but it is our obligation to impose it" (p. 75). The author admitted that those who espoused socialism at the time were in no position to impose it. Socialism, weak and confused in Colombia, still was in a doctrinaire stage (p. 74), and Colombians, with their traditions and religious preferences still intact, were far from communism.[22] In other words, conditions were not yet propitious. What was required in the intermediate stage was the development of protective institutions and laws to ensure the rights of workers while educating them in their class interests.

In the chapter "The Problem of Capital," Gaitán, following Marx, established his belief in the materialist conception of history. "History is the analysis of economic elements, almost always obscure, but always evident, that determine the social dynamic in all its manifestations" (p. 111). According to this theory, the economic elements, or more precisely wealth and who controlled it, were the decisive factors in determining the structures of society. Wealth itself resulted from labor, the natural elements, (such as land), and capital. But labor, operating upon the natural elements, was the only producer of capital (p. 85).

Capital evolved in history through various stages: simple individual capital; the beginnings of the concentration of capital; concentrated individual capital; and the present stage, capitalist production (p. 114). In the final stage, individual labor has coalesced, because of the requirements of capital concentration, into collective social production; in other words, the capitalist means of production require central control over the individual productive forces. Thus capital becomes capitalism when it is not the direct product of personal labor. "Capitalism is the concentration of capitals, socially produced, for the individual benefit of those who control the labor of others. It is a form of wealth born of a certain form of the exploitation of labor" (p. 89). Labor, therefore, is made the slave of capital. "Capital is a fact of the natural order. Capitalism is an established fact created by the dominant classes that has achieved a specific form within the judicial relations imposed by those same classes. Under capitalism the workers have been prevented from laboring for themselves, and have been forced to sell their labor to others. Under capital in its natural form man sold the fruit of his labor. Under capitalism he has to sell his own body, sell himself" (p. 90).

Gaitán concluded from this analysis that capitalism indeed existed in Colombia despite its relative weakness when compared with the advanced capitalist states. The majority of Colombians were not owners of the things they directly produced but worked for others for wages. Further, the social means of production were monopolized by a small minority of owners in industry and in land. As a result there was a proletariat and hence a social problem because of the inequality between owners and labor, between those who owned the means of production and those who were forced to sell their labor for wages. And the great concentration of individual capital cannot "be considered as a benefit for the national wealth; it, on the contrary, introduces a disequilibrium and an injustice that is the source of social injustice" (p. 85). The poverty in which the majority of Colombians lived was not caused by some "natural order," but by capitalism: the few expropriated the capital of the many.

In 1924 Colombian industrialization was in its initial stages. The economy was primarily agrarian. However, Gaitán found that the capitalist mode dominated the agrarian economy through its monopolization of the most productive lands. Again, following Marx, he wrote that this monopoly was the result of the individual usurpation and concentration of land ownership as private property. The rent (profit) of the land derived from this monopoly: "Rent is that which is paid for a monopoly born from the conversion of the land to individual property" (pp. 150–53). Gaitán objected that the large landowners benefited almost exclusively from their ownership. They derived profits from the production of the land and also from the increase in value over time of land not in production—the result of society's efforts and not theirs.

The land problem was further aggravated by the conditions of the rural workers, many of whom still were dominated in a quasi-feudal system by absentee landowners who controlled their labor force to a degree that far exceeded that of industrial owners. Gaitán believed that the three million of six million Colombians who were rural laborers or their families were the pariahs of the country, without even the basic rights of citizenship. He wrote:

> The ignorance in which they exist makes them unconscious of their rights. . . . Their food? The most miserable that can be conceived. . . . Illnesses undermine them without the least scientific help. Their

homes are so dispersed that they cannot associate for their own
defense. Their sons are slaves for whoever wants them to work,
despite their young ages and naturally weak constitutions. Their
daughters are the living victims of the *patronos*. . . . Their dwellings,
their houses, are tiny hog sties . . . Meanwhile, the man of the city,
the tycoon, wasteful, drinks in the bubbles of his champagne the
anguish of his slaves. . . . Undoubtedly the life of the city worker is
superior to the cold misery of our rural laborers. All this confirms that
among us the agrarian aspect of the social problem is the most acute.
(Pp. 176-77)

As the start toward a solution Gaitán called for the abolition of monopoly over
agricultural lands (pp. 163–64). He meant by this not the abolition of private
land ownership, but the elimination of large landholdings and limitation of the
size of private holdings. He recognized that redistribution was but a beginning.
A further necessary step was to enforce productive employment of occupied
lands, thus attacking a major problem in Colombia: the existence of large tracts
of well-located, potentially productive lands that were held without utilization.
Nor did he believe that distribution of the vast areas of land held by the
state—the *baldíos*—was a solution to the land problem. These lands were, by
and large, marginal to the national economy, undeveloped, and outside of the
exploitative capacity of the rural population (pp. 170–75). What he intended
was the distribution of lands within the national economy with the provision for
effective utilization: roads, credits, technical improvements, sanitary and
educational facilities, etc.[23] This remained the basis of the land policies that he
elaborated in all of his future programs.

Gaitán recognized that a sound agricultural policy was but one aspect of
development. And he realized that the economic and social improvement of the
Colombian population, rural as well as urban, was linked to technological
development. Therefore, he supported industrialization as the best method for
improving the lives of the people. In his view there was a functional relationship between an industrial revolution and an agrarian revolution in Colombia.[24]
The two were inseparable. Without the capital and technical benefits provided
by industrialization, an agrarian revolution would fail; industrialization without
an agrarian revolution would result in an "artificial process, precarious,
reduced to the limited area of the cities, without a countryside to provide
foodstuffs and primary materials at low cost, and employment for those not
occupied in primary production."[25] But industrialization must occur within a
socialized means of production.

From this review of several of the principal issues discussed in *Socialist
Ideas*, it is obvious that Gaitán advocated the establishment of a socialist

system, both as a means to develop the country and as a step toward social justice. First and foremost, he was a socialist. The programs he developed throughout his career only can be understood within this classification. The problem, which Gaitán recognized at the outset, was that he was operating in a country where "socialist ideas" existed, but not yet the conditions for the implementation of socialism. In his political activities, the tactics he utilized were a reflection of that fact. Further, he did not regard his programs as a culmination, but as a stage in an ongoing process that logically would evolve into communism. Gaitán hoped to put Colombia "on the road to socialism."

Many of Gaitán's critics have insisted that there was a fundamental contradiction in his seeking revolution while advocating social reform. And yet it is questionable if he saw it that way at all. He regarded himself as a revolutionary. But he brought to the term an interesting definition. To be a revolutionary, he wrote in the final section of *Socialist Ideas*, "is to fight against what one judges to be absurd and prejudiced, but seriously, methodically, wholeheartedly. The revolutionary knows that the path is difficult, arduous, that the goal will not be reached in a day, that the pyramids are not built from the top. The ideological revolutionary understands that the revolution is the culmination of a preceding evolution, organic and formal" (p. 199). In his discussions of the types of land ownership throughout history, of the utilization of capital, of the development of social thought, of judicial relationships, he emphasized their evolutionary aspects. His instinct and his study—not to mention his experience—taught him that history could not be rushed. And this knowledge governed his approach to politics.

The final chapter of the thesis, "Evolution and Tendencies of the Socialist Schools," presents a discussion of what Gaitán called the struggle for social equality, which must occur in four stages: the prehistory of socialism, social reformism, utopian socialism, and scientific socialism (p. 182). He believed that the masses remained untouched by social movements until the middle of the nineteenth century. The European revolutionary movements from the French Revolution to 1848 were democratic struggles, but not socialist: "bourgeois democracy, democracy of hierarchies" (p. 185). However, these movements were indispensable because they allowed the masses to begin to perceive their condition and slowly develop a consciousness of their rights. Yet the liberty that was the result of these revolutions was inadequate: "We do not need the liberty that makes slaves; we need the liberty that makes men, in the sense of being an end in themselves" (p. 184).

The social reform movements that emerged in the second half of the nineteenth century likewise were limited. They accepted the existing social order while asking for remedial reforms of the injustices that it had created (p. 186). They were inadequate because they could never relieve the basic class condition of the proletariat. What they asked was charity, and charity was a perverse and dangerous virtue, "perverse because it humiliates, dangerous because it does not lend its favors from a base of rights, but a base of piety. We do not want charity for men who by virtue of their work acquire the right to justice" (p. 194). After briefly describing the ideas of the utopian socialists from Robert Owen to Charles Fourier, Gaitán pointed out that their weaknesses resided not in their correct identification of the individualist system as the enemy of the proletariat, but in their idealism. Utopian socialists "think that in order to renovate society constant propaganda and a good dose of strong will is enough" (p. 196).

Gaitán regarded himself as a scientific socialist within the Marxist tradition, as one who had dialectically analyzed social relationships based upon a materialist conception of history. He explained that a scientific socialist believed that there was a "profound law" that directed men: economic interest (p. 197). From this Gaitán drew three conclusions: first, that the interests of the dominant class and those of the proletariat were in open conflict, and that the class struggle was inevitable. Second, the interests of the dominant class were maintained by the force that economic determinism has established; therefore, only by force would the workers be able to achieve social equality. "We refer to organized and conscious force, to the force that the oppressed classes, by uniting their interests and persons, should employ to contain the powerful advances of capitalism. And this in the political struggle, in the trade union struggle, in all social activities" (p. 197). Third, Gaitán insisted that the triumph of socialism was only possible through evolution and could not disregard factors of the material world, its geographical characteristics and the historical development of the country (p. 197).

Thus was established the basis of Gaitán's thought and the first outline of the political tactics that he was to develop in the following years. In *Socialist Ideas* he had, considering the time and circumstances, written an original and provocative thesis that with remarkable intuition and insight uncovered the gravest problems affecting the country. If the analytical method he utilized was derivative and often mechanical, it nonetheless focused attention on the source of the Colombian dilemma: the monopolization of economic and political power by a small ruling class. While he was not the first to recognize this, he was the first of his generation to explain it so clearly and to point the way to a solution.

Socialist Ideas was received with much praise by the Colombian left.[26] Dionisio Arango Vélez wrote a preface to the printed edition and proclaimed it a miracle that such a work could have resulted from the "lamentably anachronistic and deficient" National University School of Law.[27] He praised the author as one of the most brilliant members of his generation. Ricardo Jordán noted that it was a new and unusual departure from traditional theses, but proclaimed it a remarkably mature work.[28]

European Study

Following the awarding of his degree in November 1924, Gaitán practiced law—rather unsuccessfully—for a year and a half.[29] However, he had set his mind on studying in Europe, and much of his effort was spent working toward that end. He wanted the prestige associated with having a degree from a European university, prestige that might provide easier access to the higher circles of Colombian society;[30] but he also was motivated by the desire to study under one of the great scholars of penal law, Enrico Ferri. Since he had almost no financial resources, he devised a scheme that would provide funds for his passage and a minimal amount for subsistence in Europe. Aided by his family, he found enough money to open a pharmacy to be operated by his younger brother Manuel, then a medical student.[31] Manuel was to send a monthly stipend to Jorge in Rome while he utilized the remainder for his own education.

In July 1926 Gaitán sailed for Rome where he enrolled in the Royal University. His life in Rome was difficult, a repetition of the financial hardships he had faced in Bogotá. He lived in the cheapest *pensiones* and changed addresses frequently, probably in order to evade paying bills. As was the case in Colombia, he compensated for his poverty and feelings of inferiority with displays of intellectual brilliance performed with the usual arrogance. He sought out the company of upper-class acquaintances, even when this meant real sacrifices of his living standard.[32] However, his exotic appearance— flashy clothes and dark complexion—coupled with intelligence made him the center of attention, a position he both relished and nourished.

Following a year of diligent study Gaitán was graduated magna cum laude and first in his class.[33] After presentation of his thesis on premeditation, Professor Ferri, overcome by emotion, rushed from his chair to embrace the young Colombian lawyer, declaring him to be one of the most extraordinary students he had ever taught. The great penalist insisted that Gaitán be awarded the Ferri Prize, which was granted to the most promising criminal law graduate.[34] Not long afterward Gaitán was the first Latin American to be elected a member of the Italian section of the International Society of Penal Law.[35]

Gaitán's hard study in Rome did not interfere with his interest in politics. He attended the mass Fascist rallies when Mussolini spoke, in order to study the techniques that the Italian dictator practiced. He observed the theatrical gestures, the vocal modulations, the manipulative mannerisms,[36] and learned to tighten and systematize his own speeches and utilize oratory as a series of emotional exchanges between himself and his audience. But he was not attracted by Fascist ideology. Indeed, Gaitán claimed later, after his return to Colombia, that Facism had no ideology.[37] It had emerged in a wave of violence that resulted in the cancellation of human liberties. Mussolini, taking advantage of the masses in the disarray following World War I, could jump from one doctrine to another without losing authority because he held power through fear and intimidation. He had betrayed his own ideas and his followers once in power, with disastrous results for Italy.[38] Gaitán characterized Il Duce "as a sad exhibitionist. . . . In his discourses he is picturesque [but] the trouble is that the Italian people do not know how to distinguish between the serious and the ridiculous."[39] Nevertheless, Gaitán was impressed by Mussolini's energy and manipulative skill, and the lessons that the Fascist taught were learned well and applied no less successfully in Colombia.

With the funds from his prize, Gaitán made a trip through Italy and to Paris following graduation, visiting museums, buying prints and sculptures to adorn his office and study at home, acquainting himself with the monuments of European culture. The man who returned to Colombia in 1928 was no longer the tropical "exotic," but a polished, sophisticated professional of serious countenance. Armed with degrees from two universities, praised and befriended by one of the greatest legal minds of Europe, informed in art, philosophy, literature, and politics—the "negro Gaitán," the short, dark, mestizo from the streets of poverty, was ready to enter the world of the privileged and powerful. In a few brief years Gaitán had accomplished much. He had acquired a university education despite enormous obstacles; he had used his imagination to secure the means to study in Rome, where he had won high honors. He had written a provocative and controversial thesis which demonstrated his acute grasp of Colombia's problems. In this work he had laid down the socialist principles that would guide him in his future career as a populist leader.

II

Testing the System, 1928–1944

5

Early Politics

Upon his return from Europe in early 1928 Gaitán made two important observations about Colombia: that the country had been heavily penetrated by foreign capital and had come under the influence of foreign interests; and that the benefits of economic development during the 1920s had not been evenly distributed but had been monopolized by the few. In an interview with *El Espectador* Gaitán deplored what he termed the "subservience of the country to foreigners."[1] He said that he didn't wish to see foreigners excluded, but believed that Colombians ought to be equal to them. What he wanted was not an aggressive European nationalism, but "an integral nationalist orientation" that would defend Colombia's interests, especially her economic interests. He wished to conserve the national "personality," apparently from foreign cultural domination, but he also chastised his countrymen for not setting about the task of building their country rationally through sustained hard work. For example, he deplored the fact that Colombians talked passionately for two or three days about building a railroad, then forgot about the project.

He had hard words for the country's "directing class." He accused it of looking after its own interests while ignoring the suffering of the people— "there is progress for the rich and poverty for the poor."[2] Yet he admitted that the lower classes had no class consciousness and didn't know how to go about solving their problems. They had no sense of method and organization. But he was not without hope. Obviously pointing the way to his own future activities he concluded, "If I am a socialist I ought to be a socialist in and for Colombia." Events soon provided him the opportunity to act upon his observations.

Gaitán's successes did not automatically open all doors to him. He could be praised for his European achievements, interviewed by the newspapers, give well-attended lectures on fascism, but he was not elevated into the ranks of the oligarchy. What he needed was an issue to attract attention and support, a base from which he could launch his attack on the prevailing social order. Fortunately both were provided ready-made as a result of the strike against the United Fruit Company that broke out in November 1928.

The Banana Debate

United Fruit had been operating banana plantations in the area of Santa Marta on Colombia's north coast since early in the century.[3] Within its concession the company was practically autonomous. It owned its own transportation and communication networks and stores and held a monopoly over the irrigation system in the so-called banana zone. Because of its control over transport and water, national producers were forced to sell their produce to the company's agents at low prices.[4] The result was a continuous conflict between national producers and the company. Additionally, the company's practice of issuing script as part of wages for use only in United stores antagonized local merchants, who initially actively supported the strike when it broke out. Since in certain areas United was the sole employer, their interest was in breaking the trade monopoly of the company.

The principal conflict, however, was between the banana workers and the company. Since the first labor trouble erupted in 1918, United had consistently refused to bargain with its workers. In this it had the tacit support of consecutive Conservative governments, which always found in favor of United.[5] Until 1928 the unorganized workers had been powerless against the company supported by the government; in that year the situation changed dramatically.

As early as 1925 foreign workers with anarcho-syndicalist sympathies had been organizing workers in the banana zone.[6] The communists also were active there. When agitation increased in October 1928, the procommunist Partido Socialista Revolucionario (Revolutionary Socialist Party—PSR) sent several of its top organizers into the zone, and after the strike broke out on November 11, a PSR member, Alberto Castrillón, became a leader of the banana workers.[7] With this kind of support the workers were able to launch a well-organized effort that shut down almost all company operations.[8]

The strikers presented nine demands to United,

> the principal one being the recognition by the company that it had employees. In order to evade all of the existing labor legislation, the company did not contract directly with the workers but went through labor contractors. This meant that it did not have to pay for collective insurance nor did it have to meet the housing standards required by legislation. The subcontractors, because they had no capital, were not

required to pay these benefits. Thus when the workers demanded collective insurance, payment for work accidents, Sunday rest, housing facilities, and hospital facilities, they were simply demanding that the company keep the spirit of the labor legislation on the books at the time.[9]

Other major demands included wage increases, recognition of collective contracts—thus implying union recognition—and an end to company stores. On all of these the company refused to bargain; on the major issue the company referred to a prior finding by the government that since it did not hire workers directly it did not have to meet the existing labor legislation requirements.

In this atmosphere of intransigence the Colombian government dispatched troops to the banana zone under the command of General Cortés Vargas. He immediately jailed hundreds of workers—to obtain a settlement, he said—arrested a government labor inspector who had found in favor of the strikers, and provided labor troops for the company while protecting strikebreakers and United installations.[10] The result was a series of disruptive and violent acts by strikers against the company and army. General Cortés Vargas responded by declaring a state of siege and unleashing the army against the local inhabitants. In the reign of terror that followed at least one hundred persons were killed and more than twice as many injured, with property damage to United Fruit and workers of more than a million pesos.[11] Thirty-one participants in the strike received jail sentences in highly irregular courts-martial.

When news of the atrocities and arbitrary legal procedures spread, there was an explosion of demonstrations, strikes, and violence that lasted through the spring of 1929 and gravely undermined the prestige of the government. However, it was Gaitán who delivered the mortal blow during the 1929 sessions of the House of Representatives with a series of revelations that electrified the country.

In the months after his return from Europe, Gaitán had made an arduous campaign in the lower-class neighborhoods of Bogotá and the villages of Cundinamarca that resulted in his election to the House of Representatives on a dissident Liberal list.[12] Thus Gaitán had a national forum from which to attack the government and demonstrate his championship of the workers' cause. As Urrutia noted, the debate of 1929 was probably one of the most important in Colombian history because it brought Gaitán into the national limelight and convinced him that his future popular support was based upon his ability to defend the interests of the working class.[13]

Gaitán began his efforts with a series of articles published in the magazine *Universidad* in which he questioned the government's handling of the entire banana-zone affair. He attacked the government for deliberately maintaining its state of siege in the zone in order to continue persecutions of strikers whom it was afraid to deal with legally. He refuted the government's characterization of the strikers as common delinquents by claiming that common delinquents could not be tried under military law: "if the workers are common delinquents and do not come under military jurisdiction how is it that they are submitted to military justice?"[14]

In mid-July 1929 Gaitán traveled to the banana zone where he conducted an investigation of the army's activities during the strike. Characteristically, he gained wide interest with his mass interrogations, speeches before huge crowds, and publicized field research that attracted large numbers of people.[15] On July 19 *El Espectador* reported that he said, "If I stay here where there are so many horrors, I will end in an insane asylum!" But his return to the capital was even more spectacular. He stopped at every major populated area along the way, attacked the government for its illegal actions and corruption, and urged the people to give him their support in the coming congressional debate. In one speech he said that the department of Magdalena where the strike occurred was the Nicaragua of Colombia. He compared the struggle of the workers with those of Sandino and his followers against the Yankees.[16]

Gaitán began the debate in the House of Representatives on September 3, 1929, in an atmosphere of intense excitement. The galleries were filled with spectators; crowds waited outside in the Plaza de Bolívar to accompany Gaitán home after each session; newspapers carried full accounts of the speeches. The orator, who had done so much to generate interest, did not disappoint. He played to the sympathetic audience in a masterly performance designed to draw maximum attention to himself. For fifteen days of consecutive sessions he mixed learned discourses with sensational disclosures, analytical recitation of evidence with emotional outbursts, pompous boasts about his achievements in Europe with self-effacing statements that he was speaking only out of the deepest patriotic sentiments. When he sensed that attention might be diverted from him by attempts to cut off the speeches, or when he was attacked for personal vanity in the Conservative press, he switched tactics by charging Conservative representatives with irresponsible absenteeism, and by a dramatic donation of his legislative salary to the widows of strikers. Judging from press reports, the spectators loved every minute of it.[17]

A reading of these speeches discloses an interesting technique, a mixture of intellectuality, fact, threat, indignation, and sensationalism. For example, he opened the first address with a discourse on the role of law in a civilized society, worked his way into a discussion of the responsibility of parliament in maintaining justice, and described what revolutionary sentiments were aroused in passive people when they sensed that grave injustices had been done them.

Following this provocative opening, he stated that he would not start a political debate, after which he praised the patriotism and high moral standards of the army, and immediately read a letter from a priest in the banana zone describing the rape of a mentally retarded girl by soldiers.[18] He then launched into a highly emotional description of the army's imposition of fines, taxes, and bribes on civilians in order to finance orgies of the soldiers.

Day after day the revelations of atrocities, corruption in government agencies and the army, denunciations against the president, the minister of war, and the "drunken" General Cortés Vargas went on. When Gaitán sensed that perhaps the audience's interest was beginning to lag, he introduced gruesome stories, photographs of pitiful widows and children and, at one point, the skull of a child he disinterred in the zone, which he asked the hapless minister of education, a physician, to verify as indeed the skull of a child. He especially brought to the fore the role of United Fruit in the affair, charging it had "bought" the army: 500-peso bills for officers, quantities of food, beer, and cigarettes for the troops, a banquet for General Cortés Vargas.[19] He directly implicated the ex-minister of war, Ignacio Rengifo, who had resigned under pressure, as responsible for the massacre:

> We are going to prove that ex-Minister of War Rengifo, in order to obtain the declaration of the state of siege and impose it, did not address himself to the [civilian] governor of Magdalena or to the thirty-two thousand Colombians interested in the problem, but to the enemy of the Colombians, to their extortioner—the director of United Fruit. And this despite the fact that he had received telegrams from the director in which, as I will demonstrate with official documents, the truth was falsified, thus creating a situation that previously didn't exist, so that the serious problem of salaries could be solved by the bullets of the Colombian army.[20]

He then went on to attack the government for seeking a pretext for the massacre as its only means of dealing with the grave social problems represented by the strike.

Gaitán had discovered one of the important elements of the populist formula that would carry him to one success after another: a blend of moral outrage and emotionalism. Fortunately for him, the government had done its utmost to outrage both national pride and the human sensibilities of its own citizens.

How many of Gaitán's charges were true and how many false it is impossible to verify. Certainly his analysis of the events placed all of the blame on the government and the army and none on the actions of the strikers. He even dismissed the government's charge that the strike was actively supported by the communists, although he must have known of their part in it. Perhaps an important indication of the total truth of his charges can be found in his closing statement, when he refused the use of his evidence to bring criminal prosecution against those he indicted because "there can be no justice under so shameful a regime."[21] In the final analysis, the speeches were intended not only to discredit an already tottering government, but to introduce the new hero of the Colombian masses, a hero who had managed to marry his personal cause with that of social justice. In this Gaitán's efforts succeeded admirably. The Liberal newspapers printed scores of letters from all parts of the country applauding his work. Telegrams and letters poured into his office. As late as September 1930 a group of women from Cartago wrote hailing him as the "defender of humanity."[22] Colombians began calling him the Tribune of the People.

The Banana Debates were but one of a series of events which doomed the Conservative party's hegemony and in which Gaitán played a part. In early June 1929 a scandal had erupted in the Bogotá municipal administration over misuse of funds and nepotism. In demonstrations a student was killed by the police. Gaitán was one of the directors of the protest meetings that resulted. He delivered a series of speeches on June 7 in which he attacked government corruption and police violence.[23] In September 1929 another scandal erupted involving corruption by former War Minister Rengifo. Gaitán was appointed vice-president of an investigating commission. When the commission came under attack by the president amid rumors that the congress might be suspended, Gaitán delivered a heated defense of that body. For the first time he also directed his attack against what was to become a favorite target—the oligarchy.[24] Gaitán explained that in the postwar period, when fascists and communists were doing away with representative bodies, parliament was the best defense of the liberty of the people. He claimed that as a moderate socialist he could only defend the "democratic" legislative body despite its defects. He then charged that the "bankers and plutocrats" who were attacking the congress, and who applauded it when it defended their own interests, could not stand the efforts of young congressmen like himself who were restoring the "moral and democratic physiognomy of the country."[25]

Amid these political scandals, the world economic crisis broke upon the Conservative government. Rising unemployment, workers' demonstrations, and the collapse of the Bogotá stock market came within weeks of each other in the fall of 1929. When a faction of nationalist Conservatives, disgusted with governmental impotence and corruption, decided to put up its own candidate for the 1930 presidential election, the Conservative party assured its loss of the presidency.

The Liberal Politician

Gaitán had played a major role in undermining the Conservative government. His position as an important figure in the Liberal party thus was guaranteed. And in the two years after 1930 he rose to the highest positions of leadership in the party, a substantial achievement for a man still in his early thirties. He also became the chief spokesman for the party's youthful left wing in the congress and was elected president of the House of Representatives. But his major legislative efforts were frustrated, so that he turned away from the party in bitterness when seemingly at the peak of prestige and influence.

The circumstances under which the Liberal party elected a president in 1930 almost guaranteed the defeat of the kind of renovating social reforms Gaitán wanted to implement. The Liberal candidate, the aristocratic diplomat Enrique Olaya Herrera, refused to run unless supported by moderate elements of the Conservative party. Once elected, he instituted a Government of National Concentration that provided prominent places for Conservatives. As a practical politician he realized that his administration would be ineffective without the support of the opposition, who still controlled the legislative and judicial branches, and most departmental administrations as well. Himself a man of moderation, Olaya sought to balance the contending parties and ameliorate somewhat the growing tensions between the social classes, now aggravated by severe economic crisis.

His approach was eminently cautious. He eased the anxieties of the upper-class leaderships of both parties by assuring them that there would be no blatantly partisan politics or radical departures in program. For the fiery young leftists of his own party, like Gaitán, there were prominent positions in the government and promises that their time would come. For the discontented masses there were minimal programs of land distribution, public housing, investment in education and health facilities; for the growing middle sectors and those with capital there were debt and mortgage foreclosure prohibitions and new government institutions to provide financial support.[26] All of this was designed to cool heated political passions and calm social unrest. Olaya merely followed the formula devised by him and others in 1910 during another national crisis, when the Republican Union brought together the moderates of both parties to preserve the status quo then threatened in the aftermath of civil war, the dismemberment of Panama, and the dictatorship of Rafael Reyes.[27]

Despite the limitations inherent in Olaya's administration, his election caused delirious happiness among Liberals. There seemed little doubt that a new era had begun; for the first time in forty-five years the party had one of its own in the presidency. Under the dominance of a renovated Liberal party, new programs could be designed to deal with the grave ills besetting the country. In

Olaya the Liberals saw everything the Conservatives were not capable of providing: prestige, practicality, a progressive stance; the capability of forming a secure government supported by a majority; the ability to select men from both parties without factional interference; respectable authority; and a fresh approach to government.[28]

Gaitán, however, was suspicious of Olaya. He was disturbed by Olaya's upper-class background, his Conservative friends and allies, and especially his close connections with North American capital, the Mellon and Rockefeller interests he had so assiduously courted during his ambassadorship in Washington.[29] But out of loyalty to the party, Gaitán campaigned for Olaya through western Colombia. Yet his speeches, while urging votes for the candidate, contained warnings that both parties were far from recognizing the real needs of the country and even farther from possessing the will or the means to do anything about them.[30] The implication in the speeches was that the election of Olaya was but the start of a process.

Gaitán certainly proceeded on that assumption. During the four years of the Olaya administration he introduced a series of reform laws in the House of Representatives designed to deal with the gravest problems afflicting the lower classes and provide the government with the mechanisms necessary for implementing such legislation. None of the Gaitanista measures were accepted, which Gaitán must have known would happen. Therefore, his efforts must be interpreted as an educational process intended to instruct the country in the potentialities of government, and the people in their own interests. It also can be observed that while Gaitán's social legislation failed to pass, he notably contributed to the atmosphere necessary for the successful passage of the López administration reforms between 1934 and 1938.

During the 1930 sessions of the House of Representatives, Gaitán called for state action on behalf of the middle and lower classes, whom he described as almost totally without legal protection. He wanted intervention of the state to control prices and speculation, encourage industrial and agricultural production, and provide legislation on behalf of squatters and other rural workers.[31] He also suggested the lowering of tariffs on foodstuffs in order to ensure an adequate food supply and prevent high prices. A speech on August 21 directed attention to the middle classes, especially public and private employees. Gaitán noted that the existing laws covering workers were not applicable to salaried employees; as a result, the latter were not covered by any protective legislation.

What Gaitán called for was the writing of legislation that would recognize the right of employees in enterprises with more than three employees, to form councils consisting of a representative each of the employees, employer, and municipality.[32] The purpose of the councils was to mediate disputes, wages, working conditions, etc., with appeal possible to labor courts. Within the same law Gaitán asked for an eight-hour working day, accident and health insurance, paid holidays, a monthly bonus each year, and limited labor for women and minors. The law, of course, did not pass, but legislation enacting most of the provisions eventually did become law in Colombia.

Gaitán's appeal to the middle sectors was quite clear. During the speech outlining his legislation he expressed satisfaction that the middle sectors were developing social consciousness. He said that they would "form the vanguard of the socialist forces," a remarkably accurate prediction of the role middle-sector groups would play within his own movement in the 1940s. The major problems of Colombia in the early 1930s, however, were those of land ownership and the condition of the rural population. Most of the congressman's efforts in those years were directed to agrarian problems.

The Colombian land problem had its origins in the Conquest period when the Spanish crown granted land (*mercedes*) and control over labor (*encomienda*) to the conquerors.[33] Although *encomienda* eventually was abolished, the land grants remained. Over the centuries the heirs of the original grantees slowly expanded their holdings through both legal and illegal means, gradually acquiring the best lands and forcing the landless population onto the less fertile mountain slopes.[34]

After achieving its independence, the state recognized private titles while large tracts of land formerly the property of the crown became state property (*baldíos*).[35] A rational system of surveying and land deeding on property transfers had never been established, so that when population pressure in Antoquia in the mid–nineteenth century led to internal migration into unoccupied private lands in south-central Colombia, violence often occurred. However, occupation of state lands was approved if settlers cultivated holdings for a ten-year period.[36] This internal migration resulted in the development of the small-holding coffee sector in the late nineteenth century.

Farther east, in the eastern cordillera sections of Cundinamarca, coffee plantations developed early in the twentieth century, utilizing rural labor that had migrated from Cundinamarca and Boyacá for lack of food.[37] Generally, the workers were provided small plots for subsistence but without the right to plant coffee trees. During the same period large cattle ranches were developing in the Cauca Valley and along the north coast, where the United Fruit Company also became established. These units often encroached on established minifundia.

A rapidly expanding population during the first three decades of the twentieth century, coupled with problems such as erosion, resulted in large-scale land invasions by *colonos* ("squatters"). The government bought some large estates for distribution and resale to *colonos*, but the problem of unclear land titles resulted in endless litigation. However, it became clear that many lands were held without titles, with illegal titles, or conflicting titles.[38] Finally, in 1926 the Supreme Court decided that unless clear title could be demonstrated, land would revert to the state.[39]

By the 1920s peasant organizations had developed in the countryside, aided by militants of the PSR. Strikes for higher wages and better working conditions occurred not only on the United Fruit concession but in the coffee plantations of the western Cundinamarca region as well.[40] The government responded to the strikes with repression but vacillated in the face of the land invasions that were occurring in the Sumapaz region near Bogotá and in the Cauca Valley.

The economic crisis after 1929 gravely aggravated the problem. Many workers lured to the cities by the economic development of the 1920s returned to the countryside when they became unemployed.[41] There were other factors contributing to the unrest in the countryside in the early 1930s. The ascension to power of the Liberals probably stimulated expectations of favorable treatment; the PSR, reorganized as the Communist party in 1930, continued to agitate actively among the rural population in all parts of the country. Pierre Gilhodés, in his excellent account of agrarian struggles in Colombia, noted three major areas of conflict during the years 1930–1931: strikes for better working conditions in the coffee plantation regions of Cundinamarca and in the Cauca Valley; disputes over land ownership and property titles belonging to "absentee landlords who had speculated with public lands, acquired through bonds on the national debt or the special favors of the minister" located primarily in Sumapaz; and conflicts, principally in the southern departments of Tolima and Huila, and in the Sierra Nevada of Santa Marta in the north, where indigenous populations were aided by a Marxist movement "strongly influenced by the Indianist ideology of the Peruvian Mariátegui."[42] Political violence also broke out in the departments of Santander and Boyacá when Liberal politicians, attempting to win a parliamentary majority in 1932, tried to break the narrow Conservative majorities by force and were met with armed resistance.

In this atmosphere of widespread rural unrest Gaitán began a series of congressional speeches in August 1930 that focused on the problems of *colonos* and land ownership. He provided detailed information on abuses of *colonos* by private landowners who were receiving at least the tacit support of the state. He pointed out that in Caldas and the small-holding coffee areas where there was a pattern of property dispersion, there were generally prosperous and contented farmers.[43] What he wanted was the recognition that productive squatters be recognized as legitimate owners and receive the protection of the state. He warned that the continuation of the intolerable conditions in the countryside, abetted by an indifferent or hostile state, would lead to accelerating violence. He concluded by asking the government to enforce existing laws recognizing squatters' rights and support new laws extending protection.

But the problem of land ownership could not be dealt with effectively without changing the existing constitution. Article 31 of the constitution of 1886 stated that public rights had precedence over private rights, but the following article maintained that only in grave circumstances could there be "forceable alienation" of property.[44] These circumstances could only be defined by legislative action, with the owner indemnified before expropriation took place. Further, article 34 stated that confiscation could not be imposed. The state, which could not even deal effectively with the title problems of the few private lands it had attempted to buy, thus could not legally carry out a meaningful land policy based upon expropriation.

Gaitán's solution was to call for an amendment to the constitution of 1886 that would establish "the social function of property."[45] Such an amendment would provide a legal basis for state intervention not only to solve the land problem, but to provide protection for workers in their unequal conflicts with owners. Obviously, definition of property as having a social function was a radical but neat method of opening the way to widespread state intervention in every aspect of Colombian life, depending upon the inclination of the government. Gaitán, with a single stroke, attempted to undercut the legal concepts on which the property relationships of the bourgeois society rested. And in the speech in support of his amendment, he used the very arguments usually spoken by his opponents. He claimed that he wanted to help the individual compete more effectively by giving him the support of the state. He added that private monopolization of land, labor, and capital was inhibiting the natural development of the individual.

At this point President Olaya personally intervened. According to Osorio, the young congressman suddenly became the center of presidential attention. The suave, sophisticated Olaya convinced Gaitán—if he really needed convincing—that, while Olaya agreed with the proposed amendment, it was premature, the opposition was too powerful, there were political reasons why it and Gaitán's other proposals could not pass. As a result Gaitán gave up attempting to have his legislation made law; however, he temporarily accepted the friendship and support of Olaya, perhaps as a means to furthering his own ambitions. One important consequence was his election to the Liberal Party Directorate in 1931, following his reelection to the House of Representatives with the help of Olaya.[46] Viewed in retrospect, Gaitán's strategy during these years becomes clear. He was operating on two fronts: through the congress that provided a national forum for educating the people; and through the Liberal party, which he was attempting to transform into a social democratic movement from within.

Despite Olaya's dissuasion on the issue of constitutional reform, Gaitán continued to agitate for social reform legislation in the congressional sessions from 1931 through 1934. Most of his efforts were directed toward agrarian reform and related legislation to improve the lives of the rural population. He reiterated the need for land distribution, recognition of squatters' rights, equitable work contracts for rural laborers, financial credits, technical aid, and health and educational facilities. But he also spoke out on other important issues. In June 1931, during debates over oil concessions to North American companies, he condemned the contracts as prejudicial to Colombian interests because they were too liberal and posed a threat to national agricultural interests in the concession region.[47] He said that Colombia was in danger of becoming a pawn in a gigantic chess game between world petroleum powers and must defend its interests against foreign imperialism.

If he could not get agrarian or defensive economic legislation passed, what was the purpose of the agitation? In an article titled "Individualism and Socialism" he revealed some of his thoughts.[48] He pointed out that the first task in Colombia was the creation of a "state of soul" or revolutionary consciousness among the masses. In his view the three bases of revolution were: temperament, idea, and procedure. Temperament was what Gaitán was attempting to create with his agitation, an educational task that consisted of bringing to the forums of public life a discussion of social problems and methods for dealing with them. In speeches in the national congress and throughout the country Gaitán continuously returned to his theme of changing the orientation of the state from individualist to collective as the first step toward dealing with social problems, while urging the people to recognize their crucial role in that process.

The second base of revolution—idea—was socialism: "Liberalism has to become socialist or it is condemned to perish ideologically. Our revolution has to be very distinct, very different, but inspired by socialist sensibility and criteria."[49] The third base—procedure—consisted of mobilizing the masses of both parties in a class movement: "The Liberal capitalists are more conservative than the Conservatives. . . . There are conservatives in both parties. But Liberalism has moved to the left: its workers, *campesinos,* middle class, university students, and intellectuals are sincere leftists, passionate in their socialist beliefs, and nothing will detain them. And to their ranks will come the phalanx of Conservative workers."[50] He continued to believe in the revolutionary potential of the Liberal party and as a member of the directorate worked toward that end. While political education defined his activities in congress, transforming Liberalism was his goal as a party leader.

In a speech given shortly after his elevation to the directorate, Gaitán defined the tasks of Liberalism. He wanted the party to organize itself with special reference to the masses and orient its platforms to what he called the "new social and economic realities." Because politicians had no sense of the electorate except during elections and soon forgot their responsibilities, he wanted to impose a permanent organizational structure that would put the party in continuous contact with the people. He suggested the reorganization of the leadership on a general staff system, from the national to the municipal levels. At the local levels, militia-type units would be developed for purposes of discipline and a sense of collectivity. He went so far as to suggest a hymn, uniforms, insignias, and decorations to stimulate a constant sense of the cause. Further, he wanted the establishment in Bogotá and all important cities of *Casas Liberales* for offices, conferences, and educational programs, where party leaders would be available for daily contact with members. He suggested a national Liberal census to determine the true strength of the party and aid it in its work. Finally, he called for the establishment of a national Liberal fund to provide financial support for the party's organization and electoral efforts.[51]

These ambitious schemes were patterned after practices he had witnessed in Italy; although they may also have been borrowed from the Peruvian APRA, with which he was familiar. He managed to put some of them into effect when he formed UNIR and, later, organized his movement during the 1940's; however, there was no notable response from other Liberal leaders. They probably understood that within the kind of party Gaitán was attempting to create there would be a diminished role for them.

There were good reasons for them to believe this. In his capacity as a member of the Liberal leadership Gaitán made trips through western Colombia in December 1931, January 1932, and to the north coast in July 1932. While he continued his usual pleas for substantial economic and social reforms, much of the content of his speeches had to do with renovating Liberalism. In Barranquilla he said that he wanted to rid both parties of "notables" and make them truly mass democratic organizations where there would be no place for personal aggrandizement or ambition.[52] In Cali he appealed to the youth of the party to support the programs that the old leaders were incapable of implementing. He deplored the fact that the old leaders were attempting to cover up the great ferment in the party.[53] In a letter to left-Liberals Plinio Mendoza and Darío Samper, Gaitán wrote that the time was ripe for rebuilding Liberalism "with new ideas and a sincere devotion for practicing them."[54]

Provincial newspaper accounts of Gaitán's trips indicate that he was succeeding in arousing the support of the traditional Liberal electorate for his ideas.[55] Wherever he spoke he managed to attract sizeable audiences. Editorial comments generally were favorable; according to *El Ideal* of Tumaco, "Gaitán is the precurser of a new Liberalism, more humane and more sincere . . . he is the defender of the people, the passionate condemner of slavery, who has broken the hereditary prejudice of the middle ages, of the feudal lord, and who teaches of social horizons free and just."[56] Several dozens of letters from this period in the Gaitán Papers applaud and encourage his efforts to reconstruct Liberalism. The source of this correspondence was significant: usually not party chiefs but local groups of party members and workers. For example, a letter from the rural Liberal Committee of Tequendama thanked him for his work in support of the proletariat.[57] Another letter from the Workers' Directorate of the Department of Atlántico pledged Gaitán "all possible help in his political struggles."[58]

By the summer of 1932 it was evident that Gaitán was causing widespread ferment, and the threat of division, within the Liberal party. His activities and the support he received in the congress and party from other members of the Liberal left brought a sharp reaction from party regulars.[59]

When on June 28 at the opening session of the House of Representatives he issued a "Manifesto to the Leftists," calling for their support to amend the constitution, claiming that "the majority of the people support me in this effort because now they have consciousness," *El Tiempo* responded for Gaitán's opposition within the party. An editorial warned that Gaitán had sown the seeds of division between the Liberals and the proletariat. It claimed that his trips through the country had been directed against the Liberal bourgeoisie, "precisely those who for the past twenty-five years have generated the wealth of the country." The party had lost its unity because many of its members were seduced by leftism; Gaitán was going dangerously far on the road to communism, but the nonsocialist Liberal party would not accompany him. Finally, the editorial called for a convention to define the programs of Liberalism. Even if Gaitán were left out, the party would be unified.[60] Another newspaper, *El País*, mentioned the danger of a Liberal split because if Gaitán were expelled from the party, twenty-nine congressmen would follow him out if necessary. *El País* also noted that the president was displeased with the party activities of Gaitán and wanted a convention, presumably to discipline or expel him.[61]

The rift between Gaitán and the Liberal leadership, despite public accounts to the contrary, deepened through the summer of 1932.[62] In August, Gaitán launched a direct attack on the government in the House, accusing the administration of the massacre of *campesinos*. He called democracy in Colombia a farce and claimed that the true country was not in the government but in the provinces with the people. And, for the first time, he publicly defended the communists, despite the fact that he was "an enemy of their ideas." Once again he made an impassioned plea for the transformation of Liberalism into a "revolutionary party."[63]

The Gaitanista attack was but one of several problems that affected the stability of the Olaya administration at midpoint. Agrarian unrest continued despite harsh repression by local officials. A Conservative party increasingly under the influence of right-wing nationalists was attacking the government. In

1932 Laureano Gómez returned from his ambassadorial post in Berlin to add his voice to an aggressive Conservatism. In July, from his seat in the Senate, he launched a campaign accusing the Liberals of "selling out the national interests" and of widespread corruption in administration. Gómez very shrewdly refrained from attacking the president directly, but focused his attentions on the Liberals and especially their Conservative allies. His intention was to weaken the Conservative party internally so that he could gain control of it and install his virulently rightist, nationalist line.[64]

The Gaitán and Gómez attacks from left and right contributed to a polarization of political forces in the country, and by the fall of 1932 the survival of the government was in question. Fortunately for the Olaya administration, a conflict broke out with Peru over territory in the distant Amazon region. Gómez gave up his attacks with the proclamation, "War, war externally; peace, peace internally."[65] Gaitán conveniently accepted a diplomatic mission to explain Colombia's position in Central America, Mexico, and the United States.[66]

With all political groups in the country except the Communists rallying to the national cause, Gaitán could hardly do otherwise, especially when his nationalist sentiments had been expressed so often in the congress and on the hustings. However, his absence from the country enabled his opponents within the party to move against him. The Liberal leadership removed his name from the electoral lists for 1933, and Gaitán was forced to run for departmental assemblies in Antioquia and Cundinamarca on dissident lists supported by workers, revolutionary socialists, and anarcho-syndicalists.[67] By the time of his return to Colombia in the spring of 1933 he was beset on all sides: he had fallen out with Olaya over Bogotá municipal planning (Gaitán had been a member of the city council almost continuously since 1930); he was opposed by Alfonso López within the Liberal directorate because López feared that Gaitán might interfere with his presidential ambitions; he was under attack by Eduardo Santos, director of *El Tiempo* and leader of the Liberal moderates; and was opposed by the right-wing Conservative, Laureano Gómez, who was in total ideological disagreement with Gaitán's socialist leanings.[68] Accordingly, Gaitán decided to launch his own political movement. The idea had been germinating since his trip to Mexico, where he had been impressed by the workings of the Mexican Partido Nacional Revolucionario.[69]

In his early political years, Gaitán found his constituency and developed his basic political techniques. The strike against the United Fruit Company provided him with his first major opportunity to attract attention. After he had exposed the scandalous measures used by the administration to repress the strike, the debate in the House of Representatives gave him national prominence. He first developed here part of the populist formula of blending moral outrage and emotionalism, using the congress for educational purposes, and concretizing issues to erode the authority of the oligarchy. Though he began during this time to see the middle sectors as allies, he recognized the land problem—and that of the rural population—as the most burning issue. In connection with that problem he broached his idea of the social function of property. Another strategy formulated during these years was the aim of molding the Liberal party ideologically from within. Finally, he had focused his thinking on three active principles: (1) the creation of a "state of mind" or revolutionary consciousness among the broad public; (2) the positing of the idea—socialism; and (3) the procedure of mobilizing the electorate of both parties into a mass movement.

6

The Revolutionary Leftist National Union

Gaitán's decision to move outside of traditional political entities was not impulsive. It was the result of his frustration at having failed to effect any significant internal transformation of the Liberal party. Though he knew, as a result of his trips throughout the country, that popular sentiment existed within the party for a fundamental reorientation of its leadership and programs, he understood that the entrenched, traditional groups who dominated Liberalism at all levels made such an initiative impossible. Further, Gaitán's isolation within the party and the open hostility of its national leaders to what he had come to represent meant that he would have to seek an alternative if he wanted to remain politically active and continue his educative efforts to raise the popular political consciousness.

In late April 1933 Gaitán, Carlos Arango Vélez, a longtime admirer of Lenin, and other left-Liberals held a series of meetings to determine what political course to follow.[1] On April 29 they issued a manifesto expressing dissatisfaction with the existing Liberal leadership and called for the creation of a national, radical-leftist leadership independent of the other political entities.[2] What they intended was the establishment of a federation of departmental groups of progressive Liberals and sympathizers headed by local leaders such as Gaitán in Cundinamarca, Arango Vélez in Tolima, and Plinio Mendoza Neira in Boyacá. The goal was to establish the "base for a campaign of social agitation that would develop in Colombians a class consciousness."[3] However, the scheme fell through because several of the participants did not want to lose their official positions, the result of their Liberal affiliations. Plinio Mendoza wrote to Gaitán from Tunja, Boyacá, that he would maintain loyalty to the Liberal party although in accord with Gaitán's objectives.[4]

Although more isolated than ever, Gaitán went ahead with his efforts to organize an independent movement. In cooperation with close friends and associates, who formed the movement's leadership, Gaitán began the organization of what became the Revolutionary Leftist National Union (Unión Nacional Izquierdista Revolucionaria—UNIR).[5] The founding "Acta" of UNIR announced the "struggle for socialism, because the country cannot be developed on the basis of individualist criteria," and the struggle against all unethical systems or parties in the country. It was to be not a political party but a "free organization tending only to the realization of its ends," which it defined as building cooperation and solidarity in the country. The slogan "Death to the past, revolution toward the future," was adopted.[6]

With his usual enthusiasm Gaitán began feverishly to build the movement. He gave up his now lucrative law practice, contributed all of his available funds, and set out on an extensive organizing tour to explain the nature and objectives of UNIR. He aimed his appeals primarily at workers, *campesinos*, small merchants, students, and disaffected intellectuals—the same groups whose support he later would seek in his presidential campaign.[7]

UNIR had little difficulty attracting members. By the end of 1933 Gaitán claimed that the movement had twenty thousand members in Cundinamarca.[8] Although that figure perhaps was exaggerated, the numbers of telegrams and letters in the Gaitán Papers proclaiming "adhesion" to UNIR indicate that the membership in Cundinamarca, where UNIR was strongest, exceeded seven thousand. Other strongholds were in the departments of Huila, Tolima, Caldas, Valle, Antioquia, Santander del Sur, and Atlántico on the north coast. These were areas that were experiencing rural unrest or where there were sizeable concentrations of industrial, transport, and port workers.

Although small groups, generally numbering ten to thirty persons, affiliated themselves with UNIR independently, many joined as members of an occupation or organization. In June 1934, 2,000 workers from Socorro in Santander joined UNIR and established a center there. Six hundred *campesinos* from Tolima joined as a body, as did 120 miners from Antioquia. In Bogatá, UNIR organized all of the 150 workers of the National Chocolate Factory, more than 150 garment workers, and the workers of the electric generating plant. In cities such as Girardot, Neiva, Ibagué, Cartago, Santa Marta, and Buenaventura, UNIR attracted teamsters, shoemakers, laborers, and dock workers—many of whom declared themselves disenchanted with Liberalism. In Cali, UNIR established a National Transport Federation for the entire department of Valle, an organization that was strong enough to send support to striking UNIR-affiliated laborers in Girardot.[9]

UNIR organizers did not limit their efforts to occupation groups. Attempts were made to establish UNIR *casas* in the poorer neighborhoods of towns and cities. In Antioquia, under the leadership of Luis Emiro Mejía, UNIR made organizing efforts in almost every populated area. In the northern port of Barranquilla, UNIR propaganda and organization committees were established in the popular neighborhoods and were attracting small merchants and students in addition to workers. By April 1934 the secretary general of UNIR for the north coast, Dr. Ramón Castro González, said that UNIR there was strong enough to put up candidates for the departmental assembly, and possibly for the House of Representatives in alliance with Liberals.[10] A UNIR newspaper, *El Socialista,* also was being prepared for distribution on the north coast.

According to one critical author, UNIR also attracted many Liberals who were sympathetic to communism but did not join the party for "sentimental or bureaucratic motives, or out of human respect."[11] However, there was no love lost between UNIR and the Colombian Communist party. They competed for members among the same social classes, and frequently fought. UNIR activists battled Communists in the coffee-growing regions of western Cundinamarca, where they both had strongholds.[12] In Girardot, UNIR workers fought to prevent Communists from taking over the railroad workers' union.[13] In August 1933 the Communist party stated, "Our principal enemy is the so-called leftist tendency of the Liberals and Uniristas."[14]

In organizing UNIR, Gaitán closely followed techniques he had witnessed in Fascist Italy.[15] The techniques provided for discipline, ease of communication, and the capacity for rapid mobilization. The organizational style was new in Colombia and apparently effective, especially in matters of discipline, according to a member of the UNIR directorate. The basic unit was a team consisting of five members who elected a captain to represent them before the UNIR legion, made up of ten teams. Each legion elected its own captain.[16] Orders came down to the legions from the Central Committee, comprised of national representatives of UNIR. However, the work and discipline of the committee was controlled by the Directing Commission, the real center of UNIR power, headed by Gaitán and his lieutenants. Other commissions reporting to the Directing Commission were: Organization, responsible for memberships, statutes, and internal control; Defense, to protect members against reprisals from employers and other political groups; Agitation and Strikes, to study working conditions, organize and promote strikes; Propaganda; and Education, charged with "establishing a class consciousness and providing a revolutionary orientation."[17]

An important part of the UNIR organization was the *Casa Unirista.* The one in Bogotá had a library, lecture rooms, and administrative offices where Uniristas could gather and meet with the leadership. Eventually UNIR managed to establish *casas* in cities where the movement had major strength, such as Barranquilla, Medellín, Pereira, and Cartagena. In addition to movement activities, the *casas* provided services to members and their families. The Bogotá *casa* had a day school for children; provided free professional services; taught workers to read, write, and do simple arithmetic; developed a special course for elementary teachers; and provided activities oriented to the "economic liberation" of Colombian women through the UNIR Feminist Legion, which had 220 members.[18] All of these activities were supported by funds contributed by members according to financial ability.

Gaitán was the principal leader who gave UNIR its direction, supported by loyal lieutenants like Guillermo Hernández Rodríguez, Roberto París Gaitán, and F. López Giraldo.[19] These men were members of the middle class who did not have national political followings prior to their association with UNIR. Leaders with similar backgrounds were selected to head the organization in the provinces, although Gaitán made an effort to choose provincial leaders with some reputation such as Dr. César González Londoño, who represented railroad workers in Antioquia, and directed UNIR in western Colombia; and Dr. Trino Mantilla Gómez, a well-known lawyer who headed UNIR in Santander del Sur.[20]

There is evidence that Gaitán ran UNIR with a heavy hand. He dismissed members when they openly questioned his policies and imposed a strict regime on all employees. Most of the Friday "educational" conferences the movement provided in Bogotá were conducted by Gaitán himself.[21] Directives to movement members published in the newspaper *Unirismo* were sharp statements on the necessity for increased organizational work, discipline, and study.[22] Democracy within the movement appeared to function primarily at the local level. Indeed, as will be seen, it was Gaitán's attempt to impose a particular line that was a factor in UNIR's dissolution.

UNIR's primary medium of communication and information was its weekly tabloid newspaper, *Unirismo*. Although it did not appear until a year after the movement was founded, *Unirismo* rapidly reached a circulation of 15,000 and a claim to being the third largest newspaper in the country in terms of national readership.[23] *Unirismo* carried regular national and international news, political commentary, articles by guest columnists like Vicente Lombardo Toledano, revolutionary drawings by David Siquieros and other painters, and large amounts of UNIR news sent in by correspondents from throughout the country. Significant space was devoted to the printing of letters and telegrams of adhesion, with full lists of names included. This obviously was an appeal to the pride of local readers who could see their messages and names appear in a nationally circulated newspaper. In addition to *Unirismo,* which was distributed from Bogotá , regional UNIR newspapers were published under various names in Socorro, Santander; Medellín, Antioquia; Barranquilla, Atlántico; Campoalegre, Huila; and Pereria, then a part of Caldas.[24] All of these regional papers, like the organizational work, were funded locally. They were perhaps the best representations of the local enthusiasms of UNIR adherents.

During a March 1934 session of the Cundinamarca assembly Gaitán said, "Unirismo is not a political party. Unirismo is an autonomous, independent force of preparation and struggle, guarding the firm principles of the left."[25] However, despite Gaitán's disclaimer, UNIR developed all the trappings of a modern political party, including a program. *The Manifesto of Unirismo,* developed entirely by Gaitán, was a refinement and elaboration of many of the ideas expressed in *Socialist Ideas*. Gaitán started with the premise that the "individualist criteria" that governed Colombian society no longer were tenable, especially in politics.

> Political activity today is not based upon the philosophical postulates which describe the differences between the great historical forces of conservatism and liberalism, but upon distinct problems; the economic and the social. Regarding these, liberal and conservative leaders are in agreement, creating enormous discord and confusion of ideas. For under different names, that formerly corresponded to different ideologies, struggle two forces that are basically equal; politics and the rotation of parties in power concern merely possession of government office, a simple bureaucratic change.[26]

In Gaitán's view this self-seeking but deceptive politics practiced by a small minority of privileged individuals and interest groups, the directing class and owners of capital, had to be replaced. The task of UNIR was to educate the people toward that end. The program and platform of UNIR embodied the "socialist criteria" that were to replace the discredited, archaic "individualist criteria."

In *The Manifesto of Unirismo* Gaitán made a distinction between program and platform. The program "is the overall orientation; it outlines fundamental criteria on fundamental issues" (p. 219). It was a guide to action. The political platform, on the other hand, listed specific activities to achieve specific ends, stages that would be superseded in the progress toward fulfilling the overall program.

The fundamental points of the program were: (1) realities determine concepts, not the reverse; (2) the basic reality is economic; (3) the bases of politics therefore are economic relationships and not abstract principles; (4) there are two contending forces—the owners of the means of production and those who possess only labor; (5) in this struggle the state is the arbiter that intervenes in the economic and social process to ensure social justice and prevent exploitation of man by man; (6) the state must function according to the democratic principle, in favor of the majority, who in Colombia are the dispossessed, and provide equality for all; (7) the realization of equality, especially in the all-important economic area, requires a planned, regulated economy and the intervention of the state; (8) the intervention of the state is based upon a social criterion, that is, socialism of the state (pp. 220–24).

The UNIR platform as elaborated by Gaitán followed closely the lines suggested by the program. It had three parts: economic life, social life, and state structure.

Economic life. The state was to be the decisive element in the economic life of the nation. Its function was to provide overall planning and direction of the economy, intervention and investment when necessary, and regulation and supervision of the various economic components, such as private corporations, banking and credit institutions, and commercial and agricultural enterprises. An important role was that of ensuring the balanced development of the economy throughout the country. Although private capital was not excluded, it was to be restricted. The state could intervene in the financial operations of private enterprises, regulate and control profits, and establish price controls on foodstuffs and basic commodities. Additionally, transport and communication systems and public services were to be nationalized. Taxes were to be levied upon inheritance, income, land, and unutilized wealth (pp. 237–38, 241–42).

Two related primary concerns of the Uniristas were the system of land tenure and the condition of the rural population. The first was to be reorganized by a sweeping agrarian reform based upon the principle that the land belongs to those who work it. Noncultivated public and private lands were to be distributed; *colonos* who had worked land for five years or more without challenge were to receive title. Extensive labor legislation was to be passed protecting the rights of rural laborers. Land ownership was to be limited to 1,000 hectares or less, depending upon the geographical region. Additionally, the state was to provide technical and financial support for farmers, develop the economic infrastructure of the countryside, organize cooperatives, and provide for the education, health, culture, and general welfare of the rural population (pp. 238–39).

In relation to labor the state also had a central role. It was to organize a social security system funded by a percentage of the profits of economic enterprises. In its labor legislation it was to provide recognition and protection of the right of workers to organize; establish labor courts with worker representation; and establish workers' councils to participate in management (pp. 240, 245).

Social life. In this area Gaitán's primary interest, as might be expected, was education. He developed an ambitious plan that would affect virtually the entire population. First, he sought to reorient education to technical, vocational, and professional training to provide the kind of personnel necessary for a modernizing country. Second, he would centralize control over education by the state, which would provide supervision and orientation. Third, education would be free at all levels, and mandatory through primary grades. Fourth, a national university would be established with departmental divisions, primarily devoted to technical education; special educational institutes would include popular universities, traveling libraries, health centers, etc. (pp. 243–44).

In other areas of social life, the manifesto called for the centralization and control of social welfare by the state, abolition of legal differences between legitimate and illegitimate children, establishment of divorce, and the legal recognition of women's equality with men (pp. 244–45).

State structure.   A major contention of Uniristas was that the state was a prize to be sought and won for the wealth and benefits that derived from it. In the first stage, Gaitán wanted to change this bureaucratic orientation and make the state not only the representative of all classes, but especially the defender of those who needed it most. He wanted to provide it with an economic rather than a political character by having representative bodies elected by economic units, such as trade unions and production associations. To ensure the highest technical capacities, a civil service based upon merit and experience would be established, not only for the executive agencies, but for the separate judicial branch. However, in a departure from nineteenth-century liberal philosophy, he called for a centralized state that could carry out effective planning and implementation of policies, above all in the economic area.

Following the Mexican model, he called for new legislation establishing, for example, commercial codes that allowed rapid state intervention as needed. There also would be separate penal, labor, and *campesino* codes, which did not exist under the present system. Finally, constitutional reform was proposed that would limit presidential power in Colombia, forcing governments to be more responsive to the public interests represented in the congress and to live up to the programs of the political parties. Further, ministers and the heads of high public agencies would be accountable to the congress as well as to the president. The essence of the constitutional reform was to make all governmental agencies directly responsible to the representatives of the economic classes and sectors (pp. 245–51).

The UNIR program and platform reflected diverse ideological currents, an indication of the multiple influences working upon the author. While the basic assumptions were Marxist, according to Gaitán, there were elements of Italian corporatism and, in the judicial approach, positivism. Peruvian APRA influences were discernable in the agrarian proposals; the ideas on legal codification were borrowed from the Mexican experience. Finally, even the "socialism of the state" concept had been proposed early in the twentieth century by the Colombian liberal thinker, Rafael Uribe Uribe. What Gaitán did was adapt from all of these what he thought would fit the Colombian reality. The originality of the proposals was that they offered for the first time a comprehensive alternative to the established ideologies. What the effects would have been had they been implemented can only be guessed at; undoubtedly, they would have been revolutionary. If in fact the program and platform could have been implemented in Colombia of the 1930s, is another question. Many of the proposals, especially concerning the role of the state, required a higher level of technical competence than the society then was capable of producing. It probably is correct to regard the manifesto as an educational document, a blueprint of possibilities, an answer to critics that UNIR had no program, and a guide to action.

The influence of the manifesto upon Uniristas is debatable. Although *Unirismo* discussed aspects of them in its columns and editorials,[27] the newspaper devoted most of its space to current politics and UNIR activities rather than to ideological debates. The day-to-day problems of the movement —absorbing enough—occupied most of the attention of active Uniristas. The membership, disenchanted with the existing parties, was attracted by the personality and reputation of Gaitán. For the majority—the rural Uniristas— the attraction of the movement was its willingness to struggle for their concrete interests.

The UNIR convention that met in April 1935 did not deal extensively with ideology, but concentrated on tactical problems.[28] Although in his address to the convention Gaitán said that "the forces of the left in Colombia lacked a concrete revolutionary program," he devoted most of his speech to analyzing the political situation in the country, which he described as favorable to the growth of the movement.[29] The resolutions that resulted from the convention dealt primarily with organizational matters. Emphasis was to be placed on the establishment of departmental UNIR organizations, the formation of "revolutionary unions," the training of cadres, and the political education of adherents.[30] Since the delegates to the convention were almost entirely *campesinos* and workers, this was the most practical approach. The major concern during the convention sessions was the land problem which, of course, was the central issue for UNIR.

Since its founding in 1933 UNIR had devoted most of its energies to dealing with problems of land tenure and rural welfare. By the spring of 1935 Unirista influence was strong in several coffee-growing areas of western Cundinamarca and eastern Tolima.[31] The movement had successfully organized agitation, strikes, land invasions, unions, and *campesino* pressure on landowners in the region. Although only one of their land invasions resulted in legal recognition with title, Unirista success in stirring the population of the region, combined with Gaitán's agrarian proposals in the legislature that gained national attention, brought support from agrarian unions throughout the country.[32] Conditions were ripe for the kind of agitation the movement practiced. The coffee-producing region where UNIR was strongest was characterized by large-scale production units that monopolized the best lands. During 1933–1935 UNIR supported the demands of tenant farmers on these units to grow their own coffee trees, a demand refused by owners who feared the effect of a cash crop upon their labor force.[33] The Uniristas also supported the efforts of laborers brought in during the harvest to obtain better wages and working conditions.[34] Another major area of Unirista activity was encouragement and support of the numerous squatters on unutilized private lands who had returned to the countryside following the economic collapse of 1929.

The result of this activity was what Albert Hirschman termed a "revolution." In the eight years following 1932 the number of coffee farms in Cundinamarca and Tolima more than doubled as big landowners abandoned their properties, made settlements with *campesinos,* or saw their lands seized. Although not all of this was directly attributable to UNIR, there is no question that the movement played a large role in encouraging the *campesinos* in their quest for land.[35] However, these successes were not without their price. From the late twenties through the mid-thirties the coffee zone was the scene of widespread violence. The landowners, usually aided by the police, resisted the efforts of the *campesinos* to plant coffee trees, forceably expelled renters who declared themselves settlers and refused to pay rent, and evicted *colonos* who had settled on private —and sometimes public—lands.[36] Interviews by Gloria Gaitán de Valencia with *campesinos* who lived in the zone at the time revealed that in several areas a veritable state of terror existed. *Campesinos* were forced to meet secretly at night out of fear of landowner reprisals; the coffee-growing corporations that employed large-scale labor during the harvest sometimes forced *campesinos* into work gangs, while providing minimal food and shelter.[37]

Uniristas naturally were attacked. *Campesinos* organized by UNIR attempted to occupy the hacienda Tolima in the department of that name in early August 1934. Most of the 60,000-acre hacienda was unused. The police intervened, killing seventeen and forcing the others off the land. An editorial in *Unirismo* denouncing the massacre noted that thirty-four Uniristas had been killed and hundreds hurt, with many houses burned and property destroyed, in various rural conflicts.[38] In Socorro the UNIR secretary general of the city, Pedro Elias Jurado, was assassinated and several other Uniristas wounded.[39] *Unirismo* reported in various issues attacks on *Casas Uniristas* in Baranquilla, Cartagena, Ibagué; injuries and destruction of property; the intimidation of members; arbitrary arrests; and the disruption of the circulation of *Unirismo*.[40] These incidents often were supported by the police. However, not all of the action appeared to be the responsibility of police and landowners. *El Espec-tador* reported on June 25, 1934, that a battle took place between Uniristas and police on the hacienda El Chocó near Fusagasugá. Uniristas allegedly cut telephone lines, blocked roads, and attacked the police.[41] On this same hacienda the *campesinos* later received titles through court action.

The major conflict between Uniristas and the authorities occurred in the town of Fusagasugá on February 4, 1934. The town was the main center of Unirista activity in the coffee zone, and several Uniristas sat on the municipal council. On February 3, the area's UNIR leader, the attorney Dr. J. A. Concha y Venegas, asked Gaitán to attend a rally in the city to shore up the morale of Uniristas, who were experiencing difficulties with the police, and to rally support for the paving of roads.[42] Two thousand *campesinos* from the surrounding region assembled in the town square the next day, a Sunday, to hear Gaitán. Although the assembly technically was illegal because the governor of Cundinamarca had prohibited Sunday political rallies around election time, Gaitán considered the decision arbitrary. As he began to speak the police intervened. The Uniristas protested and refused to leave the square. Then groups of Liberals rushed into the square and attacked the Uniristas. In the ensuing battle four Uniristas were killed, others were wounded, and Gaitán was beseiged in the house of Concha, where a gun battle took place between Uniristas and Liberals.[43] According to Gaitán, the reason for the attack was Liberal dismay over UNIR's success in the municipal elections, which had provided the council with enough votes to take over the direction of the town's finances "from the few notable citizens who had been accustomed to administering them," and allowed a lowering of taxes.[44]

The battle of Fusagasugá and the near assassination of Gaitán caused shock throughout the country. The size of the confrontation focused attention on the agrarian problem as no series of small incidents could have done. The secretary of Cundinamarca, Carlos Lleras Restrepo, urged parcelization in the area despite the resistance of landowners. In the hope of cooling the situation, the national congress was moved to act on some agrarian legislation that had previously been shelved.[45] But the greatest impact of the battle was upon UNIR itself. New pledges of support came in from all over the country, and the membership increased after the incident.[46]

Although UNIR concentrated most of its attention on rural problems, it was to a lesser degree involved in urban labor activities, organizing workers in Bogotá and other major cities. In the capital, Uniristas supported strikes by brewers and laborers. During the summer of 1934 Gaitán himself led a major strike of UNIR-affiliated railroad workers in Medellín, Antioquia, that was accompanied by violence. After strikers had been fired on by police, the workers sent an empty locomotive under full steam crashing into the railroad station, causing a scene of "spectacular fire, smoke and noise," according to a witness.[47] In August and September 1934 Gaitán attempted to organize another railroad strike in Cali, Valle. However, that effort failed when only 30 percent of the workers supported the strike after the company increased wages and benefits.[48]

The lack of more than marginal success in organizing urban workers reflected a serious weakness of UNIR. Most of its resources were concentrated in rural areas, and those within a limited geographical area. As a result, urban workers in the movement felt ignored. One delegation of teamsters from the town of Armenia who visited UNIR headquarters complained to Gaitán that their interests were being forgotten as a result of UNIR's attention to *campesinos*.[49] Similar grievances from other worker groups are found in the Gaitán Papers. Gaitán, in attempting to reach both urban and rural workers, extended the movement beyond its capacities. He seemed content to recognize UNIR affiliates without concern for their ability to function effectively.

Another major internal problem was lack of firm direction from headquarters in Bogotá to the more distant affiliates. The highly centralized direction worked effectively where Gaitán was able to oversee day-to-day operations and had a personal knowledge upon which to make decisions, especially in Cundinamarca. However, when he could not provide this leadership, but still insisted on close control, serious difficulties arose. The poor communications system in the country was partly to blame, but apparently the leadership did not take this into account. The highly personalist nature of Gaitán's style and the impossible demands upon him to perform in all areas at once occasionally caused confusion and paralysis in the provinces. Letters from UNIR departmental leaders in Cartagena, Bucaramanga, and Medellín attest to this problem. They complained of "lack of orientation" and "lethargy" in the central leadership.[50]

These problems may have been symptomatic of a graver problem: the long-term commitment of Gaitán to UNIR. As early as October 1934, less than a year and a half after the founding of UNIR, rumors began circulating about Gaitán's reintegration into the Liberal party. He believed the rumors serious enough to repudiate them in the November 1, 1934, edition of *Unirismo*. He repeated his frequently stated claim that UNIR and its leadership did not have electoral ambitions. He said that the purpose of UNIR was to study, analyze, and agitate, and he believed that the movement had succeeded in considerably altering the national perception of policies which differed from the outworn conservative formulas. However, he also claimed that there were enemies within UNIR and that the movement was experiencing economic difficulties, in part caused by fraudulent use of *Unirismo* funds. The editorial of the same day also denied that UNIR "would play the electoral game." Yet the very next day, in an interview with *El Tiempo,* Gaitán obliquely suggested that the basis for an agreement between the Liberals and Uniristas existed. He thought the country was ready for making substantial reforms and added that in a country where there was no informed public opinion, a government could not be made of the people, but for the people.

It was apparent by the winter of 1935 that Gaitán was seeking an alliance with the Liberals. The real question was on what terms. And what would become of UNIR? There was a sizeable faction of Uniristas, headed by Fermín López Giraldo, which either wanted to keep the movement out of elections it could not win, or insisted that any political alliance had to be made on the basis of guarantees of honest elections and progressive programs.[51] Although Gaitán had kept UNIR out of major involvement in elections, there was some precedent for entering them. In municipal elections in October 1933 Uniristas had won three of seven council seats in Fusagasugá and had made a considerable show of strength in other municipalities of Cundinamarca.[52]

The issue of elections was widely discussed at the Unirista convention in April, and the sentiment was for participation. This view also prevailed in Antioquia and on the north coast.[53] But despite majority opinion Gaitán insisted on abstention because "there are authorities in Cundinamarca and Tolima who do not offer UNIR any kind of guarantees." However, majority opinion prevailed and the movement ran candidates for departmental assemblies on May 6 in Antioquia, Tolima, and Cundinamarca. But the split was evident in UNIR's poor showing. Its candidates secured only 3,800 votes out of more than 475,000 cast in the country.[54]

In the congressional elections on May 26 Gaitán ran on a Liberal list, despite the fact that UNIR ran candidates separately. Although his candidacy was approved by the UNIR Cundinamarca directorate,[55] the split in UNIR now was fatal. On May 14 Fermín López Giraldo had resigned from the movement, claiming that Gaitán had betrayed the founding principles of UNIR.[56] However, Gaitán insisted that UNIR was intact and even better organized following its internal difficulties. He also maintained that he had made no commitments to the Liberal party and in congress would continue to support Unirista viewpoints.[57] But this could not disguise the fact that Gaitán had been reincorporated into the mainstream of Colombian politics.

What had happened? According to López Giraldo, Gaitán had secretly accepted the Liberal offer of a seat in the House. His dissidence over the assembly election of May 5 and his waiting to begin the congressional campaign until only five days before the election on May 26 were intended to prevent UNIR from making serious inroads into Liberal votes. Even the agreement of the UNIR Cundinamarca directorate to have him run for congress on a Liberal list was rigged, because the directorate was comprised totally of Gaitán's personal friends.[58] Gaitán, in effect, had abandoned UNIR to further his personal ambitions.

The answer is more complicated than that. When Gaitán founded UNIR in 1933 the country was in turmoil because of the land problem and the failure of the first Liberal administration in almost fifty years to carry out substantial reforms. UNIR, along with the Communist party, provided a willing mechanism and voice for protest against the indifference of the traditional parties. But with the advent of the Alfonso López administration in 1934 on a platform that embodied most of the reforms that Gaitán had been advocating for years, the hold of the Liberal party on the groups most likely to support UNIR was reasserted. Gaitán was the first to understand this. His decision to return to the Liberal ranks was based, in part, upon the practical realization that no third party in Colombian history had been able to break the monopoly of the Liberals and Conservatives. When it became clear that López had succeeded in attracting a majority of the voters and would push through substantial reforms, including an extension of the franchise, Gaitán made the decision to return to Liberalism, reestablish his prestige as a Liberal leader, and await his opportunity to capture Liberalism from within.[59] The López administration coopted and absorbed much of the UNIR program and impulse, a fact which did not entirely displease Gaitán. The regular Liberals were becoming more democratic, as later extension of the franchise through electoral reform suggests. UNIR did not succeed in radicalizing and socializing the masses, but it did succeed in pushing Liberalism to the left. This fact accounts, at least in part, for Gaitán's decision to rejoin the Liberal party.

Antonio García noted that UNIR was not abandoned by its followers, but by its leaders.[60] This was substantially correct. Yet it is highly questionable, as García also suggested, that abandoning UNIR was Gaitán's greatest tactical error. Considering the decrease in rural unrest after 1935, the magnetic attraction of urban labor to López, the internal problems of UNIR, the return of all the leading young radicals of Gaitán's generation to Liberalism, it seems certain that UNIR would have diminished to an even more marginal grouping, surviving, if at all, on the very fringes of political life. Furthermore, awaiting the collapse of López reformist Liberalism was an uncertain proposition at best, and Gaitán, with his personal ambitions, his quest for fame and power, despite his belief in evolution, was not prepared to wait indefinitely on the sidelines. His ideology after all allowed him to reconcile an infinity of tactical maneuvers. And so, in that spring of 1935, the opportunist and the political realist reappeared. The Tribune of the People prepared to become the *Caudillo Popular*.

What, finally, was the balance of Gaitán's UNIR experience? Gaitán set up UNIR because of his inability in the early thirties to transform the Liberal party from within. His primary purpose was to create consciousness or, as he himself put it, to study, to analyze, and to agitate. His success in UNIR did put leftist pressure on the Liberal party, as the presidency of Alfonso López in 1934 attests. In UNIR, Gaitán demonstrated his populist inclination for patriarchal leadership, middle-sector lieutenants, and the nascent political activity of *campesinos* and workers. Aided by the world depression, he found most of his clientele in rural areas. His populist approach was well reflected in the very structure of UNIR: a partriarchal leader dominating an organization devoted to mass-mobilization techniques.

7

The Professional

With his election as a Liberal to the House of Representatives in May 1935, Gaitán reentered the mainstream of Colombian politics. He stayed within the party for the remainder of his life; during the following nine years until his decision to run for the presidency in 1944 he worked to rebuild his prestige as a Liberal leader, especially among the rank and file. His strategy, according to his widow, was to continue agitation for an authentically popular, democratic Liberalism armed with a reformist program that would benefit the majority of nonelite Colombians, while educating the masses in political consciousness preparatory to taking over the party from within.[1] This marked a return to an earlier position that Liberalism, due to its strength among the most modernized sectors of the Colombian population, was the logical agent for the social and economic transformation of the country. Gaitán singlemindedly pursued his goal both in the political forum and in various administrative positions, and despite a series of seemingly sharp reversals of political fortune—all of which worked to his ultimate advantage.

Gaitán and the Revolution on the March

Gaitán's return to Liberalism was based upon a realistic assessment of the political situation in the country. In 1934 Alfonso López was elected to the presidency, pledging to deal with the economic and social problems that had become so acute in recent decades. With the help of the Liberal generation that had come of age in the twenties he elaborated a reform program that aroused expectations and generated broad support among the populace. When he encountered initial resistance from Conservatives and moderate Liberals in congress, he went to the country to mobilize support. In the congressional elections of May 1935 the reformist Liberals achieved a majority and thus assured passage of the López reforms. The effect of a reformist president and a congress willing to pass his program was to undermine and coopt the UNIR constituency. Colombians were willing to support concrete actions in the present by those who possessed real power. Gaitán, outmaneuvered by events which his previous activities had, in part, inspired, returned to Liberalism, where he could at least maintain a visible public image and wait out the López impulse.

The decision to include Gaitán on a Liberal electoral list was made by López.[2] He undoubtedly calculated that this would deal a fatal blow to UNIR, already internally divided over the question of electoral abstention or participation. But López, an extremely astute politician, also probably recognized that Gaitán, who still possessed a considerable popular following, was more useful and less dangerous within the party than outside of it, and that the Tribune of the People could provide substantial support for the López program.

This is, in fact, what occurred. Gaitán put aside any personal rancor he might have felt toward López and his disappointment that the reforms for which he had fought were now being introduced by a certified member of the establishment. Instead, during the congressional sessions of 1935 and 1936, Gaitán worked quietly and effectively in support of the innovative legislation of the Revolution on the March. When Conservatives and moderate Liberals mounted a campaign of opposition to the López administration, Gaitán defended its legislation in the congress and on a speaking tour throughout the country. He added, however, that the government's initiatives were only a beginning toward the realization of social justice in Colombia and warned that there were many leaders in both parties and in the congress who were opposed to the new direction and would do all in their power to sabotage it.[3]

Gaitán's motives for supporting the López reforms combined self-interest and idealism. He believed that they represented a step forward for the Colombian people. But there is evidence that he was mistrustful of the genuine commitment of the administration to authentic change and its technique of reform from above. Gaitán recognized that there was a great desire for transformation on the part of the people and that López had successfully taken advantage of this popular sentiment, but he doubted that the result would be the profound alteration of the national consciousness which he regarded as vital for any significant historical progress. Although the people were becoming conscious of their own best interests—and in their clamor to realize them were becoming an undeniable, energetic force—they had no leaders to orient and guide them with new ideas or concepts, to point out the direction that the country should take and what the final goals would be.[4] Instead, Gaitán found that the politicians, especially those in power, engaged in the usual practical politics of the moment. Although they were passing potentially revolutionary legislation, they were not encouraging, by example or leadership, the education of public consciousness that would ensure its success. If the politicians did not seek to change ideas, attitudes, and behavior, none of the advanced legislation of the Revolution on the March could really be effective and would only frustrate the expectations of the people. National transformation, as Gaitán saw it, had to be an organic process involving the mind, spirit, and actions of its participants, and not merely an exercise in form. The latter was but the practice of demagoguery.

Gaitán's return to Liberalism had not been greeted with enthusiasm by the party's leaders.[5] After his abandonment of UNIR he had been subjected to charges of betrayal and opportunism by some of its former adherents and had to endure the abuse of the Liberal press as well. In the following period, while working for the López program, he was generally ignored by the Liberal leadership, a fact that was reflected by scanty coverage in the party press. Yet his qualities as a political activist were such that he could not long remain in the background. He relied upon his long-standing popularity to win a seat on the Bogotá Municipal Council in October 1935.[6] His work in the council, the congress, and the country in support of popular programs gradually attracted wider national attention and resulted in the restoration of his prestige.[7] By 1936 he was once again a political figure of considerable importance.

The Emblems of Prestige

Gaitán had, characteristically, contributed all of his money as well as his time to UNIR. When the latter was abandoned he was left virtually penniless, according to Osorio.[8] Fortunately, his reputation as a first-rate lawyer was intact, and gradually he began to rebuild a lucrative law practice. This allowed him to indulge his taste for the fine things he had dreamed about in his youth: expensive, tailored suits; large, late-model American automobiles; and membership in the Country Club (he was denied admission to the exclusive Jockey Club, despite a custom of granting membership to the mayors of Bogotá). In time he acquired a limited number of stocks in several corporations. He also purchased a few properties in new residential developments, including an attractive, well-appointed house that he lived in after his marriage.

These desires for the material signs of affluence undoubtedly grew out of the rather deprived circumstances of his childhood; but he also certainly understood that to be thought of as important it was necessary to have the furnishings of importance. The accumulation of wealth and possessions, however, never became of overriding importance. During these years, for example, the United Fruit Company offered him $10,000, a substantial amount at the time, to represent it in a case involving its director in Colombia. Gaitán refused this offer from his old enemy on ethical grounds.[9] He turned down similar offers from other large enterprises, including the Bogotá telephone company, whose workers he had represented in grievances against that organization.

Nor did Gaitán's life-style interfere with his affection for the people. Friends report that his law offices were filled with the humble and poor who came to him with their problems and in search of advice, which he gave without charge. Wealthy clients often had to wait long hours while he met with those who could not pay for his services. He frequently found time to talk on the street with workers, many of whom he knew by name, and to meet with the people in the numerous cafes that were so much a part of the political and intellectual life of the capital.[10] Other small touches which may or may not have been calculated—he drove his own automobile when many men of his position employed chauffeurs—undoubtedly impressed the common man. He also met with aspiring young writers and artists for lengthy discussions on art, literature, and other cultural subjects.

One of Gaitán's youthful dreams was of marrying a woman of the upper class. This he achieved when, suddenly and unexpectedly, he married Amparo Jaramillo of Medellín in May 1936. Gaitán flew to the Antioquian capital in that month accompanied by several dignitaries, including Eduardo Santos, the publisher of *El Tiempo* and future president, who served as Gaitán's *padrino*, or best man. The marriage followed a secret courtship of two years, initiated, astonishingly, when Gaitán was in the city directing striking railroad workers. The two had met at a social club dance. Amparo, a woman of intelligence and beauty, launched the courtship when she revealed that she knew more about him than anyone else because she had been clipping newspaper articles about him for some time.[11] Such forwardness was unusual for a young society woman of the time.

Osorio somewhat cynically reports that the marriage was at least partly the result of certain calculations by Gaitán. Antioquia was a populous department, a wealthy center of Colombian commerce and industry. Its votes were an important factor in any national election. The department, however, true to the strong regionalist tradition in the country, had a reputation for delivering its votes primarily to candidates from the region. According to Osorio, Gaitán through marriage could at least lay claim to some relationship with An-tioquia.[12] In any case, Gaitán later developed a strong following in the department; to this day his daughter Gloria reports strong Gaitanista sentiments there.[13]

The marriage between Gaitán and Amparo, according to various informal sources, was often stormy but mutually stimulating. Gaitán apparently attempted to play the domineering role expected of him in a machismo culture.

Amparo, however, had a strong character like that of her husband and was not always inclined to be the submissive wife. Unlike most women of high society, Señora de Gaitán took a keen interest in politics and developed a strong social consciousness, which is still manifest.[14] She often accompanied her husband on his political campaigns and undauntedly met the hostility of opposition political crowds.[15] Her rebelliousness, which very nearly matched that of her husband, was finely developed. Following Gaitán's assassination, she refused to allow burial of the corpse (which was laid out in the family dining room) until the government of Ospina Pérez was overthrown; after agonizing over the problem for several days the government nationalized Gaitán's house and declared it—and the corpse—a national monument. Later, when Carlos Lleras Restrepo, the future president, attempted to deliver a funeral oration at the house, Señora de Gaitán literally threw the diminutive Lleras and his microphones into the street.

The Mayor of Bogotá

By the spring of 1936 the general direction of the López administration was arousing considerable apprehension among the Colombian oligarchy. The Olaya Herrera and Eduardo Santos faction of the Liberal party exhibited considerable coolness toward López, as demonstrated in the pages of *El Tiempo*. The Conservatives, now under the leadership of Laureano Gómez, threatened to incite civil rebellion against what they regarded as the increasing subversion of the social order. Gaitán took advantage of this situation by launching an unsolicited speaking tour through the country. His motives were to warn the people to be vigilant against the threats to peace and the reformist initiatives of the administration and to once again bring himself into the national limelight as a champion of the poor and oppressed.[16] In these efforts he succeeded admirably. The controversy surrounding his abandonment of UNIR began to recede in the public memory; the crowds he attracted indicated that once again he was developing a substantial popular following that provided him with a degree of independence within the Liberal party.

This success posed a dilemma for López. Gaitán's reemergence as a popular force threatened him personally; it also endangered the system of oligarchical power. Yet Gaitán was defending the administration's program effectively in the congress and in the country, and López could not openly move against him. The president therefore hit upon the expedient of appointing Gaitán to the important post of mayor of Bogotá, with the obvious intention of showing up the Tribune as an inept administrator and then disposing of him.[17]

Gaitán obviously was aware of this ploy. When his friend Ricardo Jordán voiced concern about the president's maneuver, Gaitán responded, "And what does it matter? If I last a month I'll do the work of thirty days. If I last a day I'll do the work of twenty-four hours."[18] He apparently felt confident that his actions as mayor would stand on their own merits. Further, the appointment would give him a chance to demonstrate his administrative capabilities, which had not yet been tested.

But he also carried out a maneuver of his own designed to give the impression to the people that his appointment was not merely the result of the whim of López. He planned to take office on June 8, 1936, the seventh anniversary of popular demonstrations against the Conservative government in which he had played a prominent role. On that day he had his friends organize a demonstration in Santander Park, after which Gaitán, surrounded by the crowd, led a march to city hall, which he then "occupied," in a manner reminiscent of Mussolini's March on Rome. After the occupation an unknown speaker from the crowd gave a "spontaneous" speech declaring that Gaitán was now mayor as a result of the popular demand of the people.[19] There was no comment in the capital's press on López's reaction.

Gaitán did not arrive at his new post without prior experience in municipal affairs. He had been a member of the Bogotá Municipal Council almost continuously since 1930. As a councilman he had supported such projects as public housing for workers, city welfare projects of benefit to the poor, electrification and street paving in worker neighborhoods, and had opposed the city's financial bailing out of the foreign-owned (by U.S. interests) municipal electric company.[20] In 1935, as a council member, he had resisted the contribution by a wealthy Bogotá landowner, Luis Camacho Matiz, of land to the city for the purpose of constructing a municipal stadium. Gaitán argued that the drainage of the low land, the extension of sewage and electric lines involved, would cost the city too much in the long run and would primarily benefit Camacho, who planned to sell surrounding lots at inflated prices after the city had made land improvements and put in utilities. For his concern Gaitán was castigated for a lack of civic spirit by the local press.[21]

Once in office, Gaitán moved quickly with his customary vigor and enthusiasm. He took steps to de-politicize the administration and improve municipal efficiency and services. Three relatively unknown young men were appointed to important municipal posts on the basis of technical ability and experience rather than political affiliation. An economist, J. R. Salazar Ferro, became secretary of government; the secretary of hacienda (treasurer) was Carlos Uribe Prada, another economist; and Dr. Enrique Garcés, who had fifteen years' experience in the field, became secretary of public works.[22]

In his first decrees as mayor Gaitán established a mandatory forty-four-hour week for municipal employees, to be enforced with time clocks, centralized the internal communication system of municipal offices to provide the mayor with closer control, and took other measures to improve overall efficiency. While offering to work in full cooperation with the city council, he decided that municipal contracts, especially those involving minor sums, would in the future move through the mayor's office. He also declared that the council would have to meet in extra sessions to deal with the multiplicity of urgent municipal problems. Additionally, he decreed a general clean-up campaign in the city, including the removal of much obnoxious advertising (all business signs—and names of establishments—had to be in Spanish), the construction of sidewalks (to be paid for by those whose property they fronted), the planting of trees, the repainting of business establishments, additional lighting, and the removal of vagrant children to children's shelters. These initiatives, announced all in one day, led the *El Tiempo* columnist "Calibán"—no friend of Gaitán— to announce that "Bogotá finally has found a mayor!"[23]

One of Gaitán's first efforts was an attempt to appoint fifteen Conservatives to important municipal posts. This aroused considerable surprise, because traditionally the dominant party excluded all but its own from bureaucratic positions. After the Conservative leadership forbade its members to accept the posts, Gaitán expressed regret and explained he was only attempting to remove politics from municipal government.[24] Nevertheless, he did undertake to reduce patronage posts by firing or ordering the reassignment of employees from positions in which they had little to do.

Gaitán's major work as mayor was in the interests of the less affluent of the city's inhabitants. Bogotá at the time was experiencing rapid population growth, and the city's physical growth had outrun the availability of public services. Previous municipal efforts had been concentrated primarily in the commercial center and in the better neighborhoods. Gaitán reoriented the municipal administration's activities. During his eight-month period as mayor he extended sewer and electric lines to lower-class neighborhoods, improved transport to those areas, and started extensive street paving and tarring. He began the construction of public housing in two new working-class neighborhoods, including housing for municipal workers. One of his primary concerns was improving sanitary facilities for the poor: he began the construction of public baths and started a campaign of public health education in lower-class neighborhoods.[25]

The plight of lower-class children received priority attention by Gaitán, who undoubtedly was recalling his own youthful experiences. In order to get vagrant children off the streets and into proper institutions, he enlisted the aid of numerous charitable organizations, and upgraded the activities of city agencies concerned with welfare. He also opened "school restaurants," later extended to municipal workers, to provide the children of the poor, especially those in school, with a nutritious breakfast. He inaugurated a factory to provide free shoes for poor, school-age children and extended school bus service for those attending public schools.

These schools, generally attended by the poor who could not afford the usually superior private schools, were in a deplorable condition when Gaitán took office. He immediately closed the worst schools, began the construction of seven new ones, and upgraded others by putting in electricity, water, and sewers, and carrying out renovations.

To improve the cultural level of the lower classes, Gaitán inaugurated free, public, open-air concerts, started a mobile library service, and launched an annual book fair—all of which still are in existence in Bogotá. Finally, he clamped down on speculation in city markets and established a standard fee for stalls according to size and the quantity of merchandise sold.

Bogotá was preparing for the celebration of its four hundredth anniversary when Gaitán assumed office. In order to improve the city, elaborate plans were drawn up for the construction of a wide avenue passing through the city's center up to the house of Simón Bolívar, which nestles below the imposing mountains that tower over the capital. A new water treatment plant also was planned. To reduce congestion in the business district, trolley tracks were torn up and redirected and extensive sidewalk construction begun. Several unsightly heroic monuments were torn down, despite the anguish of local patriots, most of whom seemed to be gathered in the offices of the Conservative daily *El Siglo*.

All of this unusual activity aroused considerable public enthusiasm, and not a little opposition. Gaitán felt compelled to hold a public meeting (that *El Tiempo* reported was jammed) in the Municipal Theater on September 18 to explain his work and counter the criticism that was being directed at him. That he chose a mass meeting to explain himself was evidence in itself that criticism was coming from influential quarters. In his speech he listed the works that his administration had initiated or accomplished. He claimed that his administration was making a revolutionary constructive effort and that the public opinion against it was the work of a small but influential minority. The reasons for this adverse public opinion were suggested by what he had to say about the city's finances: for the first time there were no exceptions to the payment of taxes, arrears had been collected from merchants under threats of fines, and the collection system was functioning effectively and efficiently This had substantially raised the city's revenues and allowed the administration to acrry out its ambitious programs.[26] In effect, city government was working impartially and not merely ior the benefit of the privileged.

In order to underscore popular support for his administration Gaitán allowed a mass demonstration to be held for him on September 25. Labor-union and working-class leaders, including the Communist Gilberto Vieira, spoke in praise of Gaitán, who said that nothing would interrupt the progress being made, especially those works designed to improve conditions of life for the poor of the city.[27] But by the end of the year it was clear that a campaign of opposition to the mayor was building. *El Siglo* was openly hostile, and the Liberal press was printing more and more criticism. On January 22, 1937, Gaitán was compelled to defend his innovations—the municipal employment agency, the antipatronage policy, and even the quality of the shoes and clothes he ordered municipal workers to buy (at cost) and wear—from open attacks in the Municipal Council.[28] Two days later a small group of public conveyance drivers announced they were going out on strike because of their opposition to a recent decree by the mayor that public drivers wear uniforms. This seemingly insignificant incident heralded Gaitán's downfall.

Gaitán had issued Decree 425 of 1936 establishing that "public taxi and bus drivers wear shoes, hats, prescribed shirts, and overalls."[29] The decree was part of the campaign to clean up public service employees and provide them with a sense of decorum and responsibility. The Asociación Nacional de Choferes (ANDEC), which claimed to represent one thousand drivers in the city, refused to comply, on the grounds that the decree was an infringement of personal rights.[30] ANDEC also called upon unions throughout the country for support. When the union struck, Gaitán obtained a declaration that its action was illegal and ordered the police to prevent demonstrations. A clash between strikers and police occurred, however, and the affair assumed national importance when other transport unions declared solidarity strikes throughout Colombia. These included railroad workers who refused to move trains carrying provisions into the capital. Gaitán then went to the president, seeking support in what he regarded as his own legal action, and asked for army troops to move the trains. Gaitán apparently believed that he received the president's assurance of support and agreement; but a day later, on February 14, he was unceremoniously ousted as mayor—which could only have been done by López.[31]

What had happened? Osorio claimed that López had chosen this particular moment to embarrass and discredit Gaitán, who was succeeding all too well as mayor.[32] Through his influence over the organized labor movement—which he had been the first to recognize officially—López mobilized national opposition and made it appear that Gaitán was acting against the very people he claimed to champion. Certainly, Gaitán believed that the entire affair was the result of a maneuver by López.[33] There are interesting suggestions in the Gaitán Papers that this was the case and that the Conservatives were involved as well. For example, a letter to Gaitán on January 28, 1937, from Enrique Galvis, secretary general of another Bogotá drivers' union, the Sindicato Central Nacional de Choferes, stated that his union would abide by the decree and charged that ANDEC was controlled by Conservatives and "rightists" who wanted to undermine the mayor. The Confederación Sindical de Colombia, in a letter to Gaitán dated February 13, was as direct. It blamed a "subversive movement" directed by unnamed Liberals and the newspaper *El Tiempo*. Finally, a police report sent to Gaitán on February 10 about the clash between strikers and police stated that 35 of the 150 detained were not drivers and that almost a fifth of the 250 who signed the ANDEC public demand for Gaitán to rescind his decree were not drivers or members of the union.[34] Nor was the entire organized labor movement in Colombia against Gaitán's actions. Among the many messages of support he received from throughout the country were numerous communications from labor unions applauding his position. It would seem that Gaitán was again the victim of the oligarchy, which could not abide the populist politics he practiced. But he obtained a kind of revenge a few months later when, in September 1937, he was reelected to the Municipal Council from the working-class neighborhoods over the opposition of *El Tiempo* and the city's merchants.

Minister of Education

Gaitán was once again playing a marginal role in Colombian politics. During the next three years, while the opposition to López mounted among moderate Liberals—who found a new leader in Eduardo Santos following the death in early 1937 of Olaya Herrera—Gaitán remained an outsider. He had developed a personal antagonism to López as well as the conviction that the latter (already preparing for a second term) was essentially a demagogue who, if he returned to the presidency, would only defraud the Colombian people. In relation to Santos, despite his friendship and respect for the integrity of the newspaper publisher, Gaitán simply was far removed from him ideologically. Santos represented a return to the old Liberalism of the Generation of the *Centenario*. Santos could not be expected to carry forward the reformist impulse initiated by López in his first administration.

In the spring of 1938 Gaitán opposed the nomination of Santos for the presidency (under Colombian law López could not succeed himself). He took part in a brief, abortive campaign to secure the nomination for an extremely reluctant Darío Echandía.[35] When Santos was elected Gaitán had fallen out with both major factions of the Liberal party. His plight was demonstrated when he failed to secure a place on a Liberal electoral list for the House of Representatives in 1939. Despite an independent campaign as a dissident, Gaitán was not elected. Even the people, it seemed, had abandoned him.

Once again, in the summer of 1939, Gaitán set out to rebuild his prestige. He began a nationwide speaking tour to explain his position to the people. In his first speech in Bogotá's Municipal Theater he indicated the direction he would take after 1944. He attacked the Liberal leadership, especially the López group, for cheating the people behind the rhetoric of reform. He claimed that López's "Revolution" had neither head nor feet and that the former president's promise to continue it was mere demagoguery designed to get him reelected. He charged that the institutional structures developed by López and continued by Santos to help the people were in reality bureaucratic organisms masking fraud and speculation for the political allies of the privileged.[36]

Gaitán's campaign naturally brought retribution from the Liberal press, which united to denounce him. The dark-skinned, lower-middle-class upstart, who presumed to enter the privileged ranks of the wealthy and powerful without asking their permission, again was assailed on all sides. The attacks upon him were not only political, but personal, too; allusions to his race appeared as asides in discussions of his politics. Again Gaitán was described as the leader of the *chusma,* the ignorant street mob, in language clearly suggesting that his political behavior, like his followers, came from the gutter. The sneering disdain of the upper class for the "negro Gaitán" appeared in direct proportion to the threat he was mounting against them. Nevertheless, Gaitán had an effect. Once more he was incorporated into the system in order to silence him. President Santos, whom Osorio claims was personally offended by the vehemence of the attack on the "literate Negro," first appointed Gaitán chief justice of the Supreme Court.[37] When Gaitán turned down that prestigious post because it would remove him from active politics, Santos appointed him minister of education in mid-February 1940.[38]

The appointment surprised the nation, especially because *El Tiempo* had led the attack on Gaitán, and it was taken as a direct insult by López. But obviously Santos had his reasons, other than the personal. The Liberal party was being wracked by the vociferous nature of the López-Santos split. Further, the first effects of the world war were being felt in the Colombian economy as trade with Europe dropped off precipitously. Santos was heeding the advice of his minister of government, Carlos Lozano y Lozano, to attempt to strike a balance between the left and right wings of the Liberal party during a difficult time.[39] Having Gaitán in the moderate Santos administration might possibly work toward that end.

Gaitán accepted Santos's offer for the same reasons he had accepted the mayorship of Bogotá. However temporary the post, expediently given, it offered him a chance to engage in some positive popular actions in an area of great need and to demonstrate what he could do as an administrator.

Gaitán had a great interest in education. He believed that it was essential for democracy and would play a crucial role in economic development. In one respect, his entire political career was a process of educating the Colombian people. He had much practical experience in the field. In the early 1930s he had been elected rector of Bogotá's Universidad Libre, and throughout most of his career he taught in its law school and that of the National University.

Gaitán had certain definite ideas about Colombian education. He regarded it, especially at the higher levels, as too academic, too oriented to traditional professions such as law that provided an overabundance of talents not necessary for an underdeveloped country. As rector of the Universidad Libre he had inauguarated reforms designed to bring about a "scientific investigative" spirit, and do away with the old rote educational methods. He established new fields of specialization in law, the social sciences, and administration, and developed technical fields as well as evening programs for workers and the middle class. [40]

Once Gaitán took possession of the ministry he moved with customary speed. He declared that his goals as minister were to democratize the culture and nationalize primary education. [41] He made two extensive trips through central and southern Colombia, visiting schools and explaining before education groups and municipal councils the orientation of his ministry. [42] He usually managed to get the councils to commit funds for school construction or renovation.

In the area of higher education, leading scholars and scientists were appointed to the Ateneo de Altos Estudios, created for the purpose of advancing research in the natural sciences, mathematics, ethnography, Indian languages, etc. Another principal concern was industrial education, because of the low technical level of Colombia. The curriculum of the government's industrial schools was upgraded, new subjects added, and renovations were carried out in the shops. Gaitán made a great effort to expand industrial education and he founded several new schools, including agricultural institutes. He also moved to upgrade the normal schools, or teacher-training institutes. In order to improve the professional qualifications of teachers, he created correspondence courses in education and the natural and social sciences. [43] In the fourteen high schools directly controlled by the ministry the curriculum was reorganized to provide more mathematics, sciences, social sciences, and languages, as well as alternate courses for technical and academic students.

Gaitán pushed hard in the area of popular culture by greatly expanding the activities of the Cultural Extension Institute. A literacy campaign was started, mobile libraries put into service, book fairs held in major cities, open-air concerts and movies held, and traveling exhibitions of art organized. Much of this was paid for by contributions from private business. Finally, the ministry organized a factory for the manufacture of shoes for sale at cost to school-age children. [44]

Gaitán failed to achieve one major goal, the nationalization of primary school education. Traditionally, the central government had supplied certain funds and supplies for primary schools, with responsibility for teachers' salaries falling upon the departments, and school construction and maintenance on municipalities. The results had been deplorable. At the time approximately 60 percent of the population was illiterate; few attended school beyond the second or third grade; the vast majority of children, especially in the rural areas, did not attend school at all; and teachers, partly as a result of political patronage, generally were poorly trained. Gaitán's intention was to centralize the system and make the national government completely responsible for primary education. Correspondence in the Gaitán Papers indicates that many teachers' organizations and individual educators were in favor of this. However, when Gaitán introduced the nationalization law in congress he was attacked from all sides. The opposition in the House was led by the delegation from regionalist Antioquia, with the Conservative, and former Leopard Silvio Villegas at its head. Villegas, who was supported by the church, saw Gaitán's measure as a sinister assault on the freedom of education.[45] But much more was involved. The old issue of centralism versus federalism was revived. And through it all ran the specter of local politicians being deprived of their control over patronage and contracts. Conservatives and Liberals alike joined forces to reject Gaitán's proposal, despite his eloquent pleas that his measure represented a rational approach to one of the nation's gravest problems. Faced with such adamant opposition, Gaitán resigned in October 1940, less than a year after taking office.

Gaitán was to occupy, for a few brief months in late 1943 and early 1944, the ministry of labor. He was appointed by Acting President Darío Echandía during a period when López, in office for the second time, was out of the country. During his brief tenure he attempted unsuccessfully to get health legislation for workers passed, and he succeeded in carrying out some administrative measures that favored unions in disputes with employers.[46] But it was a bad time for Colombia, and Gaitán already was preparing to launch his campaign for the presidency. He accomplished very little except to demonstrate, as he had done as mayor and minister of education, that he was on the side of the less privileged. After 1940, the poor needed all the support they could find. The economy was increasingly affected by the world war and the dislocations it caused. Political polarization increased; social unrest intensified. Colombia was sliding into a profound crisis and the people, as usual, were its principal victims.

The reformist administration of President Alfonso López (1934–1938) had raised the expectations of the majority of people without satisfying them. During his administration the principles for reforming the laissez-faire state and the mechanisms for creating a welfare state were established. The constitution had been revised to recognize that the ownership of property was a social function that implied obligations. A limited land-reform law intended to benefit the landless had been passed. The tax structure had been revised and modernized to place more of the financial burden of the nation upon the wealthy. Workers' organizations were encouraged and protected, and social services, as well as a minimum wage, were established for the working class. The national education system, from the university to the elementary levels, was reformed, and greater access provided for the middle class. Government measures were employed to spur economic development. But all of this, intended to modernize the nation, encountered resistance among traditional groups who feared the effects of social mobility on their position. During the administration of the Liberal Eduardo Santos (1938–1942), the reformist impulse ended. The moderate Santos did not revoke the López reforms, but he ceded before the desires of Conservative and Liberal landowners and businessmen who feared the effects of land reform and the new-found strength of the workers, and who wanted to enjoy the new prosperity engendered for them by the protectionist measures of the state.[47]

But the Santos "pause" caused dismay among the elements of the population who had had their expectations raised by the López reforms and now discerned that they might not be fulfilled. A split developed in the Liberal party between those who wanted to push on and those who believed that the reformist impulse had gone far enough. The former backed López in a second, successful bid for the presidency, but the bitter Liberal battle that resulted exposed irreconcilable differences between groups whose basic interests were far apart.

The second López administration was anticlimactic. If López had any intention of renewing the Revolution on the March he found himself blocked on all sides. Moderate and rightist Liberals and Conservatives joined in the congress to halt his legislation. Powerful interest groups of landowners, businessmen, and industrialists who had organized into protective associations brought intense pressure against him.[48] Furthermore, López himself had changed. During his second administration he did not surround himself with the young leftist Liberals of Gaitán's generation who had served him in the 1930s, but with financiers and entrepreneurs—men interested in figures, not reform.[49] There were other factors that worked against the reformist impulse: what Fals Borda described as the "tendency towards inertia produced by the institutionalization of innovations (trade unions, for example) made in prior years";[50] and the rise of a vitriolic, reactionary right personified by Laureano Gómez, admirer of Franco's Spain, who charged López's private and administrative families with corruption and malfeasance, and who wanted to return to a prerepublican past with "Spain, marching forward as the sole defender of Western Civilization, leading the Western nations in the reconstruction of the empire of Hispanidad . . . we inscribe our names in the roster of its phalanxes with unutterable satisfaction. . . . Up Catholic, Imperial Spain!"[51]

The coming of World War II brought other problems. Shortages of commodities, the disruption of markets, and the accumulation of foreign exchange resulted in severe economic disorder. Speculation and inflation thrived. Although Santos's minister of finance, Carlos Lleras Restrepo, had created various state agencies to provide intervention in and control of the economy, they functioned ineffectively and without central direction in the decaying political atmosphere.[52] Black markets in import licenses and exchange permits flourished as the rich used official channels for private gain.

Under these multiple blows public disenchantment and restiveness grew. In violation of union leaders' pacts with the government, wildcat strikes multiplied as workers protested the precipitous rise in the cost of living. Employee groups petitioned for relief. Rural violence occurred, in part stimulated by Gómez Conservatives, in part due to the subverting of the agrarian reform.[53] In July 1944 elements of the army staged a coup and briefly held the president prisoner. Even the Communist party, formerly abjectly loyal to López, agonized over continued cooperation with the regime.

Finally, López, assailed from all quarters, resigned. In a dramatic departing address to the nation he said, "The branches of government do not function with regularity. Their interrelationships are profoundly disturbed. The parties do not faithfully represent the will of their members. Opinion varies radically between the political hierarchy and the people, between the city and the countryside, between the capital and the rest of the nation."[54] He went on to admit that he could not reconcile the antagonistic forces contending in the republic, and he warned of the threat that the reactionary Gómez posed for the country.

López was succeeded in 1945 by the caretaker government of Alberto Lleras Camargo (a cousin of Lleras Restrepo). He would do nothing but hold the presidency while the storm raged around him. The savage assaults on the constitutional order by Gómez continued unabated, as the reactionary right began to mobilize the traditional rural sector against the modernizing thrust of the urban and industrial sectors.[55] In the cities the plight of the workers was met with hostility as Lleras waned that he would not tolerate illegal strikes.[56] True to his word, he broke a strike of workers on the Magdalena River with force. Even the Liberals, it seemed, had turned against the people.

During these years of mounting crisis Gaitán again sought his way in politics as an outsider. In 1942 he helped lead an unsuccessful "anti-reelectionist" effort against López. The latter, in turn, managed to keep Gaitán off the Liberal electoral lists in the capital and Cundinamarca; however, provincial opponents of López in the Nariño assembly elected Gaitán a senator from that department in 1941. From his seat in the Senate, Gaitán attacked the corruption and scandals that beset the second López administration. As he watched that administration dissolve under the blows of economic disruption, growing discontent on the part of the impoverished masses, widespread fraud and speculation, and the savage attacks of the reactionary Laureano Gómez and his rejuvenated Conservatives, Gaitán judged that conditions finally were ripe for his great crusade.

One of Gaitán's major problems during the years 1935–1944 was to increase his national prestige. His work as administrator succeeded admirably in doing this. If bourgeois politicians had hoped to reveal his incompetence in a new realm, they failed. He demonstrated imagination and talent in administration and remained faithful to his populist stance by using his authority in behalf of Colombia's less affluent citizens. Most eloquent in this regard is the literacy campaign he launched as minister of education. He had spent his time well. When the gathering clouds of inflation and instability darkened Colombia during the later years of World War II, Gaitán was ready.

III

Gathering Momentum, 1944–1946

III

8

Building the Populist Movement

In 1944 Gaitán began an important task viewed in the perspective of his life: the campaign for the presidential election of May 1946. Though testimony from his wife indicates that Gaitán did not expect to win,[1] the campaign saw the emergence of the mature man: the mover of masses, the popular caudillo who lashed a corrupt and exclusive oligarchy with the whip of savage eloquence, who stirred bitter country people and city dwellers into a frenzy with passionate oratory, who shouted the emotional slogans in the town plazas and squares of Colombia that convinced the *chusma,* the despicable poor, the forgotten ones, that he was their only hope, their savior, that his cause was their cause. "I am not a man! I am a people!" "The people are superior to their leaders!" "For the moral and democratic restoration of the republic!" "People! To the attack!" And slowly, but certainly, the fabric of a society that had remained intact for centuries began to unwind. The manipulated, exploited masses, the *campesinos,* workers, anxious shopkeepers, frustrated professionals, disillusioned youth began to shuffle tentatively for the first time toward the center stage of the Colombian drama, seeking their role in history.

The campaign for the 1946 election began in an atmosphere of political polarization and economic disruption, ideal for the type of populist campaign Gaitán was to make. The second López administration was a disappointment and disillusionment to the people because it did not continue their forward progress. In the midst of disillusion, despair, worsening conditions for the people, enrichment of the few, political corruption, governmental inefficiency, ideological hatred, emerged Gaitán. He was not to correct the process of polarization, diminish the passionate hostility, or repair the tottering structure, but to render them worse. He was to mobilize hitherto powerless social groups in a vast popular movement designed to incorporate them at last into the Colombian nation, a work without precedent in the country's history.

The Decision for Candidacy

As previously explained, Gaitán had utilized his post as minister of labor to travel through the country sounding the public opinion about his candidacy. He found initial support among the Magdalena River workers who had a strong tradition of political activism but who were suffering the economic decline caused by erosion and the development of other methods of transportation.[2] Other workers' groups that had benefited from his prolabor decisions as minister proclaimed their support. But Liberal groups also found satisfying the prospect of his candidacy. An independent organization of young leftist Liberals, the Comando Nacional de Izquierdas, sent a letter to Gaitán and the Liberal directorate stating that the economic crisis brought on by the war and the failure of congress to support the government required the rejuvenation of Liberalism along "democratic and popular lines" and the integration of the people into the country. The Comando called for Gaitán's candidacy.[3] Another letter sent by a group of Liberals in mid-February expressed dismay with rampant corruption and the procession of party candidates who were "representatives of foreign houses, mercenaries who traffic with the public conscience and legal institutions." They asked for Gaitán as "the independent man who could save the country."[4] From Tumaco came a letter reporting widespread confusion in the party there. The writer noted that "here old and young believe that the electorate is not made of flesh and blood but is the powerful electoral machine you have analyzed so masterfully. . . . The local people are devoted to López, but they know that the superior man for this moment is Gaitán."[5] Jorge Villaveces in Ibagué wrote: "The people are Gaitanista from the small businessman and employee to the most humble worker."[6]

If Gaitán had any doubts about pursuing the presidency, his trip through the country and the inpouring of correspondence like that quoted above convinced him. Indeed, he found among those proclaiming their support the principal issues of the campaign. As these few letters—and there were numerous others—demonstrate, Gaitán built his campaign around issues that were agitating the people. They were not, as some of his opponents pointed out at the time, artificial. There was genuine popular concern for the democratic reconstruction of Liberalism, the breaking of the economic and political oligarchy's hold on the country, the institution of a popular government representing the interests of the majority, and the integration of the people into the nation.

The Gaitanista movement that developed after 1944 became the expression of resentment against the existing system. It capitalized on the discontent of the masses who witnessed enrichment and speculation in the midst of their misery and who, as a result, were beginning to develop a "revolutionary consciousness."[7] The movement was profoundly popular and antiparty in that it appealed to the masses over the traditional leaderships of both parties—the Liberals, whose record Gaitán had to attack, and the Conservatives, whose ideas he opposed. The movement appealed to the basic interests of the workers of the large cities, the most radical sectors of the rural population, the most progressive of the small bourgeoisie, and the youth.[8] These were precisely the groups who had been created by or benefited most from economic development, who sought new status, who expected social mobility and individual improvement, and who now found themselves frustrated by their collision with a "closed club" that effectively monopolized state power and, through it, wealth.[9] The nature of his constituency and its relationship to existing conditions defined the major themes of Gaitán's campaign: against the economic and political oligarchy; and for the moral and democratic restoration of the republic.

In the opening speech of his campaign at the Municipal Theater in Bogotá, Gaitán discussed what he meant by oligarchy and how it interfered with the development of the people. He noted that there were people who worked, who labored in the interests of their families, who sought the education of their children, who were concerned with real, daily problems of living, whose lives were involved in a constant struggle; and there were others—a minority—who were not concerned with these things, who were above the daily battle for existence, concerned only with more votes or less votes, the size of a contract, appointment to an ambassadorship. From this he deduced that there were two countries in Colombia: the national country consisting of the people; and the political country consisting of the oligarchy and its retainers. He went on to describe the oligarchy as being divided into three parts. First, there were the directors who owned and dominated the country and who made all the important decisions. Second, in the intermediate structure, were those who served as lines of communication, "men of intelligence who had the souls of secretaries." Third, there were the "arms" that penetrated into the neighborhoods, the towns, the assemblies. These were the local bosses who arranged elections for the benefit of the political country in exchange for profits.[10] The people of the national country felt a great repugnance for the "deep putrefaction that hangs over Colombian life," when public morality has disappeared.

> What is the future of our children if they continue to live in the present state of affairs? Can you be sure that they will advance because of their merit, their ability, their studies, or their efforts? No. If our children want progress, they will have to walk in the shadow and by a back road, which we do not want for them. They will suceed not by

hard work, or by being technicians, farmers, engineers, knowledge-able in their professions, but by being base and servile to the political bosses.[11]

In closing, Gaitán called upon the people, the national country, to join him in the struggle against the political country. He ended with the slogans of the Gaitanista movement: "People! For the moral restoration of Colombia, to the attack! People! For democracy, to the attack! People! For victory, to the attack!"

Gaitán's populist campaign was a new phenomenon in Colombia. By mobilizing the urban masses away from the Liberal party, by attracting certain Conservative groups, by eroding the Liberal and Communist leadership of the labor movement, it undercut the traditional political structure. By constructing an alliance between the middle and lower classes which cut across the traditional, hereditary, party allegiances, Gaitán attacked the very basis of Colombian politics. He began to turn the traditional, horizontal antagonisms of Colombian society into vertical ones, making middle- and lower-class people see their similarities rather than their differences. He began to focus the attention of the people upward upon their true enemy: the oligarchy.

Yet Gaitán did not choose to abandon the Liberal party openly. He recognized that most of his supporters were Liberals and that there was a tradition within the party that attracted them. In a manifesto of the Gaitanista movement,[12] and in his campaign speeches, he claimed that the authentic Liberalism, the popular Liberalism represented by Benjamín Herrera and Rafael Uribe Uribe, had been violated by the professional politicians who had converted the party into an electoral machine for themselves. Gaitanismo now represented legitimate Liberalism, with its present leaders cast in the role of usurpers. According to one of his collaborators, Francisco José Chaux, Gaitán understood Liberalism as a political instrument for serving the people, for raising their standard of living, and for realizing an egalitarian society founded upon study, work, competence, and the responsibility of each member.[13] Another Gaitanista, Jorge Padilla, asserted that Gaitán's movement served to rally the masses within the party so that they would not have to seek another outside movement.[14] And yet there is evidence that Gaitán saw the mobilization of support through Liberalism as only one stage in the development of his movement. When asked during the campaign why he did not stress nationalism instead of Liberalism, Gaitán answered that the former would come in time and that as his movement developed the parties would disappear. "Elements of all the parties will participate in the fundamental transformation that the country needs," he said. "But this will happen later, when the popular movement that I am leading assumes the functions of the old parties."[15]

The Gaitanista phenomenon included personalism, a political movement, and an electoral machine, all simultaneously present. This might be considered paradoxical, but it was a testimony to Gaitán's array of skills. He did not view his campaign as culminating specifically in a presidential election. Although it might have an electoral end, he was willing to destroy the traditional leadership and risk the loss of the presidency, in order to capture the party from within and use it as the base for the popular movement he was building.[16] Yet despite the popular base of the movement, despite its themes of democracy and mass participation, the movement was essentially personalist; that is, it was a movement in which Gaitán was the center, the matrix, the voice who gave the movement its definition and form. As Antonio García pointed out, in UNIR Gaitán was but the first among equals, the leader surrounded and circumscribed by a general staff.[17] But in the Movement for the Moral and Democratic Restoration, Gaitán was alone; or, as he undoubtedly would have put it, one with the masses. As it turned out, this was both its greatest strength and its greatest weakness.

By early 1944 the first Gaitanista organizations began to form in the larger provincial cities, notably on the north coast. On January 28 the Sociedad Jorge Eliécer Gaitán, forerunner of the Comité Departamental, was founded in Barranquilla. As was characteristic of provincial Gaitanista organizations, it was the result of local initiative. Although it solicited advice on organization and direction on issues and campaign themes from Bogotá headquarters, it carried out work autonomously under the direction of a local attorney, Dr. José Esmeral. By early April the Barranquilla organization was planning to establish ten local sections in the city, was distributing campaign literature throughout the department of Atlántico, had contracted for a one-hour radio program each evening, and was organizing mass demonstrations for a visit of the candidate to the city.[18]

The official candidacy was not launched until early March at a picnic given by Gaitán's friends for him on a farm outside Bogotá.[19] There the broad outlines of the campaign were discussed and plans laid for the development of an organization. By late March the Gaitanista committee was functioning in Bogotá, and Gaitán supporters were establishing organizations throughout the country.

Leadership of the Movement

The top leaders of the Gaitanista movement were men with similar ideological sympathies who discussed tactics, provided advice, wrote campaign propaganda, and handled the myriad details involved in a political campaign. The group was known as the JEGA (the initials of Gaitán's full name) and was made up of men from all social classes, although the majority were middle-class professionals and businessmen.[20] JEGA was not organized as a formal group, but functioned as a "kitchen cabinet" of confidential and intimate friends and followers. As the movement evolved it developed a more formal structure to which Gaitán appointed men with national reputations. Dr. Jose María Córdoba became secretary general of the Gaitanista National Liberal Directorate. Córdoba's files in the Gaitán Papers indicate that he operated efficiently and effectively, handling most of the details of internal organization, overseeing the operations of provincial affiliates, and providing day-to-day direction. Another important member of the Gaitanista directorate was Dr. Luis Eduardo Gacharná, an eminent jurist and lawyer.[21] The brain trust of the Gaitanista movement, which provided the candidate with ideas and detailed information on national taxation, agrarian problems, trade relations, tariff policies, etc., was comprised of Guillermo Hernández Rodríguez, a friend of many years and an expert in finance; Antonio García, a socialist economist; another socialist, Gerardo Molina, an ex-rector of the National University; and Luis Carlos Pérez, a politician.[22]

The Gaitanista provincial organizations, especially those in the departmental capitals, generally were directed by middle-class professionals and businessmen. In Medellín, they were young professionals like Jorge Ospina Londoño; in Neiva, capital of Huila, where Eliécer Pinilla directed the movement, they were old UNIR leaders. However, most of the departmental directorates had worker and small businessman representation; in the smaller towns Gaitanista committees were often entirely made up of workers and *campesinos*.[23] At every level of the Gaitanista movement a conscious effort was made to assure representation and a voice for the popular classes.

Gaitán took a personal interest in organizing. In Bogotá, where a special effort was made to win the capital, he devoted much time to the mundane tasks of politics: he addressed rallies, attended dances, bazaars, and other fund-raising activities, and met with voter delegations.[24] He insisted, however, on the importance of the autonomous local effort and refused to get involved in internal squabbles and personality conflicts. In his correspondence, he repeatedly counseled harmony and unity within the movement.[25]

Gaitán's concern that the movement have a popular, grass-roots character was reflected in his instructions to provincial organizations for the municipal elections held nationwide in the fall of 1945. *El Tiempo* had challenged the Gaitanistas to enter the elections and show their true popular appeal. After at first refusing with the argument that his movement was not interested in mere office-seeking, Gaitán acceded to internal pressure to allow Gaitanista candidates to appear on lists where they believed they had sufficient strength to make a good showing. However, he urged that local candidates be known and respected, have a good knowledge of local problems, and declare that they were not running on a plebiscite, but as independent candidates on the Gaitanista list.[26] He refused to name local candidates—a departure from usual practice—but left it up to local organizations to decide upon candidates after careful study of local conditions.[27] The results were mixed. Gaitanista candidates had won seats in numerous municipalities throughout the country, but dominated none. However, the character of the movement was preserved.

The Organization of the Movement

By mid-1945, after a year of organizational effort, the movement became fully operational. Plans were made for a national Gaitanista convention, and the national directorate began sending specific instructions on organization. Generally, Córdoba did not discriminate in his directives between Liberals and Conservatives. He sent them to whatever group declared "adhesion" to Gaitanismo. His instructions called for: regular correspondence with national headquarters; dissemination of oral, written, and radio propaganda; conducting a Liberal census; establishing sector organizations for professionals, employees and workers, *campesinos,* women; organizing a local financial arm; and setting up an agency and correspondents to handle the Gaitanista newspaper, *Jornada.*[28]

The provincial Gaitanista organizations operated with varying degrees of effectiveness and efficiency, as might be expected. The departmental and large city committees, with their larger pool of financial resources and talent, functioned better than the small town and rural groups. The Gaitán Papers show better operations, determined by the volume of correspondence, in areas of traditional Gaitanista strength, like Tolima, Valle, Antioquia, and the departments on the north coast.[29] These were areas of former UNIR strength or where economic development was most advanced. However, there also were pockets of Gaitanista strength in traditional departments like Boyacá and the Santanders, but located primarily in the larger cities and towns.[30] In these departments Gaitanista organizations were subjected to more than the usual amount of harassment and intimidation.

By the late summer of 1945 the campaign, according to Córdoba, had reached into nearly every municipality in the country. Although he gave no figures on the number of Gaitanista committees operating throughout Colombia, the size of the organization was substantial if judged by the number of people (200) working at headquarters in Bogotá.[31] Further, the volume of correspondence in the various departmental files increased markedly during this period.

In the provinces the Gaitanista organizations were supervised from the departmental capitals, where a directing committee made up of representatives from all the social sectors met regularly to provide overall coordination. For example, in Villavicencio, capital of the intendency of Meta, the Dirección Intendencial Gaitanista, headed by a local physician, Dr. Guillermo Umaña Rocha, was elected "popularly," with representation from all social groups, but with a predominance of urban workers and *campesinos*. In other municipalities and *corregimientos* of the region, committees were formed on the same basis, with their leadership ratified by the Dirección Intendencial. Thus there was some control by the provincial leadership over the composition of local committees.

The Dirección Intendencial organized in this province: urban sectors, with a chief responsible for each urban zone and for subdividing zones and designating subchiefs; rural sectors, with a chief responsible for each *vereda* ("rural area") or finca; and work sectors, with a chief from each industry or union, who also acted as representative before the directorate. There was no indication of how the chiefs were selected.[32]

The Dirección Intendencial followed in all departments the outline for organization provided by Córdoba, with commissions of agitation and propaganda, finance, *cedulación* and *revalidación* (responsible for voter registration), and transport. A strong effort also was made to constitute effective feminine committees, assigned the task of "working closely with the commissions of agitation and propaganda and finance to spread the ideals and program of the Movement for the Moral and Democratic Restoration into all the homes, especially those of *campesinos* and workers, and to make known publicly the demands for the rights of women."[33] Although women could not vote and remained within the rather narrow confines of a machismo culture, Gaitán, long a champion of women's rights, insisted that they be given an active role within the movement.

In the national capital, where the Gaitanistas made an extremely intense effort, the movement was organized along the lines already suggested. There were functioning committees in most of the barrios or neighborhoods of the city. The strongest were located in working-class neighborhoods such as Boyacá, Florida, Primavera, and Paris.[34] Efforts were made to organize the workers in commercial, industrial, and service industries. For example, the brewery workers of the large Bavaria Company, which Gaitán had represented as an attorney during the 1930s, had a committee; nurses and trainees of the National Nursing School, an affiliate of the National University, also organized a Gaitanista committee.[35]

A reading of the minutes of the Bogotá Gaitanista committee indicates that the major preoccupation was finances. This also was true in the provinces. Although Gaitán, as he had done with UNIR, devoted all of his personal funds to the movement, these fell far short of the amounts needed in the nationwide campaign. Therefore, the Gaitanistas made elaborate efforts to set up a sound financial structure. Every committee had a financial group that reported through departmental committees to the national finance committee in Bogotá.[36] Funds were raised by assessing dues from activist members, the sale of "Pro-Candidatura Gaitán" bonds, public festivals, dances, and bazaars. Monies raised were distributed to Gaitanista organizations as follows: 50 percent for the national directorate, 25 percent for the departmental or, in the case of Bogotá, city directorate, and 25 percent for the local organization.[37]

Unlike the regular Liberal and Conservative parties, who had access to funds through party treasuries or, more usually, through personal funds available to candidates, the Gaitanistas could not fall back upon either personal fortunes or an established treasury. Gaitán attempted to turn the chronic financial problem into political gain by playing up the support he received from the common people. One rather moving story told by Luis David Peña described how a badly dressed boy of about ten came to Gaitán's office and insisted on donating a peso for the movement's newspaper, *Jornada*. Gaitán gravely accepted the donation and then delivered a short lecture to his staff on the generous spirit of his *pueblo*.[38] However, the Gaitanistas were not above receiving financial support from their ideological opponents, the Conservatives. Laureano Gómez naturally encouraged the Gaitanista movement in order to widen the Liberal division, but he did so in more than verbal ways. In a 1947 speech Gaitán admitted receiving 3,500 pesos from Conservatives out of total contributions to his campaign of 300,000 pesos.[39]

Popular subscriptions were the principal means of financing the major propaganda and information medium of the movement, *Jornada*. The paper appeared as a weekly in March 1944 and was converted to a daily in January 1947. Under the supervision of Darío Samper, *Jornada* became one of the top circulation newspapers in the country. It was distributed nationwide from Bogotá. Peña claimed that *Jornada* was one of Gaitán's "loves." He took a personal interest in its technical and editorial production and provided definite ideas on how the news should be presented. He said, "We have to call things by their names. We cannot speak in euphemisms, nor hide the real intentions of our thoughts behind useless words. We must speak a direct language to the people; that is to say, tell the truth. . . . We must have sincere journalism." He added that a newspaper has the task of orienting, teaching, and informing about "great works, of being a valid force for history."[40]

One of the important reasons for founding *Jornada* was the lack of favorable coverage in existing newspapers. Although some Liberal papers supported Gaitán,[41] the Liberal press generally remained faithful to the traditional leadership. Many provincial papers, especially those of Conservative affiliation, at least provided campaign coverage. But this was not true of the great Liberal Bogotá daily *El Tiempo,* nor the rightist Liberal *La Razón,* both of which noticed Gaitán only to attack him.[42] Gaitán therefore encouraged, as he did during the UNIR period, the establishment of provincial Gaitanista papers. These local weeklies were funded by subscription, as was the case of *Restauración* of Buga, Valle, or through personal financing of an editor, such as *Campaña* in Tolima.[43] They were of limited scope and coverage but were another indicator of Gaitanista support.

Another medium utilized rather widely by the Gaitanistas was radio. The Ultimas Noticias station in Bogotá, owned by Rómulo Guzmán, frequently broadcast Gaitán's speeches, especially those he delivered on Friday evenings from various theaters in the capital.[44] By using the new technique of recording speeches and distributing records to sympathetic radio stations, Gaitán managed to reach a wide national audience. Many stations provided free time to broadcast these recorded speeches. One Bogotá station, Emisora Panamericana, played free every thirty minutes part of the record "A la Carga!" and had a special noontime program, "El Tribunal del Pueblo," that allowed Gaitanistas to express their opinions.[45] Gaitán also made use of the new electronic media by speaking to midday crowds through loudspeakers mounted on the balcony of his headquarters that fronted on the vast Plaza de Bolívar in central Bogotá.

Campaign pamphlets and broadsides also were widely used. These followed the Gaitanista themes of attacking the economic and political oligarchy and denouncing the traditional Liberals, with explanations of Gaitán's program included. One pamphlet, *Ten Reasons Why All Good Liberals Should Vote for Jorge Eliécer Gaitán*, describes the candidate as a "just, earthy, and superior man whom Colombia needs in order to save itself from the economic oligarchy and the Communist phantom." The pamphlet noted that Gaitán would carry through a bloodless revolution of "work and order" that would develop the country and provide the people with adequate food, clothing, shelter, education, and medical facilities.[46] This type of straightforward, direct appeal, playing upon both the hopes and the fears of average Colombians, with emphasis upon orderly revolutionary change, characterized the propaganda printed and distributed by provincial committees.

The Popular Convention

In September 1945, when the organization of Gaitán's movement had been fully elaborated, the popular convention was held to launch formally his candidacy. The modern campaign techniques that Gaitán introduced to mobilize the masses were best exemplified by the events surrounding this great convention, called to ratify Gaitán's candidacy, in the tradition of Bonapartism, by the direct participation of the people without intermediaries.[47] But it also was intended to be a demonstration of Gaitanista strength, an inspiring emotional experience for those involved, and a vivid contrast to the closed-door method used to choose the regular Liberal candidate for the 1946 election. In all of this it succeeded admirably. For the first time in Colombia's history, tens of thousands of its lower- and middle-class citizens participated directly in a major political event and had at least the illusion of power and influence. Some commentators have suggested that Gaitán had an affinity for fascism, but the truth is that the only aspects he had in common with the fascists were his reliance on the personal charisma of the maximum leader and the glamorous techniques of mass politics.

As was usual with Gaitanista efforts, the popular convention was carefully planned months in advance.[48] Instructions were sent out to provincial organizations to ensure representation from all parts of the country. Delegations had to include not only local leaders, but workers and *campesinos* as well. Every effort was made to assure that the majority of delegates come from the popular classes. Transportation was organized (numerous bus owners donated free use of their vehicles); reception committees were formed in Bogotá worker neighborhoods; thousands of flags and banners were assembled. On the Thursday before the convention a parade of vehicles emblazoned with flags and standards made its way through the capital to generate enthusiasm. On Saturday night a huge, torchlight parade organized by the committees of various worker neighborhoods marched through the main streets.[49]

On Sunday, September 23, fireworks heralded the arrival of the great day. Bands marched through the worker neighborhoods and delegations fell in behind. The crowds assembled before the tombs of the popular Liberal leaders Rafael Uribe Uribe and Benjamín Herrera, where they heard emotional tributes before marching on to the Circo de Santamaría, Bogotá's bullring, where the convention took place. Through all of this, squads organized by JEGA kept order and maintained enthusiasm by leading patriotic songs and chanting slogans.

The scene in the Santamaría by the time of Gaitán's arrival in late afternoon was one of near hysteria. When the caudillo entered the arena, trumpets sounded, flowers and streamers were thrown, and white doves were released. The many bands struck up the national anthem. This was followed by wave after wave of ovations by the people.[50] Gaitán, resplendent in a black suit, with his beautiful wife and child standing beside him, silently acknowledged the tribute from his platform above the crowd. What crossed his mind in the midst of this spectacular is unknown, but he delivered in that arena what was perhaps the finest speech of his career.

Gaitán began by analyzing the difference between his movement, representative of the popular will, and the mechanical politics practiced by his opponents, who had subverted the democratic spirit of the party by selecting candidates behind closed doors according to the whims of political bosses and special interests. What they had done, he claimed, was undermine the moral force that was the basis of society, the commonly agreed upon norms of conduct and methods that maintained an equilibrium among the various components of the social organism, that "conserved the rights, impeded the abuses, sanctified the truth, and developed work in an ascending scale of merited compensations."[51] For this reason the gravest problem confronting the country was moral. And that was why Gaitanistas called for the moral and democratic restoration of the republic.

Gaitán described the period in which they were living as one of transformation. Scientific and technical advances had provided the means for elevating the levels of existence for all men and had changed the nature of economic and social relationships. However, these advances had been usurped by minority oligarchies who had put them at the service of their own interests and had suborned the institutions of society, thus denying the majority the benefits of progress. The outstanding example of this "moral decomposition" was European fascism, which had just been defeated. But the symptoms of moral decomposition had affected even Colombia, where manipulation, fraud, corruption, exclusion, immorality, disdain, and indifference for the people had infected the institutions, especially those of the state, which were looked upon as "booty of war."[52]

In contrast, the Gaitanista movement represented a defensive reaction against this state of affairs, a mobilization of the nation when it sensed that its essential virtues were in danger. It was a movement to restore virtue to public life, to reestablish a democratic equilibrium and autonomy in all branches of government, to ensure that the state functioned in such a way as to provide equal opportunity to all its citizens, and to guide and develop the material and spiritual progress of the nation.[53]

Gaitán then indicted the leaders of the ruling Liberal regime for betraying the trust the people had placed in them and for violating the principles of the party, which he said were "defense of legality, struggle for truth, stimulation of honesty and sincerity, administrative rectitude, discipline in work, liberating action for the oppressed." He insisted that politics had to be in step with the new times, that the state now had to be, above all, human. It must be concerned that all Colombians have access to a decent life, that their material conditions be improved and secured, that they have adequate food, clothing, shelter, and health care. To do this, the laws of the state must be determined by the necessities of men.[54]

The speech was a reiteration and further elaboration of the themes Gaitán had developed during the course of the campaign. It was overwhelmingly condemnatory, anti-status quo in orientation, emotional in delivery. The programmatic aspects were generalized rather than specific, but keyed to the basic interests of the listeners. It was a speech suited to the circumstances in which it was delivered, a masterful performance designed to arouse the collective enthusiasm of the Gaitanistas.

As the final act of the popular convention Gaitán led a parade of the forty thousand delegates and spectators through the central streets of Bogotá.[55] It was a rousing finale reminiscent of the great fascist rallies the orator had witnessed years before in Italy. The spectacle, as Gaitán probably intended, provoked in his followers a sense of power. They must have felt that victory was within their grasp. Events proved this expectation to be an illusion; yet it cannot be denied that a vital, new, political force had come into being in Colombia.

Personalism: The Role of the Caudillo

In the eight months from the convention of September 1945 to the election of May 1946 Gaitán perfected, for the first time in Colombia, the techniques of mass politics. The convention had strengthened, enlarged, and focused the magnetism of his appeal. He stumped the country as a star and celebrity.

As important as the leadership, organization, and convention undoubtedly were, the primary ingredient was Gaitán, who symbolized the movement and embodied the hopes and aspirations of his followers. In this respect Gaitanismo was part of the caudillo tradition characteristic of Latin American politics. The tradition had its roots in the seignorial relationships of the hacienda culture. In its modern manifestation as Gaitanismo the patron-client relationship continued in the dependence of the Gaitanista masses upon the leader for both direction and inspiration. The masses were displaced from the old culture without having become absorbed totally by the new urban, industrial culture. They lacked autonomous institutions of self-defense, such as independent trade unions, a coherent ideology based upon their new economic and social environment, or the means for articulation of their interests. Their lack of political sophistication made them susceptible to the combination of personalism and mass mobilization techniques. While Gaitán often spoke of the necessity for developing class consciousness among the masses, and in fact carried out measures designed to accomplish that, in practical terms he continued to rely upon the personalist tradition at this stage of the movement.

The basis of Gaitán's personalism was, of course, his ability to identify with his followers. His lower-middle-class background helped in this regard, but it was not the most important reason for his ability to attract support. His education, general culture, and bourgeois life-style and achievements placed him far above the common people. But what Gaitán always was able to do successfully was demonstrate genuine concern for their welfare. He had proved this objectively by the many initiatives he had made on their behalf during his public career. However, more importantly, he had managed to inculcate among his followers a feeling, or spirit, of his concern. And there was no question in their minds that this was authentic. Gaitán remained heart and soul a part of his *pueblo,* and they responded by considering him "a son of their womb." The affection with which Gaitán was regarded by the common people was constantly demonstrated. For example, Hernández Rodríguez said that Gaitán often found his parked automobile filled with flowers, placed there by servant women on their way home from work.[56] The Gaitán Papers contain literally hundreds of letters from people throughout the country, speaking for themselves and their illiterate friends, declaring their affection and loyalty to Gaitán, often without reference to his particular politics.

One factor that worked favorably for Gaitán was his physical appearance. With his unmistakably mestizo ancestry, he actually looked like one of the *pueblo* whom he championed, a fact that was highlighted rather than diminished by his expensive clothes. His followers could see themselves in him, and could understand the meaning and scorn implied by the racial slur "negro Gaitán," as he often was contemptuously described by his high-born opponents. Yet they could take vicarious pleasure from the manner in which he forced himself upon "those of above" despite his background and appearance.

His life-style further enhanced his image. His large, modern house with its fine furnishings, the big, black, American-made Buicks he drove, the country club to which he belonged, even the beautiful, elegant, aristocratic woman who was his wife, appealed to the secret cravings of those who had come from the countryside to the cities seeking social mobility and a new life. They might be frustrated but here was one who was not. Gaitán was a surrogate for both their ambitions and their "Indian malice."

Gaitán, to be sure, was a social climber, but he also wanted to take the masses with him. He felt animosity toward the privileged strata, true, but so did his followers. Both he and his followers wanted some of the advantages that the rich and powerful were enjoying. The personal animosity arose, in both cases, from a sense of exclusion. The desire for a decent, comfortable life is universal. Gaitán symbolized these tendencies by castigating the upper classes and by personally appropriating their style of life which he promised, vicariously, to his followers. The man, like many others, was a paradox. He adopted the bourgeois emblems of prestige primarily as a larger, evolutionary plan to destroy the bourgeois concept itself. He and his followers had to destroy the citadel in order to possess its treasure.

The most important technique Gaitán used to establish his identity, his charismatic relationship with the masses, was emotional, flamboyant oratory. He was a master of it, perhaps one of the best in modern Latin American history. And once again he was following a tradition—one that placed great importance on the spoken word. But Gaitán did not utilize the aristocratic tone, the formal vocabulary, and the baroque texture of the best Colombian orators. When speaking to the semiliterate masses he spoke the language of the people—often crude, slangy, but always with great forcefulness and passion.[57] He emphasized emotion in his speeches rather than reason. A reading of his speeches reveals repetitions, contradictions, faulty reasonings, distortions, and inaccuracies; however, he understood that his listeners were more impressed by words delivered with power and emotion than with precise meaning and logic. His formal addresses were delivered in a reasoned, even tone, and were a model of erudition and logic. But in the political arena his speeches became an emotional exchange between his listeners and himself. Gaitán once said, "When I am before an audience I am fundamentally transformed. I feel an inexpressible emotion, an intoxication without limits." Peña described Gaitán's charismatic effect as that of a powerful antenna that gathered onto itself the most powerful collective emotions.[58]

In his entire career Gaitán wrote out beforehand only five speeches. The others were delivered extemporaneously, with only a minimum of preparation. Usually, before speaking, he reflected for a few minutes on what he wanted to stress, then took a little brandy with water to somewhat calm his nervousness.[59] When before the audience he began to speak slowly, in measured tones. But gradually he accelerated the flow of words. His voice became hoarse and emotional, his body tensed, his arms slashed the air. As his listeners responded with shouts and applause, his voice grew louder and his charged phrases came faster and faster. At the climax of a speech he shouted one phrase after another, building the emotions of the audience and himself to a peak of intensity. When he finished, the transfixed audience exploded with frenzied emotion.[60] His political speeches combined demagoguery, calculated manipulation of the listeners, and passionate involvement with them in an emotional experience. Customarily, when he finished speaking, he disappeared rapidly from the scene.

Gaitán had practiced oratory in his youth in empty classrooms and before mirrors. Sometimes his mother coached him in the use of language and gestures.[61] In order to build up his physique and lung capacity, he had during his university days exercised daily by climbing and jogging at nine thousand feet in the Andean foothills behind Bogotá's National Park. This he continued throughout his life. It allowed him to survive the rigorous eighteen-hour days of the 1945–1946 campaign, when he sometimes delivered eight to ten speeches daily after sleeping briefly in his automobile.[62]

Despite the extemporaneous character of his speeches and the seemingly spontaneous nature of the campaign, Gaitán developed a carefully planned and executed effort which always was directly under his control. When in the capital his daily schedule allowed time for political conferences and written correspondence, general supervision of *Jornada,* and both parliamentary and legal activities.[63]

His travels in the provinces were similarly closely planned and tightly controlled. For example, the candidate's schedule for March 1946 (two months before the election) indicated an extensive trip, often by airplane (which Gaitán was the first to utilize for campaigning on a large scale in Colombia), through the southwestern departments of Valle, Cauca, and Nariño, with major speeches in the most important cities.[64] A typical campaign visit to a city was planned well in advance by the local Gaitanistas, who received detailed instructions on procedure. Hand-painted sheets with slogans were prepared three days in advance and placed strategically around the city. On the morning of the visit, buses mounted with loudspeakers roamed the streets broadcasting announcements and music. A band was hired to perform in the major plaza, already decorated with signs and flags, where the political speech was delivered. A large hall was rented for a following "ideological" discourse, which usually was of a more specialized nature dealing with local problems. Fireworks were sometimes provided; a cheering section was recruited from among the regulars at local cafes, and the services of local photographers were obtained.[65] Gaitán usually stopped to rest at a location outside the city before entering around five o'clock in the afternoon when maximum crowds were assured.[66] Little was left to chance, and the result was an outburst of enthusiasm that often far exceeded the real support the Gaitanistas actually had in a particular place. But as Gaitán knew, the illusion of strength and vigor was often more impressive than the reality.

Nevertheless, as the campaign wore on Gaitán drew larger and larger crowds. By mid-1945 his Friday speeches in Bogotá's Municipal Theater filled the hall and the surrounding streets with thousands of spectators.[67] On June 21, 1945, a speech in Barranquilla was attended by more than thirty thousand persons.[68] *El Siglo* and *Jornada* during this period carried photographs and reports of vast crowds whenever Gaitán spoke. The campaign speeches were repetitions of themes already developed: attacks against the oligarchy; condemnations of the political country that was enriching itself at the expense of the national country; calls for a peaceful revolution by the people to prevent totalitarianism.

However, Gaitán was quite capable of delivering specialized speeches on complex, technical subjects addressed to a particular audience. Córdoba reported that in Villavicencio he delivered an informed lecture on the problems of the cattle industry that impressed even the cattlemen present. On another occasion, while speaking before a medical group in Barranquilla, he gave precise statistics concerning public health and the effects of various diseases in Colombia.[69] His attacks on the oligarchy also were backed up with statistics. In a speech in Cúcuta he mentioned that there were families in Medellín and Bogotá who, with capital of 12 million, had earned 18 million in one year through speculation. During that speech he responded to an attack by *Time* magazine on his restrictive credit proposals by stating that he preferred to mix with his own mestizo people rather than with the plutocrats of North America and their national allies.[70]

The personalist nature of the Gaitanista movement naturally aroused the opposition, who charged him with opportunism and demogoguery. Gaitán was aware of his central role and, despite his own considerable ego and vanity, made some attempts to downplay himself. He urged Peña to keep his name out of *Jornada* as much as possible, or to refer to him in somewhat oblique ways, as, for example, the "popular chief of Liberalism." On one occasion he chided Darío Samper, the director of *Jornada,* for reporting in the paper the unveiling of a bust of Gaitán in the town of Itaguí, Antioquia.[71] However, the continuous flow of requests for Gaitán's personal appearance by his sympathizers indicated the extreme reliance of the movement on him personally.

In the years 1944–1946 Gaitán took advantage of the confusion in the Liberal party. Over the heads of the parties' leaders, he heeded the people's call, hammering home the distinction between the national country and the political country. As his Gaitanista movement took shape, the personalist, concentric element emerged strongly. He had become a master rhetorician, commanding a grass-roots organization which emphasized charismatic techniques. He was, in a time of endemic crisis, convincing the masses of his authentic identification with them.

9
Followers, Foes, and the Campaign of 1946

The supporters of Gaitán were overwhelmingly members of the lower social classes. They were in the majority workers, although white-collar employees, *campesinos,* students, and small businessmen helped swell the Gaitanista ranks. Correspondence in the Gaitán Papers indicates that it was usually those without economic independence or outside the normal channels of political organization who rallied to Gaitanismo.[1] The nature of this support caused especially difficult problems for the national headquarters, because it often meant lack of experienced leadership at the local level, scarcity of financial resources, and hostility and harassment from local Liberal officials. Yet all of this was outweighed by the genuine enthusiasm generated by Gaitán among the so-called popular classes. What was remarkable was that the Gaitanistas were able to build a movement of such potency despite the enormous obstacles that stood in their path.

Unlike UNIR, which was essentially rural in its appeal, the Gaitanista movement after 1944 relied primarily on the urban masses. The key group among them was the workers. However, the most active and politically conscious workers (most of the urban masses were unorganized) were members of the CTC, dominated by Liberals and Communists and traditionally allied with the López wing of the Liberal party. The task of the Gaitanistas was to convince the leadership of the CTC to swing its support behind Gaitán, or, alternatively, to appeal to the workers over the heads of their leaders. When the democratic left of Liberalism and the Communist leadership decided to back the official Liberal candidate, Gabriel Turbay, the Gaitanistas opted for the latter strategy.

Gaitán's prolabor attitude as minister of labor, as well as his public record, convinced many rank-and-file workers that he was the logical candidate of organized labor. The difficult economic climate and the growing hostility of official Liberal circles to labor—represented especially by Acting President Lleras Camargo—hardened their position. As early as 1943 the Federation of Drivers of Colombia and other unions looked to Gaitán rather than to the CTC or official Liberalism as the best defender of their interests.[2] By 1945 Gaitán was receiving mass support, unauthorized by the CTC, from workers throughout Colombia: ten thousand workers in Barranquilla, three thousand miners in Segovia, Antioquia, and one thousand sugar workers in Tolima represented only a fraction of those who abandoned the official Liberals and ignored the CTC to pledge support for Gaitán.[3]

The widening gap between the CTC leadership and the rank and file was exploited to the full by the Gaitanistas during the Seventh Labor Congress that met in Bogotá in December 1945. Although the CTC leadership attempted to avoid dealing with political matters, its traditional use of political action instead of collective bargaining as a tactic meant that the internal division could not be avoided.[4] Further, rival Gaitanista and Turbay factions demanded to be heard. The atmosphere was so tense that elaborate police precautions had to be taken in the city to prevent open clashes. Finally, the congress broke up without resolution of the problem, and a group within the CTC joined the Gaitanistas.

While the CTC congress was meeting, the Gaitanistas decided to hold a simultaneous and parallel labor congress. The move was devised by Córdoba, who accredited discontented CTC delegates to the newly formed Gaitanista National Confederation of Workers (CNT). To give the illusion of having more delegates than the CTC, Córdoba made up credentials and distributed them among members of the Gaitanista city committees. Although Gaitán initially was annoyed by these tactics, according to Córdoba, he finally "understood the logic of weakening the official leadership of the CTC, which insisted on vigorously fighting the popular wing of Liberalism, calling it fascist and totalitarian, despite the fact that the rank and file backed Gaitán all the way." The CTC apparently now was too weak to counter effectively the Gaitanista moves: Córdoba claimed that they did not fight back.[5]

The failure of the CTC, the Liberal party, and the government to address themselves sincerely to the problems of labor strengthened the position of Gaitán among organized workers, many of whom sensed that they now had nowhere else to turn. Throughout the winter and spring of 1946 additional union support was pledged to the Gaitanista candidacy. In May 1946 the entire Workers' Federation of Tolima, dissatisfied with the CTC and the government, threw its official support behind Gaitán. The federation, which had a directive council consisting of five Communists and six Liberals, represented sixty-five unions in the department, including railroad, communication and highway workers, and *campesino* organizations nominally controlled by the

Communists. The executive vice-president of the federation wrote that the decision to support Gaitán was made because the majority of the unions' membership desired it. He also hinted that the affiliated unions might join the Gaitanista CNT.[6]

In addition to organized labor, the Gaitanistas drew into their ranks a sizeable minority of disaffected Liberals. Most of them were in urban areas not directly under the influence of local politicians. The voluminous correspondence in the Gaitán Papers indicates, however, that almost every municipality (a town and surrounding rural area) with registered Liberals had some Gaitanistas. In certain areas, like the primitive Chocó region along the Pacific Coast (almost totally rural), intelligence reports claimed that as much as 70 percent of the population backed Gaitán.[7] Although figures like these no doubt were inflated, they do demonstrate the national appeal of Gaitán and the broad base of his support. Finally, the chaos within the Liberal party certainly was a major contributing factor to Gaitanista strength.

The Gaitanistas often represented the only politically cohesive force in a region. Despite the lack of resources and the severe limitations of the Gaitanista organization, especially adequate local leadership, the movement picked up supporters. Some provincial Gaitanistas even suggested that official Liberalism was so badly discredited and there was so much grass-roots support for Gaitán that a local organization was really not necessary.[8] In many areas it appeared true that Gaitanismo was a mass without captains, as its opposition charged; but it was equally true that the Liberal politicians often were captains without masses.

The major problem of the Gaitanistas was not to attract adherents but to develop an efficiently functioning organization to bring out the vote. The lack of financial resources and the scarcity of politically experienced personnel probably had a major effect on the final outcome of the campaign. Although it might have been true, as Córdoba claimed, that there were Gaitanista organizations in almost every municipality in Colombia, the degree of operating effectiveness was another matter. A review of reports on the progress of the movement reveals the difficulties encountered by local Gaitanista organizations. To cite but one example, a report to Córdoba from Neiva, Huila, indicated that the movement there suffered severe economic difficulties because those with resources, such as local businessmen, remained with the official Liberals. Further, the Gaitanistas counted few professional politicians in their ranks. The local leaders were men who, although operating with "good will," nevertheless had to make a living and could not devote full attention to building the movement. The Gaitanistas in Huila were characterized in the report as "masses without directors."[9] Similar intelligence was received from other parts of the country up to the time of the 1946 election. Probably the one solace for the Gaitanistas was that the Liberals were in a state of disarray.

Another internal problem was the rivalry in local committees. In Antioquia conflicts within the leadership were severe enough to undermine seriously the entire Gaitanista effort in that important department. In the capital, Medellín, a group of young professionals led by an attorney, Jorge Ospina Londoño, had organized a department-wide directorate in the spring of 1944. However, generational and personality conflicts developed within the leadership, as well as disagreements over the dispersal of funds by the local Gaitanista treasurer, a Medellín merchant, who apparently engaged in the traditional practices of vote-buying and influence-peddling.[10] This contributed to the serious defeat of Gaitanismo in Antioquia, despite the fact that there were committees in all of the department's one hundred municipalities. In December 1946 Córdoba blamed Ospina directly for the defeat and accused him of "repeated demonstrations of anarchy and disassociation." In an unprecedented move, the Gaitanista high command removed Ospina from the Antioquia leadership and imposed its own director.[11]

Personality conflicts also afflicted the movement in Barranquilla and Cartagena on the north coast. However, the numbers of Gaitanista supporters were such that no serious damage was done, nor were there open splits in the leadership as in Medellín.

The Opposition to Gaitán

The regular Liberal leaders' reaction to Gaitán was understandably vehement when it became clear that he was not merely maneuvering for position within the party. They attempted to purge Liberalism of Gaitanismo and entered into a savage struggle for control of the party which continued after the presidential election of 1946. Even the naming of Gaitán as Jefe Unico of the party in mid-1947 did not end the conflict. Party regulars continued to resist Gaitán until his death.

Liberal circles supporting Gabriel Turbay did not initially view the Gaitán candidacy with apprehension. They believed that he merely was marshaling his forces to assure high positions and a prominent voice in the future administration. They expected that Gaitanismo would have to converge with Turbay on the basis of some as yet unnamed understandings.[12] This was a position that Turbay apparently held almost to the eve of the election.

However, the center and right of the Liberal party thought differently. Eduardo Santos and Juan Lozano y Lozano were critical of Gaitán from the beginning. Their respective newspapers, *El Tiempo* and *La Razón,* voiced the attacks of the Liberal center and right on Gaitanismo. For them Gaitán was an anti-Liberal demagogue who was arousing the unreliable masses in a frontal assault on the institutions of Colombian society. He was a traitor to a Liberalism that had served him well. His attacks on Liberal administrations threatened not only the party's hold on the government, but its very existence. Worst of all, Gaitán in reality was a socialist disguised as a Liberal. As far as the Liberal oligarchs were concerned, that was the most unforgivable of Gaitán's crimes. In commenting on the ideological differences between Gaitán and Liberalism, *La Razón* noted that the former by temperament, development, and attitude was a socialist and knew it.[13] The Liberals regarded Gaitán as a revolutionary who was deceiving his followers: they would abandon him if he dared to expose his ideology. Of course, this was exactly contrary to Gaitán's view that he represented an authentic Liberalism that was at least temperamentally socialist.

If the regular Liberals viewed the ideological issue as the most important reason for their differences with Gaitán, the Gaitanista methods proved to be most worrisome. In its editorial commenting on Gaitán's opening campaign speech, *El Tiempo* deplored his emotional appeal to the masses.[14] As the campaign wore on Gaitán came to be regarded as a ruthless demagogue who was masterfully manipulating the illiterate and dispossessed masses in a campaign based upon hate, fear, envy, and the antagonism of the "have-nots" for the "haves."[15] Gaitán's followers were described as the most undesirable elements of society, the worthless *chusma* who were moved by the most base emotions. A quarter of a century after the campaign one observer still remembered with horror the fear that the marching Gaitanistas struck in the hearts of "respectable" citizens.[16] The Gaitanista techniques of mass politics, unfamiliar in Colombia, and especially the use of "fighting squads" and the occasional appearance of unruly behavior, finally earned the Gaitanistas a sinister reputation in some quarters.[17] It must be remembered, however, that Gaitán never advocated brawny tactics except in self-defense. As for demagoguery, the truth is that the Liberals exhibited the understandable tendency to brand as a demagogue anyone who did not share their sense of personal contentment.

When Gaitán refused to abide by the July 1945 Liberal party convention that named Gabriel Turbay the candidate, he was in effect read out of the party. He knew that the convention, stacked mostly with delegates who were members of congress or handpicked by party bosses, would never select him to represent Liberalism. Indeed, he made much political currency out of the fact that the Liberal candidate had been chosen behind closed doors. For the Gaitanistas the convention was another example of the political country conspiring against the popular will.

With Gaitán pressing his antiparty campaign and continuing to disparage previous Liberal administrations, the Liberals disassociated themselves from him. *El Tiempo* called Gaitanismo an "anti-Liberal adventure," a new party that was not part of any political tradition in Colombia.[18] *La Razón* in various editorials echoed the same sentiment. The Liberal attacks on Gaitanismo were not merely verbal. Local bosses brought their power and influence to bear against the caudillo's sympathizers. In the rural department of Cauca the Gaitanista movement was reported to be weak because of the forceful caciquism exercised by three powerful, Liberal families—Chaux, Simmonds, and Zambranos—who carried out economic reprisals against Gaitanistas. The Liberals of that department were described as the "moral slaves" of those families.[19] There are many other reports in the Gaitán Papers of harassment by Liberal bosses. In some instances appointed Liberal officials carried out actions agains Gaitán's followers, including the firing of public employees who expressed sympathy for him.

In addition to the Liberals, the Gaitanistas had to contend with the Communists, who were openly hostile to them.[20] The Communist party leadership, which had allied itself with the López current of the Liberal party in the mid-1930s, considered Gaitán a demagogue and stated that his followers were the most backward elements of the masses. In a speech before the tenth plenum of the Communist party in June 1945, General Secretary Augusto Durán said: "We do not stop to examine the candidacy of Gaitán, because even if his anticapitalist and anti-oligarchy campaign receives some support among the most backward 'popular' sectors, he continues to be the voice of reaction against the Liberal regime."[21] The Communists initially supported the candidacy of Echandía, who had the blessing of López. When that failed they swung to Turbay, whom they previously had classified as an oligarch and plutocrat.[22] It must be remembered, however, that the Communist party was in its "popular front" phase and was paying more attention to its international obligations than to its national ones. The Communists later admitted "false" appreciation for the Gaitanista movement before 1946 and claimed that they did not think Santos would permit the split to result in the election of a Conservative.[23]

Despite the support of the Communist leadership for Turbay, many rank and file were leaning toward Gaitán. The minutes of the Gaitanista Bogotá committee indicated collaboration between its supporters and Communists in the working-class neighborhoods of the city. From Cartagena there were reports of resignations from the party in order to join the Gaitanistas.[24] It was obvious that the Communist party, like the CTC, was split over the Gaitán candidacy. The leaders had difficulty maintaining discipline over the membership, thus verifying, for the Gaitanistas at least, that "the people are superior to their leaders."

Candidates and Maneuvers

Although Gabriel Turbay had flirted with radicalism as a young Nuevo and had earned the reputation of a demogogue, by the time of his candidacy he was best known for his ability to conciliate and compromise.[25] Indeed, he saw his principal task as that of reconciling the various factions of Liberalism. In his campaign speeches he continuously stressed the need for party unity, but he also recognized the political crisis that the country was experiencing and called for renovation of the party to provide more internal democracy and a greater voice for the masses.[26] Unlike Gaitán, who attacked the oligarchy, Turbay stressed the fundamental responsibility of the "directing classes" in reforming the nation. Essentially, while Gaitán wanted to curtail or remove the oligarchy, Turbay wanted it to become accountable for the welfare of the people.

In contrast to the flamboyant Gaitán, Turbay during the campaign appeared bland and colorless. While calling for renovation and reform of the parties and public institutions, he refused to agitate the masses. He knew that he had the support of the party machinery and relied upon it to see him through. Therefore, while Gaitán was mobilizing the alienated, Turbay was mobilizing the party bosses. Though Turbay failed to realize the extent of support for Gaitán within Liberal ranks, it turned out that enough Liberals voted for Turbay to assure his victory had there not been a complicating factor.

Less than two months before the election, on March 23, 1946, a surprise candidate appeared. A Conservative party convention launched the candidacy of Mariano Ospina Pérez, a wealthy member of a prominent Antioquia family that had provided Colombia with two previous presidents. He also had the guileful and important backing of Laureano Gómez, the leader of the Conservative party, who had initially indicated support for Gaitán as a strategy in dividing the Liberals and who then chose the decisive moment to assemble the Conservative convention and to nominate Ospina. Because there had been no Conservative candidate for president since 1930, the Gómez strategy worked beautifully.

The nomination of Ospina caused consternation among the regular Liberals. This totally unexpected development almost assured a Liberal defeat and the creation of a government deeply influenced by the hated and feared Laureano Gómez. Frantically, the party chiefs began to seek a means of uniting the Liberals. All of the invective and repugnance for Gaitán were forgotten in an attempt to bring him and Turbay together. Finally, at the behest of Santos, Gaitán agreed to meet with Santos, López, and Turbay at the beginning of April, although he had declared at the end of March that he had no intention of abandoning his own candidacy.[27] At this conference Gaitán agreed to meet privately with Turbay, with the condition that the talks include specific programs of government. Gaitán apparently wanted to guarantee the strongest possible reform program even if he decided to withdraw from the race.

The Gaitán-Turbay meetings took place in an atmosphere of cordiality. Both candidates agreed on the need for fundamental social and economic reforms and increased participation by the people in the institutions of the country.[28] They explored the possibility of uniting Liberalism on the basis of an "anti-oligarchy pact."[29] Within this context Gaitán would withdraw from the race in order to assure Liberal victory. Turbay as president would carry out a reformist program while Gaitán became party chief, first designate to the presidency (literally, vice-president in the Colombian system), and the party's candidate four years later in 1950.[30]

When word of the possible anti-oligarchy pact leaked out, those party chiefs who originally had urged the meetings of the candidates quickly changed their positions. Santos informed his candidate, Turbay, that if he reached an agreement with Gaitán on the basis of their talks, not only would he withdraw his personal support and that of his machine, but he would openly declare against Turbay, as well. López let it be known that he would not support the Gaitán-Turbay agreement and would continue his opposition to Turbay. It was suggested that he even considered a Conservative victory preferable to a victory by either of the Liberal candidates.[31]

Turbay needed the regular Liberal machine, which was not commanded by him personally; Gaitán faced similar wide-scale defections from his ranks. The announcement of the talks with Turbay had generated disapproval among Gaitán's followers.[32] The tone of this sentiment was exemplified by a letter from a Gaitanista in Barranquilla: "You have no right to resign. You can't betray the multitudes. To resign in favor of the Santos clique will perpetuate the oligarchic system we have been fighting against."[33] Thus the actions of both candidates were circumscribed by the conflicting interests they represented. Turbay was a prisoner of the Liberal party machine. Gaitán was beholden to expectant followers whose aspirations he had aroused. Compromise was impossible.

Following the third and final meeting with Turbay, Gaitán went to Bogotá's Municipal Theater to deliver one of this regular campaign addresses. The scene in the theater was disorderly. Gaitán had to ask several times for silence so that he could speak. If he was wavering in his decision when he entered the theater, what he encountered there was enough to convince him to stay in the race. He probably understood that the abandonment of his movement would wreck his career as a popular leader, if not as a Liberal politician. But he also must have known that without the masses he would be another politician dependent upon the oligarchy which had shown no great inclination to accept him fully in the past.

In his speech Gaitán did not criticize Turbay. He concentrated on attacking the Liberal-Conservative oligarchy which he said was joining together to meet the threat from below. He claimed that the Liberal and Conservative *pueblo* again was about to be cheated by the ruling class, which was putting aside its internal differences in order to defend its common interests. But he vowed to continue the struggle. "A clean banner alone upon the summit has more value than a hundred flags washed in the mud!" he shouted. He predicted a revolution that would topple the oligarchy but, characteristically, urged his followers to continue the struggle by peaceful means.[34] He was bolstered in his determination to pursue his independent cause by his vision of the campaign as an instrument by which to educate the masses.

The Final Outcome

As the election returns began to come in on the evening of May 5 it appeared that Gaitán was the winner. But these early results were from the cities. With the gradual accumulation of votes from the rural areas, where the traditional parties were strongest, the regular candidates eventually surged ahead. The final tally, broken down by departments, is shown in table 4. The combined Liberal vote was 799,548 compared with the Conservative vote of 565,260. However, Ospina was the winner, and sixteen years of Liberal presidential domination ended.

A study of the voting pattern indicates that Gaitán won absolute majorities in the departments of Atlántico and Bolívar on the north coast, and additional majorities of the Liberal vote in Cauca, Cundinamarca, Huila, Magdalena, Valle, and the intendancy of Meta (which also included Vichada and Vaupés in the vast eastern plains regions). Though a complete breakdown by major cities is not available, *El Tiempo* indicated that he won overwhelmingly in Bogotá and Barranquilla, and in the most important urban centers of Cali, Cartagena, Santa Marta, Neiva, Ibagué, and Cúcuta. He also won most of the other departmental capitals, and came very close in Popayán. The only major city he lost in significantly was Medellín, Ospina's home town, where the Gaitanista organization suffered major internal problems.[35]

Although Gaitán came in third in the popular voting, he had demonstrated the enormous appeal of his movement. In only two years, with scant resources and without prominent backing, he had touched the sensitive nerve of social unrest and constructed a powerful political force out of the new groups created by modernization. As Antonio García wrote, "The Moral Restoration was the avalanche of the *pueblo* behind a messianic leader."[36] For the first time in Colombia's history the alienated had made their weight felt convincingly; it signaled a new era in Colombian politics. With his personalist style and

TABLE 4: 1946 PRESIDENTIAL ELECTION RESULTS

	Liberal		Conservative	
Department	Turbay	Gaitán	Ospina	Other
Antioquia	80,955	7,710	99,544	19
Atlántico	6,234	31,044	11,789	15
Bolívar	17,822	55,454	32,814	4
Boyacá	35,016	11,301	32,655	1
Caldas	55,734	17,607	72,075	—
Cauca	16,031	17,055	22,758	14
Chocó	4,401	3,076	2,326	—
Cundinamarca	38,131	79,655	71,287	31
Huila	5,531	14,749	22,245	—
Magdalena	17,610	20,361	19,040	—
Meta	1,072	2,163	4,246	—
Nariño	20,613	6,811	29,623	6
Norte de Santander	14,854	9,358	21,639	12
Santander	54,914	6,964	30,403	23
Tolima	31,596	29,840	34,774	41
Valle	40,077	45,809	58,042	1,866
Totals	440,591	358,957	565,260	2,032

Source: Colombia, Departamento Administrativo Nacional de Estadística, "Tendencias Electorales, 1935-1968," *Boletín Mensual de Estadística* 221 (Dec. 1969), 111–13.

populist ideology Gaitán had created the greatest threat from below that Colombia's ruling class had encountered since independence.

Commenting on the election, Enrique Santos, *El Tiempo*'s prestigious columnist, wrote that "Gaitán showed strength that was enormously surprising. . . . [He was] master of the urban masses and knew how to manage them. . . . Liberalism cannot regain power without the masses that follow Gaitán."[37] Santos made a call for immediate reconciliation between regular Liberalism and Gaitán. *La Razón* also called for Liberal unity while stating that Gaitanismo "must be recognized as a new and great social force. . . . The number of Gaitán's followers represented a great personal triumph."[38]

On May 6, the day after the election, Bototá was nearly paralyzed by spontaneous strikes of workers. Liberal party headquarters was dark and deserted. Gabriel Turbay, deeply discouraged, burned his papers and prepared to depart for Europe, where he would die prematurely at the age of forty-six. Gaitán, smiling, satisfied with his work, prepared the second phase of his campaign with the slogan, "For the reconquest of power! To the attack!"

10

The Gaitanista Program

A discussion of Gaitán's mission is incomplete without a description of the program he elaborated for Colombia during the year 1947. It contains the reforms he expected to carry out following his ascension to power and represents the culmination of his thought as it evolved from the early *Socialist Ideas in Colombia* and the *Manifesto of Unirismo*. The essentials of the program are found in two documents: the *Plataforma del Colón,* approved by the Gaitanista popular convention of January 1947; and the *Plan Gaitán,* one of the legislative measures submitted to the national congress by the Gaitanistas during the 1947 session. Although there were several contributors to each of these documents, they bore the indelible imprint of Gaitán, who provided the principal ideological source and inspiration.

The Gaitanista program was, in modern terms, reformist. That is, it would not have swept away the existing system in its entirety, but sought popular and nationalist goals such as broadening mass political participation and, through state-directed development, integrate peasants, workers, and the various middle-sector groups as active agents into the economic and social life of the nation. In 1947, however, the implications of the program were revolutionary: it threatened the political and economic monopoly of the traditional elites and gave increased power and participation to previously excluded or dependent social groups. There was no doubt that implementation of the program would have transformed the country.

The *Plataforma del Colón* was the Gaitanista version of the new Liberalism, the plan of action for the mass, democratic, and developmentalist party that Gaitán had envisaged since the 1920s. The first articles of the *Plataforma,* which declared Liberalism "the party of the people," committed it to a "permanent process of transformation, of advance and betterment, in all spheres of human activity."[1] This dynamic conception of the party's role implied a continuous adaptation through historical stages to the economic and social necessities of man, in harmony with technical and cultural development. It was in keeping with Gaitán's belief in historical evolution and the necessity for adapting political institutions to objective realities. It was far removed from nineteenth-century Colombian Liberalism, but in direct line with the early twentieth-century, Liberal-Socialist ideas of Rafael Uribe Uribe.

The subtitle of the *Plataforma* was the slogan "Political democracy cannot exist without economic democracy" (p. 329). Liberalism reaffirmed its belief in participatory democracy in which the majority expressed its collective will through the electoral process and the parties, and thus was involved in the governing of the state. In order to support the democratic process, civil rights and guarantees for all citizens were defended. The Gaitanistas did not believe that democracy existed in Colombia because, despite the formal apparatus of representative government, the economic life of the country was controlled by an oligarchy which exercised power through political and other institutions representing its interests. What was essential, in the Gaitanista view, was the establishment of economic democracy as the necessary condition for political democracy. Economic democracy meant first breaking the oligarchy's monopoly, then providing wider distribution of economic wealth and resources through broader ownership and participation in the productive forces of the nation. Only when the great majority of citizens possessed economic power was political democracy possible.

Most of the *Plataforma* was a prescription for achieving these goals. The most important role was assigned to the state, which was to intervene not only to spur balanced economic development and assure the health of all economic sectors, but to compensate for the economically weak in order to create an equilibrium among diverse economic interests—what the Gaitanistas called "equalitarian social harmony" (p. 338). Characteristically, the *Plataforma* contained the sentence, "Production is for man and not man for production" (p. 341). All social and economic policies were to be inspired by this principle. The belief that man was the primary source of national wealth and that the creation of other wealth had to be conditioned to his necessities was a departure from the much criticized "individualist criteria" in the direction of "socialist criteria."

It was recognized that the state administrative machinery was inadequate for dealing with these tasks. Therefore, the *Plataforma* contained provisions for the establishment of administrative bodies such as planning agencies and regional and municipal development institutes. Emphasis was placed upon the need for a technically qualified career civil service in all administrative bureaus of the government. The Gaitanistas sought to create a strong, centralized, state apparatus, supported by constitutional provisions and subject only to policy guidance by the political parties. It was to be technically capable of planning and implementing major economic and social policies (pp. 333–34). Essentially, this would mean a shift of responsibility for most facets of modernizations to a vigorous public sector equipped to deal with national priorities and goals.

The *Plataforma* contained numerous provisions for far-reaching economic, social, and political reforms. In the economic category, the primary goal was to spur the nation's productive forces. Progressive taxation policies were called for to encourage investment in areas that would increase national wealth and employment and result in economic growth. Nonproductive wealth and gains from speculation were to be heavily taxed, and regressive, indirect taxes were to be abolished (p. 334). National (i.e., Colombian-owned) industry was to be encouraged and protected; however, it would be required to serve the interests of consumers as well as producers, and excessive profits would be subject to confiscation by the state. Further, the state was to be represented on the directing boards of private corporations and have the power to intervene in their financial affairs (pp. 340–41). Close state control and supervision of the nation's financial system was to be inaugurated in order to provide more effective utilization of capital. The state's credit distributing powers were to be vastly expanded so as to favor economically weak sectors. The state also was to provide organizational and financial support for agrarian and small business cooperatives (pp. 339–40). Nationalization of public services such as electricity, water, telephones, and public transportation was proposed, and price controls were to be established on such essential items as food staples, transport fares, rents, etc. Legislative measures would be enacted to prohibit monopolies in areas deemed crucial to economic development (pp. 340–41). Finally, the *Plataforma* contained an agrarian reform designed to distribute land to those who worked it and provide general improvements in rural living conditions through overall development of the agrarian sector.

As might be expected, the *Plataforma* was designed to appeal to and strengthen the Gaitanista working-class and lower-middle-sector constituency. As such, Liberalism proclaimed the following objectives: elimination of salary and benefits discrimination against workers and employees except on the basis of technical qualifications; establishment of a minimum salary based upon cost-of-living and what was considered essential to family sustenance; wage supplements for each child; worker participation in the profits of enterprises; state coordination of the labor market and creation of employment agencies; state encouragement and defense of the unity, independence, and development of the labor movement and its rights, and provision for places to meet, study, and work; establishment of a labor code governing collective bargaining, and provisions for legal aid for workers at public expense; expansion of the right to strike to certain public sectors and broadened civil service coverage; extension of the social security system to all public and private workers, including *campesinos;* welfare benefits to those not covered by social security; national coordination and development of public health policies and facilities; and the establishment of legal equality and rights for women, including equal pay (pp. 342-46).

The *Plataforma* also reflected Gaitán's continuing interest in education. Liberalism promised a complete renovation of the educational system under direct state control and supervision, with education available to all citizens based upon their capacities and subject to the needs of the nation. Emphasis would shift from the predominantly academic fields into technical training. Professional university education in such traditionally oversupplied fields as law was to be strictly limited, and students were to be encouraged to seek degrees in specialized fields that would support the industrial and agricultural development of the country. Obligatory social service of graduates for a certain period was to be imposed in order to provide technical personnel for provincial development, and schools were to undertake projects in support of small industrial and agrarian enterprises. Additionally, the state was to undertake a nationwide literacy campaign and establish popular universities and mobile schools and libraries to spread the benefits of culture and education among the people. In remote areas the armed forces were to be assigned "civil action" projects, including the building of schools and literacy training (pp. 346-47). In the entire field of education the developmental needs of the state obviously were to take precedence over individual desires.

In the political area the Gaitanistas called for judicial reforms such as the modernizing of the penal law and the establishment of civil, commercial, and labor codes. An independent judiciary based upon a career civil service was to be created, with promotion based upon merit and not subject to political interference. Popular election of public officials was to be expanded to include the vice-president and the governors and mayors of departmental capitals and large cities (p. 337).

In articles pertaining to foreign policy the *Plataforma* declared Liberalism's solidarity with the leftist political forces of the continent that were struggling "to make democracy effective, liberating it from the domination of plutocratic groups that are imperialists abroad and oligarchs at home." The unity of the Latin American peoples was declared an urgent necessity; the Liberals proposed the calling of a Latin American economic conference for the purpose of establishing a common market. However, Liberalism declared itself in favor of continuing alliance with the United States, since both countries were struggling for "democratic ideals." Mutual advantages were seen for both countries in commercial exchange, with the United States collaborating in the economic development of Colombia. The *Plataforma* ratified the Good Neighbor policy (pp. 331–32).

While the *Plataforma* was a general outline of the Gaitanista program, a more detailed look at specific areas was provided by the *Plan Gaitán*. The *Plan* was, in effect, a broad program that would affect all areas of economic life and entrust to the state primary responsibility for the nation's economic development. It proposed a reorganization of the central Bank of the Republic and the creation of a Colombian Corporation of Credit, Development, and Savings to act as a central planning institute and development agency. The *Plan* was elaborated by a former president of the Council of State and financial expert, Guillermo Hernández Rodríguez; the socialist economist, Antonio García; and two other men with wide experience in fiscal affairs, Antonio Ordóñez and Luis Rafael Robles (p. 280).

The first part of the *Plan,* concerned with the reform of the Bank of the Republic, consisted of proposals to extend its capacity as a regulator of the money market, provide it with greater control over the private banking sector, and broaden its credit-granting functions. Its directing council was to be reorganized so that public interests would dominate private enterprise. The reformed bank was to act as a reserve bank, an emission agency, an import-export bank with broad regulatory powers, and an institute designed to provide and oversee credit distribution in harmony with national development goals (pp. 258–62, 281–95). In effect, its powers would be so great that it would control much of the nation's monetary resources through a de facto nationalization of credit and close supervision of private banking policies. The acknowledged intention was to marshal financial resources in support of national rather than private goals, and to ensure balanced development of all economic sectors.

The second part of the *Plan* proposed the establishment of the Colombian Corporation of Credit, Development, and Savings. This monolithic agency, that was to fuse several existing credit, industrial, and agricultural development institutes into one entity, was the most ambitious of the Gaitanista projects. The corporation, dominated by public-sector directors but with private-sector representation, was to be divided into three institutes. Their functions would be as follows. The Institute of Credit was to provide loans through its bureaus of industrial and agricultural credit to those economic sectors respectively, and through its bureau of territorial credit it was to develop urban and rural housing.[2] The Institute of Development was responsible for the fostering of agricultural and industrial development. The Institute of Savings was to serve as a national savings bank. The corporation was to be financed by a 50 million peso loan from the Bank of the Republic and by the sale of bonds to commercial banks totaling 10 percent of their deposits (pp. 263–64, 275–76).

The *Plan* stipulated that the credit policies of the corporation be subject to two general propositions: that credit was to be provided as a social service rather than as a business function and with terms and conditions that guaranteed the "sound" agricultural and industrial development of the country; and that sufficient credit be made available to provide a planned but constant increase in rural and urban popular housing (p. 271).

The *Plan* assigned the most important projects to the Institute of Development and provided guidelines for them. The Gaitanista agrarian reform intended to liquidate problems of small holdings and nonproductive latifundia held principally as long-term investments. Land that did not fulfill the constitutional provision of property providing a "social function," or underutilized land near population centers that could be dedicated to the production of primary foodstuffs, would be expropriated, the owners indemnified by bonds. Lands thus acquired were to be organized into three distinct types of agrarian units: (1) medium-sized parcels of no less than four *fanegadas* —about 6.4 acres—large enough for efficient and productive agriculture for sustenance and market uses, to be distributed and paid for by thirty-year bonds at low interest; (2) state farms equipped with machinery and employing advanced agricultural techniques that would serve as a model for the parcel holders and provide them with technological support; (3) agrarian villages (literally, collective farms) containing *campesino* housing, schools, health facilities, stores, and other services devoted to cooperative agricultural production. The key to the reform was, of course, large-scale parcelization with the state providing facilities to improve and increase production and to raise living and cultural conditions for the rural population. The intention was, through the establishment of rural cooperatives and like measures, to encourage and "conserve collective forms of work" (pp. 319–20). The reform obviously was a moderate, half-way measure between complete private ownership and full land nationalization. Large, productive private units were to be left undisturbed, although their workers were to enjoy the wage and social benefits available to all workers.

The Institute of Development was also charged with the direct stimulation of industrialization. The Gaitanista rationale was that the lack of sufficient private capital, scarce credit, and the relative weakness of Colombian industrial enterprises when faced with advanced foreign industries required the state to play a primary role. The Gaitanistas characterized their efforts as leading to a "mixed phenomenon, in that the [existing] preponderant individual initiative is mixed more and more with the initiative and intervention of the state in increasing development" (p. 325). Thus, the Department of Industrial Development within the institute was to: found factories directly, or with the partial collaboration of private capital, in those industries that were not developed in the country or that were necessary for national economic prosperity; found enterprises under the same conditions in fields where national production was not sufficiently developed by private enterprise; provide aid for existing industries by the purchase of stock until the state controlled sixty percent of those industries; establish factories in fields where the sales price of commodities far exceeded the cost of production. The overall policies of the institute were to assure state control and direction of investment in keeping with the planned industrialization of the country (pp. 274–75).

This review of the main points of the Gaitanista program demonstrates that it was in advance of its time. Only a partial implementation, as suggested earlier, would have brought about significant transformations in Colombia's social and economic structures. The program obviously was intended to establish the conditions through which socialism eventually would come about.

Gaitán argued forcefully for his program during the final years of his life. He attempted to convince the nation's businessmen that it was their duty to facilitate the development of the country through programs like his own before "the masses erupt and sweep all away."[3] He insisted that Liberalism was not the enemy of private enterprise but was interested in protecting private national industries so long as advantages were provided for owners, workers, and consumers.[4] His appeals met with some positive response. Commenting on the bank reform, *El Espectador* noted that the nation's banking laws were out of date and needed reform and that national credit moved in too narrow a circle.[5] The newspaper generally supported Gaitán's proposals. The president of ANDI, the Colombian industrialists' association, publicly announced that he was in accord with many of Gaitán's proposals, especially those establishing price controls and favoring the development of new primary industries.[6]

Viewed summarily, the Gaitanista program had as its populist goal the integration of the common people into the nation. It came out of Gaitán's evolutionary vision of economic democracy and social change. An important role was assigned to state economic planning, progressive taxation, and the role of national industry. Further, it cailed for the nationalization of public services, authentic agrarian reform, establishment of social welfare agencies, and national, centralized control of education. It sought to further democratic responsiveness by advocating direct election of mayors, governors, high public officials, and the establishment of an independent judiciary. Internationally, it accepted Roosevelt's Good Neighbor policy and urged a Latin American common market. Finally, the entire Gaitanista program was diffused with antiimperialist and antiplutocratic values.

IV

The Drive for Power, 1946–1948

11

Gaitán and the Liberals

The victory of the Conservative candidate, Ospina Pérez, in the presidential election of May 1946 caused widespread alarm among Liberals of all factions. In Bogotá workers staged spontaneous strikes; Liberal mobs surged through the streets demanding immediate action to nullify the results of the election. For many rank-and-file Liberals it was inconceivable that a party which claimed a nationwide majority of a quarter million votes should allow the Conservatives to regain control of the executive branch.

The calls for action were heard in the top levels of the Gaitanista leadership as well. Several of Gaitán's close associates, led by Jorge Uribe Márquez and J. A. Osorio Lizarazo, conceived a plan for a general strike to topple the government, "impose the will of the people, and take advantage of the agitated and seditious atmosphere that Gaitán's oratory had created." However, Gaitán rejected any suggestion of a coup with the response that he was a lawyer who respected the law and would conduct his movement within the norms of the constitution.[1] Although this position confounded many Gaitanistas, it was a simple recognition that Gaitán had come in last in the popular voting and could not count on even a Liberal majority for any extralegal adventure.

Nevertheless, the pressures on Gaitán were enormous. Changes in party government historically were accompanied by upheavals of varying degrees of intensity. In the polarized conditions of the time the worst was expected by many Liberals, especially those living outside the large cities. The rural violence of the early 1930s, much of it engendered by Liberal politicians attempting to break narrow Conservative majorities in departments like the Santanders, was still fresh in memory. Liberals in such areas had every reason to expect retaliation and many feared for their lives and property. Symptomatic of this feeling was an anguished telegram sent to Gaitán by several women two days after the election imploring him to take over the government and "save our families from Conservative persecution."[2] Numerous other telegrams described Gaitán as the only salvation for the country, while others contained offers to take up arms under Gaitán's leadership in order to prevent the Conservatives from coming to power.

Gaitán refused to be seduced by any temptation to raise the barricades. Instead, in his first major postelection address, on May 7, he called for order and organization rather than anarchy. He claimed that during the past forty-eight hours he had had the power to bring about a revolution but had refrained from doing so—an explicit bow to constitutional processes, but an implicit recognition that he held the decision for civil war or peace in Colombia. Gaitán then officially recognized the victory of Ospina. He added, however, that for his followers the struggle had just begun. He did not view the results of the election as a defeat for his movement but as a victory for the people over the political country, as a battle in which the oligarchs had been given a "hard lesson." He then called upon all Liberals to join with him in a massive effort to regain power, while warning the Conservatives that if reprisals were taken against Liberals he personally would lead a nationwide strike.[3] The speech was characteristic of those delivered by Gaitán in the post-1946 period. While he reiterated his dedication to the existing political system, he issued threats should his opponents not abide by the rules of the game. It was a ploy designed to caution the opposition while keeping his own followers in a state of expectation. It was a dangerous tactic, but it was designed to buy him the time he thought he needed.

In the same speech Gaitán suggested the strategy he would vollow vis-á-vis the Liberal party in the postelection period. He called for a provisional Liberal convention that would prepare the way for a great popular convention to restructure the party along more representative and democratic lines. Of course, he was confident that he would emerge from such a convention as the leader of Liberalism. His appeal for unity was based upon the tacit assumption that it would be on Gaitanista terms. He was convinced that the disarray in regular Liberal ranks was a fact that would not easily be overcome and that time and circumstances worked to the advantage of the Gaitanistas.

The correspondence flowing out from Gaitanista headquarters in the post-election period supports this interpretation. In his instructions Córdoba urged local Gaitanistas to make every effort possible to reach agreements with Liberals at the local level and to incorporate Turbayistas into the ranks if they were willing to recognize Gaitán's supremacy. Córdoba specifically stated that adherence to Gaitanismo by the various Liberal chieftains wasn't important but that the unity of the Liberal masses was.[4] Thus the Gaitanistas appealed to the base of the party with the expectation that it would be isolated from the leadership. In accord with this the Gaitanistas were to continue their regular organizing efforts. In a letter to local organizations throughout Colombia fifteen days after the election Córdoba wrote that "this first contact with our enemies has resulted in a partial victory and we should not be distracted from our efforts to impose our indisputable majorities in the municipal councils, departmental assemblies, and the national congress."[5] This letter also suggested that the Gaitanistas were concerned not only with unifying the Liberal masses but also with maintaining the Liberal majority in the other branches of government. They recognized the neutralizing effect this could have on the Conservative executive and on the formal power base provided for the future presidential campaign.[6]

The postelection emphasis upon unity resulted in an apparently more conciliatory and diplomatic stance on the part of Gaitán. However, this was appearance rather than reality. The savage infighting for control of the Liberal party continued, with the Gaitanistas now holding the initiative. Despite the fact that Turbay had won more votes, Gaitán held the political momentum in his hands. The tide of political feeling was moving in his direction, and he did everything in his power to aid it. He knew that he was becoming more popular each day. Therefore, while Gaitán opened his arms to all the elements of the party, he showed no willingness to share a leadership which he believed to be rightfully his.

This hard line probably was related to the internal condition of the Gaitanista movement. From correspondence in the Gaitán Papers it can be determined that the organization remained more or less intact following the election of May 5. The abrupt departure of Turbay for Europe and the confusion within the regular party resulted in immediate benefits for the Gaitanistas. Proclamations of support from Liberals of all factions poured into the movement's headquarters. In the departments where Gaitán had made a good showing the movement added strength and appeared to be stronger than ever by the end of 1946. In Tolima, for example, a new leadership consisting of Gaitanistas and former Turbay supporters was incorporated in October 1946. They carried out an organizational drive that unified the party under Gaitán's leadership even before the elections of March 1947.[7] Many Liberals began to enter the Gaitanista ranks out of necessity rather than conviction, and there were complaints by old Gaitán supporters about opportunism and infiltration. But Gaitán was more interested at this time in electoral majorities than in purity of motives. Further, many Liberals deserted the party for Gaitanismo—evidence of the growing strength of the latter. Under the circumstances, Gaitán could afford to maintain his intransigence behind a public display of conciliation.

Gaitán and the Regular Liberals, 1946

The headquarters of the Liberal party was described on May 6 as being dark and deserted, many of its windows broken as a result of attacks by Gaitanistas.[8] It was an apt description of the internal condition of the party as well. In the postelection weeks of soul-searching, Liberal leaders might have recognized this and made an effort to reconstruct the party in accord with the tendencies and desires of the membership. But that was not the case. If the "hard lesson" provided by the Gaitanistas had any impact upon the thinking of the Liberal leaders, it was to drive them farther away from a confrontation with the Gaitán phenomenon. Or, if they were willing to grant Gaitán a place within the party, they insisted that it be a minority one, hedged in by a party directorate dominated by the old leadership.[9] Temperamentally and ideologically opposed to what Gaitán and his followers represented, the old, prominent leaders of Liberalism turned away from the progressive and popular currents in their party and supported a coalition with Conservatism. As Gaitán had predicted, once threatened from below, the oligarchy began to coalesce at the top.

While regular Liberal ideologues were recoiling from the implications of Gaitanismo, the party chiefs continued to cast about for some method of healing the split. Responsibility for party affairs immediately following the election devolved upon the Liberal congressional representatives, the majority of whom were regulars opposed to Gaitán. The principal spokesman for the group was Carlos Lleras Restrepo. They met several times during June to consider the future of the party. During one of these meetings Senator Parmenio Cárdenas called for the election of Gaitán as first designate to the presidency (vice-president), while the minority faction of Gaitanistas urged the establishment of a provisional party directorate and the calling of a popular convention as mentioned earlier by Gaitán. Lleras Restrepo rejected the election of Gaitán as first designate, probably because he feared that this would make the latter de facto party chief. In answer to the popular convention Lleras proposed a Liberal convention based upon a complicated proportional delegate representation system that would have assured the regulars control of the party. At this point twenty-two Liberal Gaitanista congressmen, led by Parmenio Cárdenas, abandoned the meeting. One of this group, Representative Mario Ruiz Camacho, explained that the Liberals and Gaitanistas were divided by "two distinct political criteria" and that the issue only could be settled by the congressional elections of the following March.[10] Córdoba, in a letter to Gaitanista organizations, stated that the meetings of the Liberal congressmen failed because the regulars expected the party to continue under the control of the oligarchy. He attacked the Lleras Restrepo proposal for a convention on the grounds that it would leave the Liberal majority (Gaitanistas) in the minority.

He then reissued the call for a popular convention without the regular Liberals.[11]

Following the failure of the congressional meetings, former presidents Santos and López met with Gaitán during July in an attempt to reach an accord. Gaitán rejected their proposal for a joint party directorate with the argument that only a popular convention could select a valid party leadership.[12] Santos and López, opposed to that, then abandoned further efforts to deal jointly with Gaitán.

Increasingly desperate in the face of the continuing disunity of Liberalism, the regulars made yet another attempt to reach agreement with Gaitán and rebuild the party. In September the congressional group elected a provisional directorate, consisting of Roberto Salazar Ferro, Carlos Lozano y Lozano, Darío Echandía, Lleras Camargo, Turbay, and Gaitán, and representing all factions and ideological tendencies within Liberalism. Gaitán was offered parity and veto power within the proposed directorate, but he refused, claiming that the congressional group was not truly representative of majority opinion in the party and therefore had no power to elect such a directorate.[13] When the directorate failed soon after its election, Gaitán was held responsible by the Liberal press.[14]

Finally, in November, the congressional group appointed a commission consisting of three regulars and three Gaitanistas to organize a convention. The commission developed a conciliatory plan that would have allowed the Gaitanistas a slim majority of the delegates. But Gaitán, now in the midst of organizing his own convention, was not interested, and Lleras Camargo openly opposed any convention that would turn over the leadership of the party to Gaitán.[15] Faced with this situation, the commission soon dissolved.

As 1946 closed, the gap between the regular Liberals and the Gaitanistas appeared to be deep and irrevocable. Recognizing that the question of who controlled the Liberal majority could only be resolved at the polls, both sides began preparing for the March 1947 congressional elections. The Liberals temporarily patched up their differences and united behind the moderating influence of Eduardo Santos. But they did look forward to the elections with total confidence. Some in the party expected the Gaitanistas to be dealt a decisive, final defeat.[16] Yet while his own editorial writers and columnists were awaiting that, Santos himself, perhaps more realistic, was prepared yet again to seek some accord with Gaitán.

Gaitán and the Regular Liberals, 1947

In an effort to provide some unity within his own warring faction, Santos early in January appointed a Junta Asesora to direct the Liberals in the upcoming campaign. The junta consisted of Luis López de Mesa, representing the Liberal right; Darío Echandía who, with his labor connections, was of the non-Gaitanista Liberal left; and Adán Arriaga Andrade, a former labor minister, popular in the unions, but ideologically a moderate.[17] With this balanced leadership the Liberals began a vigorous, nationwide campaign.

Despite the red-baiting and scare tactics that the Liberal campaigners utilized against the Gaitanistas around the country, and the general feeling in the party that a final battle with a deadly foe was being fought, certain Liberals were still willing to reach some agreement with Gaitán. In late February Santos himself made overtures to the opposition. He probably was motivated in part by the internal condition of Liberalism at the time. Departmental party conventions in Santander del Sur, Cundinamarca, and Boyacá had been marked by savage infighting among politicians of various factions, and Santos was having increasing difficulty holding the party together in those places. And several prominent Liberals, among them Forero Benavides, went so far as to disclaim openly the leadership of Santos.[18] But whatever the motivation of Santos, there was no doubt that he was approaching Gaitán from a position of increasing weakness.

In his reply to Santos, Gaitán restated his public position. He claimed that Santos had refused a plebiscite over party leadership because he knew that it would mean victory for the popular forces and a radical change in the orientation of the party. The Gaitanistas had a concrete program while the Santos faction only wanted to defend previous presidential administrations. He ended by stating that Santos's politics were outmoded, and that taking Liberalism into a union with the Conservative government would end with the defrauding of the people's expectations.[19] But what Gaitán said in a private gathering at his house was perhaps more to the point. He rejected an agreement with the Liberals because "divided we will win the elections more easily than united. The reason is very simple. The masses have a mystique, they have a faith, they have a well-defined orientation. And the masses will follow us. If we compromise, we'll slow down and almost abandon the struggle, and the result will be lack of interest and abstention."[20]

As usual, Gaitán had correctly read the public temper. He knew that conditions in the country were worsening—strikes, inflation, increasing repression—and that more and more people believed he had the answer.[21] The results of the March 16 election seemed to bear him out. The Gaitanistas polled 448,848 votes to 352,959 for the Santistas. The Conservatives received 653,987. The Liberals won thirty-four seats in the Senate against twenty-nine for the Conservatives; in the House the Liberals had a majority of seventy-three seats over fifty-eight for the Conservatives. The majority of Liberal congressmen in both houses were affiliated with Gaitanismo.[22] The election confirmed Gaitán's claim that he represented the majority of Colombia's Liberals.

Liberalism's "natural chiefs"—as Gaitán saracastically called his opponents—reacted with stunned disbelief when the results of the election were known. Eduardo Santos, the respected and prestigious former president, followed Turbay's lead and announced he was abandoning politics for an indefinite stay in Europe. Santos recognized the legality of Gaitán's victory and the momentum that it portended. He warned that danger would accrue to the party if it, too, did not comprehend the essential nature and force of that victory. At the end of the month, in a poignant and somewhat bitter message of resignation from the party leadership, Santos suggested that "something" had ended in Colombian political life. He could not refrain from making an attack on a personalism that did not have the welfare of the party at heart.[23]

Numerous national leaders of Liberalism followed Santos's example and retired from active politics. They included Carlos Lleras Restrepo, Carlos Lozano y Lozano, Luís López de Mesa, Adán Arriaga Andrade, Jorge Soto del Corral, and others. However, several party leaders decided to come to terms with Gaitanismo. One of these was Darío Echandía, who said that "on March 26, Gaitán obtained a majority and the Liberal people follow him as chief."[24] Former anti-Gaitanistas Plinio Mendoza and J. Lemus Guzmán also switched positions because they felt that the party now needed unity more than ever.[25] The intellectuals José Mar and Moisés Prieto joined Gaitán because he obviously represented the true force of Liberalism.[26]

The major Liberal newspapers, *El Tiempo* and *El Espectador,* and the party's weekly, *Sábado,* reluctantly recognized the Gaitanista victory, while urging their opponent to assume a more moderate and responsible position now that he held the leadership. The López and Lleras Camargo paper, *El Liberal,* was more forthright in accepting Gaitán and calling for cooperation with him. Only *La Razón,* directed by Juan Lozano y Lozano, remained adamant in its opposition. The paper deplored the departure of Santos at a time when the country was in danger, when the democratic order was threatened by the "class-oriented current."[27]

It has been suggested that many in the party believed after March 16 that the best strategy for dealing with Gaitán was to allow him to have control so that he could discredit himself completely. They did not believe that Gaitán could reconcile his movement with the traditional groups within Liberalism, nor did they have much faith in his capacity for leadership. This view was articulated by Juan Lozano y Lozano—an avid supporter of Santos—who obviously was expressing the attitude of the latter.[28] This strategy relied upon what Santos considered the latent strength of traditional Liberalism, which would reappear at the appropriate time in the future.

Despite the withdrawal of many of the "natural chiefs" from active politics, and the collaboration of others with Gaitán, the opposition to Gaitanismo within the party did not remain entirely passive. Some, like Juan Lozano y Lozano, who declared himself one of the principal enemies of Gaitán, continued to agitate against the movement and urged the cooperation of Conservatives and dissident Liberals to prevent a future take-over of the country. Enrique Santos, a columnist for *El Tiempo* and a nephew of the former president, also called for such an alliance.[29] These disruptive tactics, during a period when Gaitán was having difficulties enforcing his leadership, resulted in a blistering attack by the caudillo on the unreconciled Liberals in mid-December. Gaitán charged that the Liberal oligarchy, with the backing of *El Tiempo* and *El Espectador,* was attempting to forge an alliance with Conservatism in order to prevent the "Liberal restoration." He said that the state, "controlled by the great economic interests," was conspiring against the interests of the middle class and the poor, and implicated the Liberal leadership in this conspiracy.[30]

Despite the vehemence of these words, however, Gaitán declared in the same speech his willingness to include Darío Echandía with him as a co-leader of the party, a fact which indicated the continuing influence of sectors of the traditional anti-Gaitanista leadership. As the Gaitanistas discovered, their victories at the polls could not by themselves ensure a unified, cooperative party. Even after the October 1947 municipal elections, which ratified once again a national Liberal majority and was interpreted as another victory for Gaitanismo, many in the traditional leadership refused to come to terms. The Liberal right, true to its ideological convictions, preferred alliance with its historical opponents despite the growing Conservative-incited violence in the countryside, the resulting threat of civil war, and the ineptness of the Ospina administration.

The opposition to Gaitán within the party also was expressed by its congressional representatives. Although 80 of the 107 Liberal congressmen elected in March met in early June 1947 and unanimously elected Gaitán Jefe Unico of the party, they did not all support his sweeping economic program in that summer's congressional sessions.[31] The result was a coalition of Liberals and Conservatives that defeated the program. Liberal congressmen were, however, quite willing to act as disruptively as possible toward the Ospina administration, activities which Gaitán did little to deter. They could not or would not unite for any positive action. The sorry record of the congress for 1947 resulted in lessened prestige for Gaitán in regular Liberal political circles,[32] a fact which Gaitán might have interpreted as a good sign. As he became less popular with the politicians he became more popular with the people.

The continuing opposition to Gaitán's leadership in the party and the undermining of his legislative program by the regular congressmen undoubtedly had a major impact upon the behavior of Liberals in the provinces. Following the March election numerous provincial Santista chiefs joined Gaitán's movement.[33] The usual large numbers of telegrams declaring adhesion to Gaitanismo also flowed into the movement's headquarters. But despite Gaitán's instructions to his followers, both before and after being elected Jefe Unico, to seek unity with Liberals, the correspondence indicated that some provincial chiefs either refused unity or simply did not recognize the new party leaders. In Cartagena, for example, the Gaitanistas complained as late as September 1947 that they did not have representation in the local and departmental party leadership and expected to go into the October elections with an independent list.[34] In December they charged that the Liberals in Bolívar were seeking a coalition with local Conservatives.[35] From Montería in December came a radiogram reporting that Liberals there, inspired by the capital's Liberal press, planned a coalition with Conservatives in order to nullify the Gaitanista majority in future elections.[36]

Gaitán's response to these and other complaints of Liberal obstruction invariably was the same: make all effort to overcome differences; continue struggling for "our democratic ideals." However, he generally refused to intervene personally in these quarrels, probably expecting that time and circumstances and his gathering momentum would force the Liberals to come around. In many of his instructions he attacked personalism, which he undoubtedly felt was the root of many of the local difficulties. In this he was substantially correct. At the local level Colombian politics traditionally had been dominated by jefes and their cliques of followers. Probably for many outsiders adherence to Gaitanismo was a means of gaining political influence or of challenging the existing power structure, which the regular leaders naturally resisted. After Gaitán captured the party leadership, many Liberals, including local chiefs with nowhere else to go, joined the Gaitanistas for reasons of political survival. The internal struggles between and among local Gaitanistas and Liberals thus were motivated by the desire for political power and influence as well as by ideology.

The result after Gaitán's take-over of the party was not, however, the integration of Liberalism into Gaitanismo. If he was recognized as sole leader of the party, he was by no means in full control of it. Rather, what existed after June 1947 was an uneasy alliance between Gaitanismo and Liberalism, with their final fusion yet to come. Gaitán fully expected to realize this; had time remained for him it probably would have been accomplished. But how he would have done this, especially in dealing with the regular local chiefs throughout the country, remains unanswered. Certainly the restraint and soft line he took toward the provincial regulars bought him a kind of unity, but it was, at best, uneasy and temporary.

12

Gaitán and the Gaitanistas

Three days after the May 1946 election Gaitán called for a popular convention to determine the leadership of Liberalism. When this was wisely rejected by the regular leadership, Gaitán went ahead with his own convention plans. The gathering would be another human demonstration of immense proportions intended to reaffirm Gaitanista power and discredit once again the oligarchs of the political country. It also would stimulate the Gaitanista masses for the final electoral showdown with Liberalism in March 1947.

Gaitán consistently had refused to trust his and the people's destiny to the regular Liberal conventions. Although the statutes of the party directed that delegates be elected from municipalities by popular vote, municipal elections were controlled in fact by local chiefs, many of whom owed their positions to departmental and national party leaders.[1] Delegates usually voted for candidates and programs sponsored by the national party directorate. It was this system that Gaitán assailed as being both undemocratic and unrepresentative. He, on the other hand, would summon an authentic convention based upon the popular will.

The resolution calling for a popular national convention stated, in brief:

> Considering that the Liberal party ought to be democratic, with directors elected by the people; and that the people have the right to a direct plebiscite to elect their leaders and ideological platform; and that the party ought to accommodate itself to the new economic and social circumstances of Colombian life: Be it resolved to convoke a National Convention of the Liberal Party based upon the votes of the citizens of the municipalities, of origin entirely popular.[2]

The resolution provided that the convention meet during a designated Week of the Reconquest of Power and that it be organized by a National Organizing Commission directed by Francisco José Chaux. Significantly, the latter was responsible for designating the departmental commissions charged with carrying out the delegate selection process, a policy for which the Liberals previously had been criticized. Apparently, the internal problems of the movement demanded closer control by Gaitanista headquarters.

As with the previous Gaitanista convention, Gaitán worked hard to ensure success. He personally made a trip through Boyacá and the Santanders, generating enthusiasm in areas where his movement had not been particularly strong. Warm-up political rallies were organized in the capital and major provincial cities. *Semana* laconically noted that the rather frantic preconvention activity was not designed to attract attention to a set of programs or a man, but merely to attract attention. The magazine wondered in print where all the money was coming from for the elaborate organization, and why it was being spent, since the result already was known—Gaitán as Jefe Unico in a movement that day by day was limited more and more to himself.[3] Gaitán, however, believed that it pays to advertise.

The convention, which opened on January 18, 1947, seemed to confirm *Semana*'s observation. The affair was above all a political spectacle that outdid all previous Gaitanista efforts. For several days prior to the convention, public rallies, dances, and festivals were held in the workers' barrios of Bogotá. Marchers carrying flags and banners paraded through the streets. Buses mounted with loudspeakers and adorned with slogans kept up a continuous din. On the eighteenth bands brought in from all over the country led masses of people carrying propaganda through the central streets of the city. By four o'clock the Circo de Toros was jammed with fourteen thousand people, including twelve hundred convention delegates. *Semana,* which devoted many columns and photographic space to the convention, reported that when Gaitán entered the Circo no one before had passed through its portals with such success.[4] The caudillo, obviously moved by this enthusiasm of his own making, delivered an emotional address on his usual themes to the excited audience. When he concluded he led the crowd in a parade through the city's streets.

The real work of the convention was carried on during the following days in the Teatro de Colón, where the delegates met to name Gaitán Jefe Unico and approve the program that became known as the *Plataforma del Colón*. There was some discussion of the form Gaitán's leadership would take. The JEGA group wanted him named sole chief of the movement, while others wanted him as leader but assisted by an advisory body. JEGA won out. The *Plataforma* was approved unanimously after some minor modifications by Gaitán designed to make it "truly revolutionary." However, the question of who would stand on the Gaitanista electoral lists for the upcoming election caused considerable infighting. In one instance (the department of Bolívar) Gaitán had to intervene personally to impose his candidates.[5] The problem of the lists was not completely settled by the end of the convention because of discord and, apparently, personal ambitions. Finally, the matter was left to Gaitán alone to decide, a decision that gave him enormous additional personal power within the movement.

For the Gaitanista "purists" the convention was not entirely satisfactory. The procedure in the Teatro de Colón was too reminiscent of traditional Colombian party conventions and not exactly in keeping with the promise of a democratic transaction. They could point, as many obviously did, to the method of selecting electoral candidates and to the candidates themselves. In Cundinamarca, for example, where Gaitán headed the list, there were included those old regulars of the political country, Uribe Márquez and Parmenio Cárdenas.[6] Old Gaitanistas began to wonder how far their leader would go for the sake of capturing the Liberal party.

Gaitán certainly was aware of this mood. As an experienced politician he knew that there were plenty of insincere opportunists around him. In private conversations during the convention he spoke often of "leashing the ambitions of his friends."[7] Yet he was willing to use these people for the sake of his objective. In the interests of harmony he refused to expel the regular Liberal chiefs as he did Santos. Although this was more symbolic than real, it demonstrated that Gaitán had an eye on the future affiliation of these now wavering, influential politicians. He also, on his own initiative, made peace with the Communists, whose leader, Augusto Durán, declared that the party would join forces with the Gaitanistas when it didn't have sufficient strength to battle alone—which in 1947 was often. The small Socialist party, in which one of Gaitán's advisers, Antonio García, was prominent, also was wooed and won over.[8] The broadening of the Gaitanista base went on despite the misgivings of many of the movement's followers.

Almost immediately after the closing of the popular convention the Gaitanistas launched their campaign for the March congressional elections. The campaign was as vigorous as that for the previous presidential election. In early February Gaitán made a tour through northern Colombia accompanied by the fanfare that now characterized his movement. In Barranquilla he spoke before an estimated sixty thousand people and also drew large crowds in other coastal cities.[9] His speeches had two major themes: the failure of the Santos faction to represent the popular will, and the necessity for sweeping reforms in the country based upon the *Plataforma del Colón*. In respect to the former, Gaitán claimed that the Santos faction did not view the Liberal party as an instrument for transformation but as an organization to defend the bureaucratic and administrative gains of the Liberal regimes. The Gaitanista movement was the only one in the country with an ideological platform based upon political realities. He said: "We want the reconquest of power through the autonomy of Liberalism as the party of opposition, not of obstruction, to the present government; the Santos faction, by supporting the politics of National Union and allowing Liberals to serve in public office unconditionally, . . . far from representing the true advantages of national solidarity . . . is merely clearing the way for the consolidation of Conservatism in power."[10] Gaitán added that Santos's politics, party to the bloody acts of violence against Liberals throughout the country, represented a grave threat to the nation. He ended by stating his belief that the internal battle of Liberalism was ideological and that the leaders of each faction were too committed to reach a compromise. Agreement between Gaitanismo and Liberalism only could take place on the local level in the form of collaboration against Conservative violence.[11]

In his references to the Ospina government, Gaitán claimed that it had neither the ideology nor the means to deal with the nation's problems. It could not follow the Catholic socialist precepts of Pope Leo XIII for fear of losing its Conservative and Liberal oligarchic supporters. It was unable or unwilling to control the increasing violence in the countryside or to carry out measures necessary to alleviate the grave economic problems.[12] In contrast, the Gaitanistas offered a concrete program of planned development, including agrarian reform and social legislation designed to improve the living conditions of the majority of Colombians, while guaranteeing democratic liberties. Finally, Gaitán proclaimed solidarity with all the forces of the left in Latin America that were struggling for democracy and against oligarchs and imperialists.[13]

The battle between Gaitanistas and Liberals was not only joined at the debating level. Clashes between the two groups were frequent. Numerous complaints arrived at Gaitanista headquarters charging intimidation and violence by Liberals in small towns and the countryside. In Cali the Gaitanista *casa* was attacked by Liberals; on February 22 a battle between the two factions there resulted in one death. This was in addition to the violence between Liberals and Conservatives that was raging in parts of the country.[14]

How much Gaitán contributed to the atmosphere of tension and insecurity is problematical. Certainly, the tone of his speeches was provocative. Increasingly he spoke of revolution, of the overthrow of the "lords" by the people, of the vindication of *los de abajo* ("those from below").[15] He issued threats not only against the government for condoning violence, but against those who were attempting to weaken the unity of his movement. The effects of his passionate and inflammatory oratory on the vast crowds—already primed by

Gaitanista mobilization techniques—can only be imagined. On the other hand, he publicly deplored violence and insisted that he was leading a peaceful movement. The night before the March election, in a radio address to the nation, he urged restraint and peace, and said that violence was symptomatic of weakness.[16] He was careful to add a subtle warning against those who interfered with the right to vote. The results of the congressional election of March 1947 affirmed Gaitán's majority within the Liberal party. *Jornada* expressed best what it meant, at least for him and his followers: the breaking of minority control over the party, the destruction of the old exclusionist political system, the triumph of the masses, and the beginning of the process of social and economic transformation of Colombia.[17] Of course, these sentiments were premature.

Throughout the spring of 1947, while instructing his followers in the provinces to negotiate unity with the Liberals, Gaitán initiated a series of consultations with regular provincial party chiefs designed to solidify his position. He knew that victory in 1950 was dependent upon the unity of *all* Liberals. The declining Liberal majority demonstrated that. Further erosion could be expected in future elections. Gaitán required the cooperation of provincial chiefs who could deliver votes outside of the large cities that were the real centers of Gaitanista strength. An alliance was possible because the chiefs knew that they had no place to go and that their hopes of sharing in any future government lay with Gaitán. On the other hand, Gaitán was quite willing to recognize their positions in exchange for their support. He apparently believed that their distaste for him would be neutralized by his hold on the party masses and that, once he was in power, they would not be able to resist the imposition of his program. The Gaitanista-Liberal alliance that emerged was purely tactical; there were no indications that Gaitán's former foes changed their convictions. The two factions continued to take advantage of opportunities to discredit one another within the party. The factions, however, realized that at this time they were dependent on each other despite their differences.

The final ratification of Gaitán's leadership of Liberalism came in early June during a series of meetings, called by Gaitán, to discuss the municipal elections of October 1947. The majority of the newly elected Liberal senators and representatives met for three days and, on June 11, elected Gaitán Jefe Unico of the party by a unanimous vote. However, as a concession to the non-Gaitanistas, the new chief agreed to the the election of an advisory commission comprised, in part, of several Liberals who had opposed him in the past.[18] The advisory commission's role, according to one of its members and a new Gaitainista, Plinio Mendoza Neira, was to prepare the party for the October municipal elections and not to serve as a check on the party leader. While this can be doubted, the advisory commission proved to be singularly ineffective. Gaitán largely ignored it.[19]

Gaitán's attitude toward his newfound Liberal allies was demonstrated during the 1947 congressional session. At the June meetings the Liberal congressmen had discussed and agreed upon a series of legislative proposals, including banking, tax, electoral, and customs reforms. The congressional session was, however, preceded by a typical Gaitanista action. Gaitán decided to put popular pressure upon the regular Liberals and anyone else who might benefit from it. He had mastered the technique of synchronizing what was going on in the street with what was going on in the capital. The week before congress met was designated another Week of the Reconquest. Once again Gaitanistas were rallied for a series of demonstrations, torchlight parades, and general fanfare. In a major address in the Municipal Theater, Gaitán described the Liberal party as a major force for renovation. He legitimized his role in the party by outlining its history and placing himself in a direct line with the party's most popular and progressive leaders—Murillo Toro, Rafael Uribe Uribe, and Benjamín Herrera.[20]

The effect of the Week of the Reconquest was to focus national attention on Gaitán and once more demonstrate his mass appeal. It also raised expectations for constructive legislative activity to deal with the severe economic and social problems. It was a means, too, of putting public pressure on the system, the political country. In his instructions to the organizers of the affair, Gaitán called for a show of strength in order to impress (or intimidate) the Liberal congressmen and the Ospina government. The instructions did not mention the legislative program, but indicated that Gaitán really was interested in convincing non-Gaitanista Liberals that they had no choice except to back him completely.[21] Gaitán gave a further indication of his thinking during his speech in the Municipal Theater when he said that those who opposed his leadership in the party would be "pushed aside."[22] Liberal unity still was to be on Gaitán's terms.

The almost total failure of the congressional session to provide anything beneficial for the nation resulted in attacks on the congress and Gaitán's leadership by both the Liberal and Conservative press. The people, however, were not fooled. The failure of the congress served Gaitán admirably. He had put forth his program for propaganda effect. Its far-reaching economic and social reforms offered promising possibilities for the Colombian people, especially when contrasted with the government proposals. Further, the failure of the program to move through congress allowed Gaitán to return to his old theme of the Liberal-Conservative oligarchy and the political country working against the best interests of the people. This put additional pressure on the Liberal chiefs to support Gaitán unequivocably.

Indeed, this was the Gaitanista line during the campaign for the October 1947 municipal council elections held throughout the country. Gaitán appealed to the masses of both parties to join him in his struggle against the oligarchs. he warned that the caciques were preparing electoral obstruction in order to defraud the people. The suggestion was that the caciques included Liberals. The columnist Jorge Padilla, writing in *Jornada,* was more direct. He blamed the congressional committees, to which Gaitán had "generously" appointed many non-Gaitanistas, for obstructing the program.[23] The implication was clear, as was Gaitán's strategy. Either he would get the legislation that he and the people desired or he would expose the recalcitrant "democratic" representatives to the scorn of the public.

The October municipal council election resulted in another victory for Gaitán. Despite widespread reports of violence and the failure of Liberals to vote in many places because they lacked guarantees of security, they managed to outpoll the Conservatives by 659,625 votes to 521,845, and to elect 396 councilmen against 273 for the Conservatives. Further, the Liberals captured every major city in the country except Pasto. They won majorities in all departments except Nariño, Santander del Norte, and Boyacá. Surprisingly, they managed to win, although by close margins, in departments formerly hostile to Gaitán: Antioquía, Caldas, and Cauca.[24] The election threw the government into another cabinet crisis; reaffirmed the Liberal majority despite Laureano Gómez's charge that the Liberals had almost two million false identification cards which they used to defraud elections; and demonstrated Gaitán's effectiveness in holding all Liberals together. Whatever the feelings of Liberal chiefs, the rank and file obviously supported him.

The election was Gaitán's final test within Liberalism. On October 24 the Liberal congressmen proclaimed him their presidential candidate for 1950. The Liberal departmental directorates did so a day later.[25] From the correspondence and newspaper reports it was apparent that the provincial chiefs finally were reconciled to Gaitán's leadership and candidacy without being necessarily over-enthusiastic about his program. In the capital both *El Tiempo* and *El Espectador* tacitly recognized his leadership, although the former believed a candidacy to be premature. Nevertheless, in a formal, elegant dinner at Bogotá's Hotel Granada on November 9 attended by Liberal dignitaries, Gaitán, in effect, opened the presidential campaign of 1950.[26]

The October election was a confirmation of Gaitán's strength in the country. His hold on the Liberal masses was secure; he had demonstrated his ability to maintain a Liberal electoral majority despite adverse conditions; he had forged a Gaitanista-Liberal alliance; and he had won at least grudging acceptance for his leadership and program among former party opponents. But what perhaps was most satisfying in terms of his personal ambitions—he had apparently secured the party's presidential nomination and could expect to go into the 1950 election as the candidate of a unified, majority party. He had demonstrated what "Calibán" of *El Tiempo* feared: that without Gaitán the Liberals could not return to power; indeed, they were unlikely to maintain their majority.[27]

The securing of the Liberal leadership brought problems of its own. As the head of a vast social movement he was free to act much as he pleased. But as the leader of a traditional political party working within an established system he was forced into quite different roles. He had to deal with his Liberal allies, over whom he had questionable influence, not on the level of personalism, but on the basis of political deals and compromise. In his capacity as opposition leader he had to formulate a policy before government, a task increasingly difficult, as will be shown. Finally, his attempts to reconcile all of his roles resulted in difficulties within his own movement.

Internal Affairs

After the presidential election many national and provincial regulars joined the Gaitanista camp. Gaitán accepted them wholeheartedly, placing many of them in important positions within the movement. By the time of the March congressional election there were two or three professional political leaders in each department who had served in high positions during the years of Liberal power and who had replaced the "primitive" Gaitanistas as leaders of the movement.[28] Correspondence in the Gaitán Papers indicates that every departmental directorate had to forward lists of candidates to Gaitán for his approval, and there was evidence that certain candidates were rejected. From the protests of old Gaitanistas it was evident that newcomers were being placed or allowed on the lists. Original Gaitanistas also were shouldered aside in the selection of delegates to the popular convention.[29]

The appearance of former foes of the political country within Gaitanismo resulted in defections and charges of treason. A letter to Gaitán from a group of his followers in Huila asked why he had betrayed them by heading an electoral list made up of "old-line party members and oligarchs."[30] Another letter from Cartagena pointed out that after Gaitán became head of the party many of the traditional chiefs in the department became Gaitanistas and managed to infiltrate into the movement and become influential. This had begun to disrupt the "iron discipline" of the movement and had resulted in "abandonment of the struggle" by many old followers.[31]

Gaitán's replies to these kinds of protests generally were conciliatory. He answered the Huila group with: "It is convenient that I continue to head the official Liberal list. I expect that all Liberals will continue fighting for the good of the party and not against each other." To the correspondent from Cartagena,

Gaitán merely wrote that there was no reason for internal party struggle.[32] He obviously was willing to accept some erosion within his movement in exchange for the political knowledge and strength brought by the regulars. He apparently believed that the majority of old Gaitanistas would follow him whatever politics he practiced. Even the writer from Cartagena promised to continue working for the Gaitanista program because "what is essential is the reconquest of power and the transformation of the country." The advantage of personalism was the individual loyalty of the follower.

Ironically, Gaitán viewed local personalism and not ideological differences as the major difficulty in forging a Gaitanista-Liberal alliance in the provinces. In letter after letter replying to his followers' complaints that local party chiefs were obstructing unity, Gaitán urged that personal differences and ambitions be put aside for the good of the party. To a group of Liberals in Montería, Córdoba, he wrote: "We do not struggle for personal ends, for bureaucratic posts in the municipal, departmental, or national governments, but for the complete overthrow of the old administrative system of the country. This is what is obstructing the country. There is no reason now for division within the Liberal party. There is a great necessity for strong unity."[33] Gaitán handled well a problem not easily dealt with in a country where the traditional reward for political service was a government position.

Gaitán devoted most of his energies during 1947 to organizing the party. In this he was generally successful, as the October election results indicated. He also began to reinvigorate the *Casa Liberal*, the party headquarters in Bogotá. The *Casa* was staffed and communications reopened with provincial leaders, who were called in for regular consultations. A bureau dealing with worker and *campesino* affairs was established. Legal defense committees were set up to deal with the growing problem of political violence, and the *Casa* became the organizational center for the "houses of refuge" established for the victims of the violence. Plans also were laid for the rejuvenation of *Casas Liberales* in the provinces. As a result of this and other initiatives *Jornada* reported enthusiastically that messages coming in from all over the country indicated that "the party is reborn!"[34]

Gaitán's preoccupation with party affairs caused other problems. He was not able to devote sufficient attention to directing the Liberal bloc in the congress and therefore left himself open to charges of ineptitude. His lack of interest in formulating a firm policy toward the Ospina government—sometimes refusing collaboration, sometimes encouraging it—sowed confusion in Liberal ranks, even among his own followers.[35] By the end of 1947 Gaitán had aroused dissatisfaction among enough regular Liberals for him to consider sharing the party leadership with Darío Echandía. But the enthusiasm of the capital's Liberal press for this quickly aroused his suspicions and he changed his mind.[36]

While changes appeared in the top ranks of Gaitanismo at the national level and in the provinces, the Gaitanista core of mass support was expanding. Gaitanismo continued largely as an urban phenomenon drawing followers from the working class and lower middle class. However, during 1947 the alliance with and assimilation of Liberalism brought additional support from the countryside; this was actively fostered by Gaitán, who, according to one of his lieutenants, was increasingly preoccupied with the conditions of the *campesinos*.[37] After the 1946 election Gaitanismo also solidified its position within organized labor and made a tactical alliance with the Communist party.[38] There was evidence too that the movement had substantial numbers of sympathizers within a crucial sector: the armed forces. According to a former Colombian naval officer, Guillermo Barriga Casalini, many officers and enlisted ranks viewed Gaitán and his program favorably.[39] Finally, despite charges that Gaitán lost whatever support he had among Conservatives when he insisted on identifying completely with Liberalism, there was no question that he retained at least potentially strong influence among Conservatives. Letters and telegrams from Conservatives after 1946 support this. And a former Conservative senator from Valle, Dr. Alfonso Garcés Valencia, stated that Gaitán's appeal among Conservatives, especially *campesinos* and other rank and file, remained substantial. He said that certain Conservative provincial leaders did not rule out the possibility of an electoral alliance with Gaitán in 1950.[40] Thus in the final years, notwithstanding charges of ineptitude as party chief and congressional leader, Gaitán—and Gaitanismo—emerged as the single most powerful political force in Colombia. With his following intact and expanded, and with a progressive, reformist program of national appeal, there appeared to be nothing that could prevent Gaitán's assumption of power in 1950.

13

Gaitán and the Ospina Government

Mariano Ospina Pérez, in a statement issued before taking office as president in August 1946, told the nation that he expected to rule with a Government of National Union involving the collaboration of both parties.[1] He also promised to guarantee civil rights and prevent political reprisals. Under the circumstances, he could hardly do otherwise. The Liberals controlled both houses of the national congress, departmental assemblies, and were the majority in the country. Furthermore, they were in an ugly mood after losing the presidency. The disorders following the election were fresh in mind; there still was talk of a coup; and Gaitán had warned the incoming government that if it initiated repressive and reactionary policies he would lead a general strike.[2]

The regular Liberals generally reacted favorably to the Ospina offer of collaboration. Half of the members of Ospina's first cabinet were regular Liberals;[3] half of the departmental governorships also went to party members. The Liberals apparently accepted because they agreed with the thesis of Alfonzo López, who argued that sharing in power was the best means for preventing a Conservative monopoly and defending Liberal interests.[4]

But the Government of National Union was not premised upon common agreement over programs; it merely involved the participation of individuals. Ospina failed to reach an agreement with Gaitán over the terms of collaboration and appointed a cabinet without consulting him.[5] Gaitán immediately refused to cooperate, leaving the government open to charges that it was a maneuver of the oligarchs of both parties for defeating the interests of the people and preventing the realization of popular demands.

In conversations with Ospina prior to the latter's taking office, Gaitán had affirmed that the only possible basis for collaboration was a common agreement over social and economic programs of benefit to the people. His plan was to

158

cooperate with the Conservatives on a platform of popular action, within well-defined areas of mutual compromise.[6] He opposed what he termed "bureaucratic collaboration" of the type favored by the Liberal regulars. As he later said to the Liberal congressional representatives, "I am an enemy of cooperation [without a common program] because it raises the danger that individuals who participate in the cabinet, instead of giving the impulse of Liberal ideas to a Conservative administration, will themselves become conservatized."[7] This general viewpoint was sustained by Gaitán until after the March 1947 elections.

Whether or not Ospina wanted a true Government of National Union was questionable. He must have realized that without the Gaitanistas he was disregarding substantial, if not yet majority, opinion in the country. Perhaps he believed that the double oligarchy of regular Liberals and Conservatives could effectively govern without considering the masses, as it always had in the past. Perhaps he had full confidence in being able to control the potentially dangerous *chusma* should the need arise. The historian Germán Arciniegas considered Ospina's intentions suspicious from the start. He believed that Ospina, by calling for collaboration and accepting it from the regular Liberals, merely was inspiring enough confidence so that he could set up the machinery behind the scenes that would prevent the majority from exercising its political rights.[8]

Whatever the reasons for Ospina's political actions, his government immediately was faced with severe economic problems inherited from its predecessors. The dislocations caused by World War II and its aftermath were straining the Colombian economy, with the effects falling most heavily on the lower classes. According to Fluharty,

> the period preceding the critical political era in Colombia [pre-1946] had been one of constrictive inflation, induced by an export surplus which stemmed from heavy war demands for Colombian coffee and raw materials; by a simultaneous piling-up of exchange (as imports were reduced below the selling volume), and the use of the unexpended balances as speculative capital; and, finally by a sharp, rapid increase in all prices, due to import controls and shortages of goods, which prevented buyers from spending and made money cheap, excessive in quantity, and ready for any reasonable venture as it had never been before.[9]

The results of this were speculative gains for the owners of capital, flourishing black marketeering, and profitable manipulations by those with political influence in government agencies responsible for import and export licenses.

For the majority without capital or influence it meant wages falling behind living costs, scarcities of staple goods, and unemployment. As Ospina came into office the situation was aggravated by a demand inflation caused by the pent-up desire for goods. Through 1947 prices continued to spiral upward as spending and speculation accelerated. The foreign exchange surplus disappeared and a deficit occurred. The cost-of-living index (1938 base year of 100) rose to 235 for July 1946. By March 1948 the cost-of-living index for a Bogotá working class family rose to 283.8. Meanwhile, real wages rose more slowly than prices and actually showed a net decline from 1941.[10]

Ospina's response was a conventional deflationary policy: cutbacks in government spending, especially in public works; rationing of dollar exports; limitations on currency issue and government bonds; restrictions of credit.[11] He did reinstitute price controls, although without much effect. Further, the government allowed price increases on certain basic staples, like *panela* and chocolate, that mostly affected the lower classes. In sum, the government's economic policy largely worked against the interests of those with great need, a growing number of people.

Partly in response to worsening economic conditions, partly as a result of a concomitant internal division within the CTC between Liberals and Communists, a series of serious labor strikes broke out in the fall of 1946. In October the Communist-dominated oil workers began the longest industrial strike in the nation's history.[12] This protest was followed by violent protest strikes of teamsters, railroad, highway, and river workers. The situation was so serious in Cali that the government declared a state of siege in Valle on November 8, an action that precipitated the first cabinet crisis of the new government and resulted in the resignation of the Liberal ministers.[13] The government continued to act firmly. Ospina said that he would adopt all necessary measures to safeguard lives and property and gave the impression that he would not go out of his way in dealing with the demands of the strikers. At the same time he called for the passage of new legislation to provide the government with more power in dealing with strikes; this request was not interpreted positively by the workers. Nor did they respond favorably to Ospina's charge that the strikes were caused by "professional agitators."[14] The government's hostile attitude and the continuing rise in the cost of food, clothing, and shelter resulted in an attempted general strike in May 1947, a political action designed to bring down the government. However, the organizer of the strike, the CTC, already in a state of internal turmoil, failed to receive the support of all Colombian unions, the Liberal party, or even the Gaitanistas. The effort failed without in the least benefiting Colombian workers.

The Ospina government's political difficulties and the peoples' economic hardships triggered a far graver outburst in late 1946: *la violencia*. This essentially rural phenomenon—in the first stages it was a partisan conflict between Liberals and Conservatives—increasingly engaged the attention of both the government and its opponents. But as it grew in intensity and spread throughout vast regions of the country, *la violencia* gathered a momentum of its own that strained the very fabric of Colombian society.

The first serious violence occurred in Boyacá in 1946. This large department to the north of Bogotá was one of the most backward, feudalistic, and cacique-dominated areas in the country. It had been the scene of Liberal violence against the Conservative majority in the 1930s. In 1946 the Liberals claimed a narrow majority and apparently expected to keep it, because violence against Conservatives was reported to be widespread during the presidential election. However, after the inauguration of Ospina the tables were turned. A Conservative governor, Rivera Valderrama, was appointed; he immediately set about the "reconquest" of the department for his party. The Conservatives reasoned that the voting pattern in Boyacá could be altered in their favor without much difficulty; since the department had the third highest representation in congress, Conservative domination would have an important impact nationally.[15] This also appeared to be a major consideration in two other departments of early widespread violence, the Santanders, located north of Boyacá.

The techniques of Conservative reconquest were direct, simple, and brutal. In swing-vote areas the national police ranks were filled with Conservative sympathizers willing to carry out the orders of Conservative officials. Liberal job holders were dismissed, holders of Liberal identity cards intimidated, Liberal peasants were dispossessed of their lands, saw their property destroyed, and often were killed. In this atmosphere old feuds over water, land, and local interests flared up and took on a partisan character.[16] According to one source, latifundistas, especially in Boyacá, took advantage of the violence to restore lands lost after the Liberal agrarian reforms or to create new latifundia.[17] Naturally, Liberals resorted to self defense and attacks upon Conservatives; thus the spiral of terror and counterterror continued upward in intensity, with the political parties adding their quotient of hatred with heated rhetoric.

The question of who was initially responsible for *la violencia* has aroused considerable debate.[18] But there is no question that Ospina's actions (or inactions) contributed significantly to it. Conservatives charged that it was the logical result of 1,800,000 false Liberal identity cards that led to fraudulent electoral majorities.[19] Liberals believed that it was caused by Conservative attempts to intimidate the Liberal majority by terror and that the Ospina government volunteered itself to this task by converting the police and armed forces into political arms of the Conservative party.[20]

With qualifications, the evidence appears to support the Liberals. Although it probably was true that the Liberals possessed false identity cards, there was no question about the party's majority in the country after 1930. There also was no question about Conservative officials' activities in the departments already discussed. The conversion of the national police into a political weapon also was a fact; the police commander since 1943, General Carlos Vanegas, resigned in late 1946 over the mass dismissal of Liberals from the ranks and the appointment of Conservatives in their places, done with the approval of the Conservative minister of government, Roberto Urdaneta Arbeláez.[21] Further, in the Gaitán Papers for 1947 there are hundreds of telegrams from all sections of the country detailing personal and property violence against Liberals, often with the assistance of known Conservative officials and police. In one folder of the Santander file there are more than fifty telegrams sent during the fall of 1947 describing acts against Liberals in which Conservative officials were involved; several of the telegrams described government-appointed investigating commissions dominated by Conservatives and highly partial to the initiators of the violence. While this type of evidence admittedly is biased, the sheer bulk of it lends credence to the Liberals' charges.

In his public statements Ospina spoke out constantly against *la violencia*. In strong messages delivered to the nation in February and September 1947 he denounced it as against the "national concord" and contrary to the politics of his own government.[22] In a directive sent to government officials prior to the March 1947 election he urged respect and guarantees for all citizens.[23] But Ospina's appeals failed to have the necessary impact. Whether by design or accident, *la violencia* accelerated in scope and intensity. Positions on both sides hardened and the government's actions appeared, to Liberals at least, increasingly partisan and repressive.

By the end of 1947 the government's control of the country appeared to be slipping away. Liberals in Nariño had demanded the appointment of military mayors in cities and towns to deal with the insecurity.[24] Arms and ammunition began to move across the frontier from Venezuela into northeastern Colombia, and Liberals were reported to be carrying long-range weapons for use against the government's newly organized political police. In Tolima organized revolt broke out, apparently with the support of the governor. And one Conservative source charged that the National Liberal Directorate issued instructions on the use of arms and promised to supply them to party members.[25] Finally, by January 1948 the violence reached such proportions in Santander del Norte that a state of siege was declared and a military governor named for the department.[26] During the same month the government placed some restrictions on radio broadcasts and the press. It should be noted here that *la violencia* began in the countryside, where Gaitán's voice had penetrated least. Beset by political instability, labor troubles, inflation and its accompanying poverty, and by ever accelerating violence, the Ospina government appeared at the end of the year to be drifting uncertainly in a sea of duress, less in control of events than a victim of them.

These events provided a challenge for Gaitán. His approach in reconciling his various roles was evident during the labor troubles of late 1946 and 1947. During the disorders that preceded the declaration of the state of siege in the Valle del Cauca in November 1946, when the popular classes and especially the workers expected firm direction from their champion, Gaitán was conveniently laid up in a hospital recuperating from a minor operation (during the disturbances following the May election he had gone on vacation). From his hospital bed he merely stated that the government's violence against workers was a repeat of the banana zone episode, and that it "gave the best results," presumably for his own cause. Nor did he attend a meeting called by Ospina with prominent Liberals to discuss the proposed state of siege declaration. And as the resulting cabinet crisis unfolded, Gaitán urged the Liberals to do nothing so that after the March 1947 congressional elections negotiations could be carried out with the government in order to define the sharing of power.[27]

As long as Gaitán was ignored by Ospina on the matter of political collaboration, he was free to maintain his opposition to the government. He took every opportunity to attack the government. *Jornada* editorials blasted away at the ineffectiveness of the government's economic policies; on the campaign trail in February and March 1947 Gaitán vociferously assaulted Ospina's failure to confront seriously or even to recognize the grave social problems the country faced.[28]

After the March election verified Gaitán's hold on the majority of Liberals, he once more demonstrated willingness to collaborate with Ospina, especially after the latter recognized Gaitan's leadership of his party. Gaitán, naturally, still insisted upon a political agreement between the parties, which Ospina refused. Hoping to gain the support of those Liberals whom he had just defeated and to consolidate his leadership of the party, Gaitán then reversed his previous position and agreed to allow Liberals to serve in the cabinet without being subject to party discipline. This represented an apparent concession that was applauded by the Liberal press, which felt that Gaitán now was accepting his "responsibilities."[29]

The May general strike demonstrated the difficulties of Gaitán's position. Once again he might have been expected by some to defend the workers' cause; but to do so would have meant contradicting the government—in which Liberal ministers were serving with Gaitán's consent—which declared the strike illegal and employed strong force against the workers. Gaitán, out of respect for the law, was reduced to maintaining silence until after the strike was over. Then, bombarded with criticism, he made an anguished three-hour speech explaining his silence. He said that the demands of the workers were justified, but not their tactics: the strike was "just but illegal." He said that he had been silent in order not to "demoralize" the workers. He then claimed that the criticism was a tactic of the oligarchy to discredit him and undermine his program in the coming congress.[30] This purist explanation only brought more attacks from the Liberal press. *El Liberal,* usually sympathetic, asked how he could condemn the general strike as illegal when he himself on various occasions threatened to use it against the government. *La Razón* noted that Gaitán "ought to speak directly and not act like an opportunist, waiting to see who wins before taking sides and covering up by making attacks on the 'oligarchy'."[31]

Not surprisingly, however, the strike served to strengthen Gaitán's position with organized labor, which may or may not have been the intended result of his stand. The CTC secretary general, Victor Julio Silva, a Gaitanista, defended Gaitán's position against the "vile" attempts of those who were attempting to compromise him.[32] The CTC, already beset by internal divisions, was gravely weakened by the strike's failure; its leadership was compromised, and it could hardly look forward to favorable treatment by the government. It also was facing competition from the newly organized Union of Colombian Workers (UTC). The Gaitanistas probably had all this in mind when they made a strong appeal to the CTC to "rectify the old errors . . . recognize the new realities" and ally itself to the dominant current of Liberalism.[33] This appeal met a very favorable response during the CTC's Ninth National Congress in Cali in December 1947.[34] Like most Liberals, the CTC found itself in the position of having nowhere to go except toward Gaitanismo.

However successful Gaitán was in maneuvering—either by design, instinct, or accident—through the dilemma posed by the general strike, he still faced serious problems: what attitude to adopt toward the government in the congress, and how to ensure Liberal support for his own program in that body; how to maintain a position of willingness to collaborate with the government while guaranteeing a Liberal victory in the October election; and what to do about the increasing violence in the face of a government that appeared unwilling or unable to deal with it.

Since he was preoccupied with putting popular pressure on the party leadership and with winning the October municipal elections with an increasing Gaitanista clientele, Gaitán bided his time in the congress. The result was the farce already described, with the Liberals attempting to disrupt and discredit the government at every opportunity. However, while the congress ignored Ospina's proposals, it also failed to act positively on Gaitán's. Since Gaitanistas in the congress worked hard in committees on their program, its failure provided Gaitán with ammunition in the October election, because the inaction undoubtedly aggravated the situation in the country. The spectacle of congressmen fighting endlessly with the executive and among themselves while failing to enact legislation beneficial to the people was hardly conducive to benign feelings in a country whose citizens already were desperate and aroused. Gaitán seemed to sense this reality instinctively.

Under pressures to win the election despite expected Conservative fraud and harassment, and to meet Liberal demands for action to stop the violence, Gaitán became increasingly emphatic and vehement. In Manizales in September 1947 he departed from usual practice and attacked Ospina personally by claiming that the president didn't have the "pants" to live up to the National Union. He also savagely attacked the Conservative caciques who were "money-grubbing at the expense of the state," and the city mayors in the department of Caldas who were practicing "vicious party sectarianism." In another speech, in Bogotá's Municipal Theater, Gaitán said that the government was too incompetent to rule the country. He then read a letter ostensibly sent to Ospina by the National Conservative Directorate asking for the destruction of "revolutionary Liberal unionism" and the "mutilation" of the labor movement.[35]

All of this was but a prelude to the sensational charges he brought against the government from his seat in the Senate in mid-September. On the twelfth he read documents indicating that arms and tear-gas bombs had been brought illegally into the country by the U.S. military attaché in U.S. Air Force planes from a North American base in Panama. The matériel was destined for the national police. This procedure violated Colombian law because such arms could be imported only by the general staff of the armed forces. The proof of the importation was discovered in the files of the national police command during an investigation by the controller general of the republic.[36]

The revelation threw the government into another crisis. The House of Representatives and the Senate appointed investigating commissions to look into the affair. In the streets of the capital antigovernment demonstrations occurred. When the explanations of the minister of government failed to calm the situation, the president was obliged to speak to the nation. He admitted that his government had solicited the United States for the arms and that they had been brought in by foreign aircraft because the Colombian government lacked the required transport. He explained his action by referring to the disturbances that had resulted in the state of siege of the previous November and defended the tear gas as a humane method of avoiding the spilling of blood. As for Gaitán's charges, he dismissed them and the investigation commissions as nothing more than political acts of the opposition against the government.[37]

The incident further inflamed the nation and brought any hope for authentic cooperation between the parties one step closer to doom. Ospina later admitted that after this he lost all confidence in Gaitán; the president believed that as the principal responsible for law and order he had the right and duty to act as he had;

additionally, he felt that Gaitán's charges were unmerited because of the Liberal representation in his cabinet.[38]

Meanwhile Gaitán was confronting his own difficulties. He undoubtedly acted both to make political capital just prior to an election and to oppose further government repression of Liberals. Yet, if he carried the consequences of his charges to their logical conclusion and broke off all collaboration with the government, he endangered the electoral victory (the firing of Liberal officials at all levels that would surely follow presented the possibility of widespread fraud); if he continued to collaborate on Ospina's terms and without guarantees for Liberal security he was failing to meet the most urgent demands of his followers for action against *la violencia,* thus endangering his hold on the Liberal masses and opening the way for actions that could result in civil war and the end of constitutional government.

In the short term, at least, Gaitán decided to allow the Liberal ministers to serve in the cabinet. He apparently wanted to get safely past the election in the hope that a Liberal victory would convince Ospina to come around; and, indeed, following the election he once more offered Ospina an "attitude of respect" and cooperation. He even urged the congress to turn from its bickering and begin enacting constructive legislation.[39] However, as he probably knew all along, Gaitán did not have sufficient control of the congress to force it to do his bidding. The chaos there continued: in early December the nation was treated to the spectacle of representatives pointing pistols at each other in the lower house.[40] Nor did Ospina change his attitude on Liberal collaboration. In fact, the government's position hardened. A new Conservative minister of government, José Antonio Montalvo, said that a Gaitanista proposal to reorganize the national police on nonsectarian lines would be met by the government "with blood and fire." He added that the president could compose a government as he pleased and told the Liberals not to expect generosity. Later Montalvo charged Gaitán with wanting to overthrow Ospina. And speaking for the government he said: "Traditional parties are one thing and caudillismo is another. The country cannot continue to look favorably on this dangerous confusion. Caudillismo or political parties? That is the question."[41]

By the end of 1947 it was evident that, though he had made progress, Gaitán had failed to reconcile completely the contradictions inherent in his various roles. His absorption in capturing the leadership of the Liberal party and maintaining it as the majority political force in the country had slowed his pace. He had not moved a meaningful program through congress nor formulated a viable opposition policy. He had not yet successfully fused Gaitanismo and Liberalism. His efforts to maintain his positions both as a mass, popular leader and chief of a traditional party over which he did not have complete influence caused him to act with great care. He knew that he could serve either the national country or the political country, but not both. He believed that the people's only hope lay in the ability of the former to free itself, at long last, from the debilitating influence of the latter.

1948: The Final Act

In his first speech after the 1946 presidential election Gaitán had threatened the incoming government with a general strike if it failed to provide the Liberals with "guarantees." In addresses after that he made frequent, if veiled and generalized, threats; for example, once when speaking about violence in Boyacá he said that "the people have in their hands the means to defend themselves."[42] But generally he took a moderate position regarding *la violencia*. As it mounted in intensity and scope in the countryside he repeatedly made efforts to deal with it by peaceful means through petition and pressure on the government, by speaking out against it, and by attempting intraparty agreements. Whether or not he fully realized the extent of his own contribution to the atmosphere that generated *la violencia* is questionable. Possibly he was so enmeshed in his long-standing role of popular caudillo that his own actions constituted a blind spot.

Throughout 1947 Gaitán came under enormous pressure from Liberals to deal with the violence. In response to an appeal by Ospina prior to the March 1947 election, he and Laureano Gómez delivered national radio addresses urging restraint and moderation by their respective followers. On April 12 Gaitán delivered a "Memorandum of Grievances" to Ospina in which he asked the president to bring an end to Conservative attacks on Liberals. He blamed not the national government but lower functionaries in the provinces "who are unable to practice or respect the most basic principles of democracy" and attached a long list of acts allegedly committed against Liberals.[43] In early June 1947 Gaitán traveled to Bucaramanga, Santander del Sur, in an effort to deal personally with the difficult situation in that department. As elected president of the Santander assembly he introduced a law for the nationalization of the departmental police as the best method for securing order, and he maneuvered Liberal ministers into the departmental cabinet of the Conservative governor as an attempt to ensure protection for Liberals.[44]

As the violence spread and engendered counterattacks by Liberals, it became obvious that the national party leaders and even the government had little influence or control. Gaitán's hold over the urban masses did not extend to the rural areas; despite his repeated appeals to Liberals in Caldas, for example, hostilities continued there.[45] Ospina's efforts were counterproductive. Within the national police he organized a political police force to deal with all violence. But under the control of Conservatives it inevitably became an arm of the

Conservative party.[46] Nor was the government's response to the "Memorandum of Grievances" and other complaints reassuring. Ospina merely stated that he would study the memorandum and consider appropriate action. National government officials denied charges of Conservative violence that appeared in the Liberal press, or claimed that Liberals were equally responsible.

The issue was taken up by the congress in July and August and resulted in nationally publicized, wild debates as Liberals and Conservatives traded charges and countercharges. Gaitán also returned to the attack. In a speech before eighty thousand people in Medellín on August 22, 1947, he said that the question of civil war or peace was in the hands of the government and warned that he would not stand for the defrauding of Liberalism or the violation of its rights.[47] But while his tone was belligerent, he had no intention of acting. The speech was designed to bring pressure on Ospina to accept the peace agreement between the parties that Gaitán was negotiating at the time with Gómez and the minister of government, Urdaneta Arbeláez.[48] Alarmed at the spread of violence and the threat it posed for the nation, the minister had brought the two party chiefs together to work out an arrangement.

A Liberal-Conservative peace pact was signed on August 29, 1947. Gaitán, once more reversing his belligerent pose, urged all Colombians to accept the pact. He said that the workers and *campesinos* gained nothing from the violence, which only served the bureaucratic aims of the petty caciques, and that it hindered the building of schools, the electrification of the countryside, and improvement of the lives of the people. He called for "passionate" ideological debate, the struggle of ideas against ideas, but political peace among men. As he had in the past, he blamed not the Conservative masses for the violence, but "little groups interested in their positions." The speech was reasonable, moderate, and conciliatory. But it had absolutely no effect. By September, Gómez was accusing the Liberals of not honoring the agreement, and Gaitán was calling on the government to send troops to Santander del Norte after the authorities there admitted they could no longer maintain order.[49]

Gaitán's public statements alternated between calls for defensive vigilance on the part of his followers and offers of conciliation to his opponents, depending upon the contingencies of the moment. In his private correspondence, however, he continually urged restraint and chastized Liberals who were threatening reprisals against Conservatives. He lamented the attacks upon Liberals but urged them to carry their protests to the authorities through peaceful means.[50] He repeated this advice in letter after letter despite the most anguished pleas and provocative charges brought by Liberals throughout Colombia. Obviously, he was willing to go to almost any length to prevent open civil war. When a newspaper editorialized that Liberals would have to take drastic measures, including a general strike, to defend themselves, Gaitán said to several of his friends: "This is absurd. We cannot commit Liberalism to anarchy and the country to disorder. Those who speak of a national strike and violent opposition do so because they do not have the responsibility of declaring them. I know that I have to lead my party to the reconquest of power by the constitutional road, . . . in the councils, in the assemblies, in the congress."[51] He remained convinced that he would take power in 1950 at the head of a constitutionally legal, mass democratic movement, and that the violence would end as his program transformed the nation.

Yet the strain inherent in his position began to tell upon Gaitán personally. He was constantly under surveillance by the secret police. Sabotage was carried out against *Jornada*, and its staff was subjected to considerable harassment by the police.[52] There were reports that Colombian secret agents were in Venezuela attempting to discover if he was receiving funds from the Betancourt government.[53] And Gaitán received many anonymous threats on his life. (He refused to have bodyguards because, he said, his enemies knew that his death would cause a national upheaval that would sweep them all away.)[54] Unnaturally, Gaitán began to spend periods when he refused to see anyone. On one of his last brief vacations in Puerto Colombia on the Magdalena River he lived completely alone, spent long hours walking on the river bank, and only spoke with local fishermen about their lives.[55]

The new year brought more violence. In addition to the refugees streaming into Bogotá and other cities, there were reports of entire families crossing the northeast frontier into Venezuela in order to escape. Gaitán sent a message to Rómulo Betancourt of Venezuela requesting his help for these forced emigrants, and the latter responded favorably.[56] At the end of January, Gaitán established a "house of refuge" in the capital funded by Liberal contributions and directed party leaders to do the same in provincial capitals.[57] In late January he traveled through the Santanders where he managed to calm Liberals who were on the verge of open revolt.[58]

Upon his return to the capital Gaitán proclaimed the right of legitimate self-defense for the masses, but he did not cease to be genuinely concerned to end *la violencia*. His trip had been undertaken at the request of Ospina and provincial government leaders; it was an indication of his willingness to cooperate.[59] However, he had only a temporary effect. At the end of January 1948 the government was compelled to declare a state of siege in Santander del Norte.

The grave situation did for the national Liberal leadership what all of Gaitán's maneuverings had not been able to accomplish: bring it together. On January 27, 1948, following meetings with prominent Liberals of the Santos and López factions, Gaitán, Echandía, and the writer Zea Hernández sent another moving "Memorandum of Grievances" to Ospina that stated, in part, "there are many abandoned towns and fields in the land. . . . Families, and entire populations, have fled from their provinces."[60] Ospina responded with another plea for cooperation between the party leaders but offered nothing concrete. He spent more time, in *El Tiempo*'s view, defending the police than their victims.[61] In this atmosphere the Liberal leaders gathered once more to decide on a course of action. For almost two weeks from mid-February they debated the issue. Carlos Lozano y Lozano, speaking for the Liberal right, urged continued cooperation essentially on Ospina's terms; López reiterated his thesis that the "frontiers" between the parties had disappeared and insisted on the National Union; Echandía vacillated and Gaitán remained silent, willing to abide by whatever decision was reached.[62] The Liberal oligarchs appeared willing to go to almost any length to reach an agreement with the government, but Ospina offered nothing more than his previous policy. He insisted that an accord be reached between the parties, rather than between the Liberals and the government—something that already had failed. Thus, reluctantly, the Liberals decided to break off all collaboration on February 28, 1948. The Liberal press blamed *la violencia* and Ospina's failure to deal with it as the cause of the rupture. It also reported that Liberal leaders now agreed that Gaitán had been correct in his original stand on cooperation and that they were uniting behind his leadership.[63]

As the violence mounted in intensity and spread throughout wider regions of the country, Gaitán decided to abandon his personal appeals to the government in favor of mass pressure. In early February huge protest demonstrations were staged in cities throughout the country. They were peaceful except in the Caldas cities of Manizales and Pereira, where recently recruited Conservative police, some with criminal records, fired into the Liberal crowds and killed several persons.[64] The greatest demonstration occurred in Bogotá, where Gaitán delivered an "Oración por la Paz" (Oration for Peace) before more than one hundred thousand silent marchers who had gathered in the vast Plaza de Bolívar. The demonstration was the last great Gaitanista rally and showed him at his most honorable.

Several members of Gaitán's staff voiced doubts about the wisdom of gathering so many people together at such a time and about Gaitán's ability to control them. They further questioned his desire that the demonstration be entirely silent. But, characteristically, Gaitán dismissed them by saying, "I am sure that the multitude will not utter one cry. Those who don't know the masses don't know their reactions. Our people are profoundly intelligent. I don't share your skepticism. The demonstration will be a success. I guarantee it."[65] On Saturday, February 7, 1948, at four o'clock in the afternoon Gaitán stood on a balcony overlooking the plaza. He was greeted only by the waving of thousands of white handkerchiefs. In his short, eloquent, emotional oration, addressed to the president, he said, in part:

> Señor Presidente: Today we do not make economic or political demands. We ask only that the actions of our country not bring shame upon us. We ask for the building of peace and civilization. We ask that the persecution by the authorities stop. Thus asks this immense multitude. We ask a small but great thing: that our political struggles be governed by the constitution. Do not believe that our silence, this impressive silence, is cowardice! We, Señor Presidente, we are not cowards. We are the descendants of the heroes who annihilated the tyrants on this sacred soil. We are capable of sacrificing our lives to save the peace and liberty of Colombia!
>
> Señor, stop the violence. We want human life to be defended, that is the least a people can ask. . . . Señor Presidente, our flag is in mourning; this silent multitude, this mute cry from our hearts, asks only that you treat us . . . as you would have us treat you.
>
> We say to you finally, Your Excellency: Fortunate are those who understand that words of peace and harmony should not conceal sentiments of rancor or enmity. Badly advised are those in the government who conceal behind kind words their lack of respect for the people. They will be marked in the pages of history by the finger of infamy![66]

There was no response from Ospina. The demonstrations, like the appeals before them, failed to have any effect. The violence continued. A committee of Liberal congressmen led by Echandía met with Ospina in March 1948 and said that they were prepared to cooperate with the government on electoral reform and police nationalization. The president reacted "coldly and correctly" and restated his thesis about party-to-party agreements. The Liberals interpreted this as deliberate rejection.[67] At the end of March, Ospina appointed an all-Conservative cabinet, which elicited this biting comment from Roberto Urdaneta Arbeláez: "The Conservatives think they have won everything; the Liberals believe they have lost nothing."[68]

While these events were transpiring, the capital was being prepared for the Ninth Inter-American Conference scheduled for the first two weeks of April. The government, concerned that the meeting be a success and that Bogotá present itself in the most favorable light, had requested and received four million pesos from congress for beautification, which was being directed by the foreign minister, Laureano Gómez. However, while the Capitol received a face-lifting and the shoeshine men new uniforms, the populace, especially the lower and middle classes, grew angry. The cost-of-living soared "fabulously" in the city in the months prior to the conference because merchants were hoarding in anticipation of higher prices and the harvest was poor.[69] Many believed that the government's works were wasteful and there were rumors that government officials and contractors were arranging mutually profitable, but fraudulent deals.

To make matters worse, Ospina named a combined Conservative-Liberal delegation to the conference comprised, as previously agreed upon, of leaders of both parties; however, he excluded Gaitán with the flimsy excuse that the latter was not an expert in international law and had never directed a diplomatic mission.[70] Gómez, the leader of the delegation, had insisted in the face of both Conservative and Liberal protests that if Gaitán were selected he would refuse to serve. He feared that Gaitán would disrupt the conference with fiery speeches. In the face of these threats Ospina complied. Although personally insulted, Gaitán gracefully accepted Ospina's decision. However, he had to restrain Liberal leaders who wanted to boycott the conference and his own followers who wanted to launch mass street demonstrations in protest.[71]

Heightening the acrimonious atmosphere in the city, numerous leftists began arriving from all over the hemisphere. They came to protest the Cold War anticommunist resolutions that were expected to be placed by the United States on the conference agenda.[72] Although there is much controversy concerning their real intentions, there is no question that they constituted a disturbing influence during a difficult time. Their presence, along with the police agents of various countries and the strengthened security forces brought into the city by the Ospina government, almost assured a provocative situation. Tension increased as protest meetings were held, wild rumors of bomb threats and planned assassinations flew about the city, and propaganda about oligarchs dining in state while the people died of hunger circulated widely.[73] Then police reported the arrest of a worker who was attempting to plant a bomb in the Capitol where the conference was meeting; and on April 7 a mob attacked an automobile of the Ecuadorian delegation in the mistaken belief that it carried Gómez. As the conference convened the historian Germán Arciniegas described the atmosphere as "a chill wind of terror blowing in from the provinces."[74] Foreign delegates and newsmen made similar observations.

While the conference met, Gaitán abstained from making any public statements and appearances. Nor did he play a role in the disturbances that were agitating the city. He devoted his time to his law practice, met only with close friends, and was seen in public only walking to and from his law office or in nearby restaurants. Late in the morning of April 9 he appeared at his office, where he jovially received the congratulations of his close associates for his successful defense, the evening before, of an army officer charged with murder.[75] Shortly before one o'clock, after bantering about where to lunch and who would pay, he descended to the street with Plinio Mendoza Neira, *Jornada* editors Jorge Padilla and Alejandro Vallejo, and a long-time friend, the physician Pedro Eliseo Cruz. Following lunch Gaitán was scheduled to meet with a Cuban student leader, Fidel Castro. At the entrance to the building the group brushed past a paunchy, unshaven, badly dressed man. The man followed them a few steps into the street, passed them and, brandishing a revolver, turned to face them. Gaitán immediately attempted to return to the building, but several shots rang out. He fell to the sidewalk, mortally wounded in the head, lungs, and liver.[76]

V

Epitaph and Epilogue

14
The Aftermath

The assassination of Gaitán set off a spontaneous uprising in Bogotá that rapidly spread throughout the country. The Gaitanista multitudes, reacting in frustrated rage to the death of their caudillo, for a few brief hours came close to overthrowing the existing social order in an orgy of violence and destruction. They completed the final, desperate act of the Gaitanista drama, the terrible vengeance of the dispossessed who had been stirred by the unprecedented campaigns of Gaitán in their name, and who now, freed from all restraints by his death, unleashed their furious hatred against the persons, institutions, and symbols of their common enemies. The *Bogotazo,* as the events of April 9 were named, ended an era in Colombian history. The long struggle of Gaitán to raise his forsaken people from their centuries-old ignorance and hopelessness finally succeeded. On that "tragic Friday" the masses turned for the first time against a system that ruthlessly exploited them and announced their irrevocable, undeniable presence in the Colombian reality. [1]

Rural violence and sustained political agitation had created an atmosphere of extreme tension by early April 1948. Foreigners who arrived for the Ninth Inter-American Conference and residents of Bogotá commented on this. The mood of the capital's citizens, especially the immense lower classes, was particularly ugly. Nor did they appreciate the expenditures for beautification of the city or the food shortages and rising prices that accompanied the opening of the conference. The shooting of Gaitán was the spark that ignited the inferno. Within minutes after he slumped to the sidewalk, the assassin was cornered in a nearby drugstore and beaten and kicked to death. Then, almost instinctively, the rapidly multiplying, hysterical mobs turned their wrath upon those whom they believed were actually responsible. As Gaitán had predicted when he refused to use personal bodyguards, saying that his enemies would not dare kill him because they feared what would follow, the catastrophe erupted.

Within an hour of the shooting thousands of enraged Bogatanos were devastating the city's center. The presidential palace, into which President Ospina barely managed to escape when returning to the city in early afternoon, was under attack by civilians armed with weapons looted from stores or abandoned by the deserting police. The mobs sought out Laureano Gómez at the Foreign Ministry. Not finding him there, they destroyed the building. His house in the suburbs also was looted and burned, as was his newspaper, *El Siglo*. The Capitol, where the conference was meeting, was overrun and damaged. The Palace of Justice and other government buildings were sacked and burned. When rumors spread that priests were firing on the rioters from church steeples, the cathedral and other churches were desecrated, and the palaces of the archbishop and papal nuncio severely damaged.

When Darío Echandía announced the death of Gaitán at the clinic to which the Liberal leader had been taken, the fury of the mobs intensified. In the streets, automobiles and streetcars were overturned and set afire. Stores were broken into and their contents emptied. Rioters armed with machetes and homemade gasoline bombs sought out convenient targets. Bottles stolen from liquor stores passed from hand to hand and increased the delirium. Lower-class women, dressed in furs and finery taken from expensive shops, raced through the streets at the side of the men. By mid-afternoon the city's center was a shambles. Merchandise and debris filled the streets; thick, black smoke rose from blazing buildings. Bogotá resembled a European city after a World War II bombing attack.

The capital's army garrison did not appear in force until almost two hours after the initial shooting. But the tanks and automatic weapons of the soldiers soon proved to be murderously effective. Despite suicidal charges by the rioters against armored units and heavy street fighting in some sectors between troops and armed civilians, the military prevailed. By nightfall the rioting had peaked as a result of both the army's actions and a steadily falling freezing rain. Flareups continued throughout the night and into the following Saturday, and there was continued fighting between snipers and soldiers, as well as a brief battle in front of the U.S. Embassy at eleven o'clock, but the army gradually regained control of the city. The arrival of more troops on April 10 meant the final containment of the uprising in Bogotá.

The cost in the capital in human lives and property damage was tremendous. Although exact figures are not available, it was estimated that several thousand died, most of whom were members of the lower class. Several hundred corpses were taken to the city morgue within hours of the outbreak. The presidential palace was surrounded by the bodies of those who had fallen in attacks there, victims of the presidential guard. Photographs display dozens of bodies dumped in the main cemetery. As for property, almost every government and church building was destroyed or damaged, as well as dozens of business establishments. Few structures were left intact on the city's main commercial artery, Carrera Septima. Historic edifices also suffered. The Colonial Museum was damaged and the ancient church of San Francisco was destroyed.

As news of the assassination spread, similar outbreaks occurred throughout the country. There was rioting, looting, and burning in almost every major city and town of Colombia. Serious fighting also erupted in the countryside and lasted for more than a month, thus adding another dimension to the destruction of *la violencia*. In Cartagena naval units took control before serious trouble occurred, but in Cali, Baranquilla, and Ibagué, Liberals proclaimed revolutionary juntas and ousted the authorities. Bucaramanga was temporarily seized by rebellious groups. The most serious trouble was in Cali and the surrounding region where only brutal repressive action by army units commanded by the future dictator General Rojas Pinilla prevented a regional revolutionary movement from gaining momentum.

The government was almost completely disrupted by the uprising. Only the timely intervention of the armed forces prevented a total collapse. In Bogotá, President Ospina was virtually a prisoner in the palace. The presidential guard barely managed to keep the building from being overrun. However, the president courageously refused to leave. He said that he was of more service to the country as a dead president than a fleeing one.

The Liberal leadership in Bototá, Gaitanista and regular, was largely paralyzed during the hours when the mobs ruled the streets. Most of the Gaitanistas, including Darío Echandía, remained in the clinic where Gaitán had been taken. There they hovered uncertainly and indecisively around their dying chief.[2] Of the prominent Gaitanistas only Carlos Pareja and Jorge Zalamea Borda went into the streets and attempted to take command; they were aided by Gaitán's socialist collaborators, Antonia García and Geraldo Molina.[3] The regular Liberals gathered in the offices of *El Tiempo* where they discussed what action to take. As it happened, they chose a political solution as befit members of the political country. They failed to understand, or pretended to misunderstand, the fact that the turbulence in the streets was a massive repudiation of things as they were. They, like the raging people around them, wanted to overthrow the government, but their motives were different: the Liberal politicians wanted political power; the people in arms wanted to overthrow an unjust socioeconomic system. But the people had no leaders and their movement dissipated and was crushed. This outcome created the opportunity for the politicians.

In the waning hours of the rebellion, when the army seemed to have regained control, a delegation of Liberals cautiously made its way to the presidential palace. It consisted of Luis Cano, Darío Echandía, Carlos Lleras Restrepo, Alfonso Araújo, and Plinio Mendoza Neira. The Liberals asked Ospina to resign in favor of Echandía, the presumed heir of Gaitán.[4] Ospina refused on the grounds that to do so would only cause more bloodshed. The Liberals then left with only the promise that the president would keep them informed.

The following morning a group of generals arrived and requested that the president step aside so that a military junta could take command and restore order in the country. Once more Ospina refused. He declared that to do so was to violate the constitution.[5] Despite reservations, the generals finally acceded.

Ospina then proposed to the Liberals the restoration of the Government of National Union. Echandía was to be minister of government and the pro-Liberal General Germán Ocampo named minister of war. To this the Liberals readily agreed. The only conditions they imposed were the removal of the hated Laureano Gómez and José Antonio Montalvo from their government posts.[6]

When President Ospina spoke to the nation on April 11 to urge peace and harmony, he did so as leader of a coalition government in which Liberals had equal representation.[7] Once more the political country had triumphed; the oligarchy had closed ranks in the face of crisis. The social and economic grievances that cried out so desperately for solution were conveniently forgotten as politics returned to normal. Even some of the Gaitanistas urged cooperation with the new government. An editorial in *Jornada* asked its readers to be "patient" with the new government; the Gaitanista Jorge Uribe Márquez in a speech only a month after Gaitán's death called upon the dead leader's followers to support the "peace and unity" of the Liberal party.[8]

The *Bogotazo* has been variously described as a social movement of unprecedented dimensions, as a caste rebellion inspired by Gaitán's hatred of the oligarchs, and as "the earthquake of a people provoked by the assassination of its own voice."[9] It clearly was a confrontation between the urban masses who aspired to the privileges of the wealthy minority, and the elite who sought to retain its prerogatives. In the countryside the conflict took on the aspects of traditional Conservative-Liberal struggles.[10] The result of the uprising was not a concerted effort to reform the system in order to meet the most urgent demands of the people, but an oligarchic closing of ranks, participated in by the Liberal leaders, intent upon preservation of the status quo.

After Gaitán's death Liberals of all factions and persuasions pledged to carry on his ideals and work for the rapid implementation of his program. These same sentiments were expressed by all the prominent Liberals at Gaitán's funeral. The principal eulogist and rising star of Colombian Liberalism, Carlos Lleras Restrepo, said that Gaitán "always believed it necessary to maintain direct contact with his people . . . and the politics of the Liberal party will not change now."[11] Unfortunately, noble words like this, spoken when the fires of Bogotá were still smoldering, were soon forgotten as the politicians returned to their old ways.

In the months and years after Gaitán's death, Colombia journeyed into disaster. *La violencia* intensified and widened in scope. Two hundred thousand people were killed. The lives of millions more were disrupted. In large areas of the countryside order succumbed to chaos. Military repression reigned in the cities. While the army and the oligarchy remained united, the rest of the country tore itself apart.

As for Gaitanismo, the personalism which was a strength while Gaitán lived was, of course, a defect after he died. His movement, like much else, fell victim to military repression and violence. Disheartened by Gaitán's death, leaderless, with no ready alternative organization to turn to, the majority of Gaitanistas stayed in the Liberal party. There they witnessed the systematic removal of the Gaitanista leadership throughout the country in the months after April 9.[12] They watched Darío Echandía, Francisco José Chaux, and Darío Samper—all former Gaitanista leaders—compete openly for the right to be called the heir of Gaitán. When the moderate Echandía entered the Ospina government, many Gaitanistas followed Samper and his *Jornada* group, which opposed collaboration with the Conservatives. This element formed the principal dissenting group within Liberalism and in early 1949 organized the independent Comando de Izquierda. The Comando, which included congressional Gaitanistas like Jorge Uribe Márquez and Eduardo Camancho Gamba, opposed the regular Liberal directorate comprised of Lleras Restrepo and Chaux who, like Echandía, opted for collaboration. But the Comando itself was attacked by former Gaitanistas.[13] In this acrimonious atmosphere many Gaitanistas turned away in disgust.[14] *Jornada* was more than correct when, on April 9, 1950, it noted that the Gaitanistas felt "frustrated" and "abandoned" and added that none of the existing Liberal chiefs had Gaitán's power over the masses, or even had the "intuition" of what to do.

An additional factor contributed to the dissolution of Gaitanismo. Supported by the military, and at least implicitly agreed to by the regular Liberals, the Conservative government carried through repressive policies after the *Bogotazo* intended to crush social unrest. The official persecution, which became in effect a counterrevolution during the Gómez presidency, fell most effectively upon the more easily controlled urban masses who had made up the bulk of the Gaitanistas. True, many Gaitanistas, especially those in the countryside, eventually formed the guerrilla groups that provided the principal armed resistance to the Ospina and Gómez governments.[15] And some of the more radical Gaitanistas found their way into the Communist party; or, like Antonio García, organized socialist groups like the Partido Popular Socialista

Colombiano (Colombian Popular Socialist Party—PPSC), which later supported Rojas Pinilla.[16] But these were either unattractive or unavailable alternatives for the majority of Gaitanistas who, perhaps hoping against hope, remained within Liberalism in the expectation that it would fight for the goals of Gaitán, or that they would find a leader who could assume the mantle of the caudillo.

Who killed Gaitán?[17] Perhaps the real question should be, Who profited most from his disappearance? The oligarchs have dropped a curtain of confusion over his death and they dare history to see through it.

15
The Legacy

For two decades Jorge Eliécer Gaitán was the foremost spokesman for those non-elite Colombians seeking participation in their national life. During the 1940s he was the only politician with a national reputation to demand democratic transformations of the country's political and socioeconomic structures. After 1944 he mobilized large segments of the urban and part of the lower rural classes into a movement without precedent in Colombia's history. In doing so he undercut the political system of elite-dominated parties that was more than a century old and challenged the heretofore unquestioned right of the upper class to rule. He introduced modern mass politics into the country and succeeded in integrating those whose cause he championed into the political system for the first time. By articulating the desires of the lower classes for social justice and sharpening their awareness of class differences, he managed to affect substantially the nature of the political cutlure. Perhaps the best comment on his impact was made by one of his contemporaries, Juan Lozano y Lozano: "Gaitán has the indisputable merit of being the first Colombian who has put the people before himself and has made their weight felt. The nonconformist ferment that he has stirred up extends farther each day and never again will be extinguished in the public conscience. . . . Gaitán has put into circulation among us a new value, the social value of politics."[1]

The final four years of Gaitán's life mark the high point of his political career; during those years conditions appeared that made possible the kind of politics he practiced. The elite, or oligarchy, having earlier experimented with reform from above now turned against it. The burdens of an economy disrupted by war and industrialization fell heavily upon the lower classes. The lower social strata brought into existence by modernization and development resented the interruption of their quest for a share of the goods and benefits and the decision-making processes of their society. They willingly listened to the moralistic and democratic appeals of Gaitán. When he recruited a leadership from among disaffected elitist intellectuals and middle-class professionals and businessmen who were frustrated by social rigidities, the Gaitanista movement was born.[2]

Gaitán was aided by the organizational weakness of the lower classes, which limited viable alternatives to him. The failure of the second López administration and defeat of reform Liberalism left the majority of that party who favored continued reform available for mobilization. The trade unions represented only a small minority of all workers, had limited appeal, and were dependent upon the good will of the state. The Communists, divided and in their "popular front" phase, were appendages of the Liberals. No other strong organizations of the left existed. A right dominated by the reactionary Laureano Gómez was a frightening threat rather than an attractive possibility.

Gaitán managed to overcome differences within the lower class—for example, between trade union, issue-oriented industrial workers and subsistence-minded urban subproletarians—and between his mass base and essentially middle-class leadership by appealing against the common enemy: the oligarchy. Diverse social strata thus joined together under the ambiguous but attractive, emotion-charged slogan, "For the moral and democratic restoration!" After the electoral defeat of 1946 additional support came from Liberals who rallied to him as the symbol of opposition to the restoration of Conservative hegemony.

Although the anti-oligarchic slogan served as a common rallying point, Gaitán's personalized, charismatic leadership provided the most effective means of mobilizing the masses caught in the uncertain transitional phase between the traditional and modern worlds. They responded to Gaitán's personalism because it was within a political tradition that went back to Benjamín Herrera, Rafael Uribe Uribe, and the Liberal caudillos of the nineteenth century. They also were magnetized by Gaitán's forceful, compelling personality and his messianic identification with them—"I am not a man! I am a people!" A humble background, similar physical characteristics, intuitive knowledge of aspirations and resentments and the ability to articulate them—all served to link Gaitán with his followers.

A decisive element in Gaitán's ability to achieve mass rather than merely class support was his enormous prestige. There are numerous reasons for it. He was active in national politics longer than other political figures, including López and Santos. Further, he had a more profound knowledge of contemporary political realities than anyone else, especially in regard to popular sentiments. Despite his education, culture, and status, which were never allowed to interfere with his political message, he eliminated all barriers between himself and the people; within Liberalism no one had a deeper understanding and knowledge of the rank and file. He communicated with the people in a crude, forceful language that reduced intellectual abstractions to simple formulas of combat and struggle. Popular aspirations, sentiments, malaise were transformed by language into elemental ideas capable of being grasped by the illiterate and unsophisticated. His speech was direct, spontaneous, frank, and usually lacking the evasions characteristic of political language. Following the political experience of 1946 Gaitán's prestige reached its highest point. When the party was abandoned by most of the regular leaders, many of those who formerly had opposed him accepted his leadership. But his greatest prestige remained among the poor, in whose name he so often had struggled.[3]

In addition to personalism, Gaitanismo offered an appealing program. Gaitán succeeded in combining his mass politics with a program that emphasized development, electoral reform, controls over societal exploitation, profit-sharing, education, housing, etc. It was devised to attract broad strata of the population, especially from the middle and lower classes. Essentially it was a moderate, reformist program designed to attack poverty rather than wealth. Nationalist and democratic socialist in orientation, it actually reflected the evolutionary ideological inclinations of Gaitán. However, when surrounded by the Gaitanista rhetoric the program took on a revolutionary hue.

The result of Gaitanista politics was the appearance, especially among the urban lower and lower-middle classes, of a collective identity and heightened class consciousness. Loyalties to the traditional parties began to be transcended; a modernized politics based upon lower- and middle-class interests began to appear. These changes represented revolutionary challenges to the established order.

Despite the stubborn capacity of the elitist hold on the Colombian political system, what was most remarkable was Gaitán's ability to mobilize and sustain the populist momentum. Though he felt compelled to work within one of the two traditional parties, he was succeeding in its inward transformation. His experience with UNIR in the 1930s demonstrated the difficulty of working outside the existing parties and influenced his decision not to establish a separate "third force" political movement. Furthermore, his personal ambition precluded any long period in the wilderness while he was building a third party. Nevertheless, his handling of his difficulties (they did slow his pace) as Jefe Unico of Liberalism demonstrated his skill in using the existing political structures and cultural traditions. With the merger of Gaitanismo and Liberalism he was at once the popular leader of a mass movement of national transformation and head of the opposition within an historic, poly-class collectivity in which much of the traditional leadership and an important minority of the membership opposed him. His political maneuverings in this period suggested an inimitable sense of timing and flexibility and a close rapport with the populace. His intention was to convert Liberalism, in effect, into Gaitanismo while retaining its name and some of its traditional functions. He expected that both historic parties eventually would disappear as a result of the realignment of class forces. He did not have time to complete the restructuring of Liberalism. This fact and the defect in personalism help explain why Gaitanismo failed to survive him.

Another indication of the strength of Gaitán's momentum was his ability to hold to the legal road to power. Fidel Castro, an admirer of Gaitán, agreed that his legalistic tactic was correct, given existing Colombian conditions. As Castro observed when commenting on this question, "Reality cannot be invented."[4] In spite of the prerevolutionary conditions that existed after 1946 and the expectations of many of his followers like J. A. Osorio Lizarazo and Antonio García, Gaitán refused to depart from legality.[5] Indeed, the mutual desire of the populace and Gaitán for meaningful law was one of the sources of his strength. Gaitanismo was not longing for violence. The nature of Gaitán's rhetoric does, admittedly, contain the threat of insurrection, but a close reading of his speeches shows that he meant an insurrection in defense of law. Gaitán fatally believed that the political institutions of the Colombian bourgeois "democracy" were still somewhat open. In 1930 and again in 1946 minority opposition parties won pluralities in national elections and were allowed to take power. Gaitán, supported by the recently enfranchised masses, fully expected to win power legally in the 1950 presidential election. Further, there were indications that the opposition seemed resigned to this probability. Gaitán believed that a majority electoral victory would legitimate his government and the reforms it would carry out. He expected that an attempt to prevent him from taking power would lead to an upheaval, which his opponents feared. Gaitán had no vested interest in *la violencia*.

The question of what would have happened had Gaitán been elected president in 1950 and allowed to take office cannot, of course, be answered. But it appears certain that Gaitán rather quickly would have had to deal with the aspirations of the lower classes that he did so much to arouse. Undoubtedly this would have generated powerful opposition within the elite and an attempt to sabotage his efforts at every level. If Gaitán persisted, and if the armed forces did not precipitate a coup, the type of regime that would eventually have emerged might have approximated some form of socialist-leaning populism. Given Gaitán's imperious personal characteristics, and the examples set by the internal structures of UNIR and the Gaitanista movement, it would have been a government of strong authority vested in a charismatic leadership. While the success of the regime would have required the distribution of substantial benefits to the lower classes, his emphasis on education makes it seem likely that their democratic participation would not have been limited to that of an approving chorus. Though Gaitán's history indicates that he reacted quickly against any dissidence or opposition no matter what the source (he was living in a machismo culture), his performance as mayor of Bogotá and minister of education and of labor demonstrated that he was a capable and even an imaginative administrator. In summary, Gaitán would have restricted or tried to break the monopoly of power by the traditional elite, as was the intention of Allende in Chile, and certainly he would have improved the conditions of the lower classes, but it is doubtful that democracy would have suffered as a result. Considering the tragedy that the country lived through in the decade after April 9, 1948, and the unfulfilled promises of every government since, Gaitán's premature death must be counted, in the words of John Martz, as "one of the most serious losses in recent Colombian history."[6]

No man's work, however, is entirely lost. Although Gaitanismo was a great hope dashed, it did leave a legacy. Gaitán is remembered to this day as a champion of the poor and oppressed. He has found a place in the pantheon of great Liberal leaders. At party conventions his portrait hangs high above the delegates and his name is invoked to stir the party faithful. On Sundays and holidays working-class families reverently visit his tomb, now a national monument, to pay homage to his memory. Seldom does an anniversary of his death pass without the appearance of newspaper articles describing his life and work and without demonstrations honoring him.

As for substantive results, Gaitán did have a lasting impact on the political culture, at least to the extent of forcing the oligarchs to address themselves to the questions he raised. He also succeeded in revealing the theatrical element in plutocratic politics. For instance, the Colombian people have demonstrated their increasing awareness by their growing abstention from the polls. With the exceptions of the 1957 plebiscite which established the two-party National Front Government and its promises, and the 1974 presidential election which ended the National Front era (and brought more promises from the contending parties), Colombians have honored the sacred right of voting more in the breach than in the observance. Certainly Gaitán left a legacy here.

But what are the larger meanings of Gaitán's legacy? Gaitán and his story have much to suggest about the nature of populism in Latin America and its inherent value. Like Víctor Raúl Haya de la Torre in Peru, Lázaro Cárdenas in Mexico, Getulio Vargas in Brazil, to a lesser extent Juan Perón in Argentina, and others, Gaitán attempted to raise the level of consciousness of the people, to educate them, and to reveal the unrepresentative nature of traditional Latin American politics. All stressed the inherent worth and value of the individual regardless of background. They attempted to induce a spirit of self-respect, high morale, and dignity. They sought, as well, to satisfy the people's material aspirations. They wished to provide schools for the masses. Their aim was authentic citizenship for their followers. They knew, however, that reaching their goals necessitated exposing the manipulation and pompous words of the privileged strata. As Fidel Castro said, "They [the plutocrats] made the *campesinos* drunk with words."

Despite appreciable differences in form, the basic challenge of populism is that it attempts to dissolve the horizontal antagonisms—Liberal versus Conservative, employed versus unemployed, educated versus uneducated, rural versus urban, men versus women, and light-skinned versus dark-skinned—induced or manipulated by the oligarchy; it seeks to unify the popular base and to cut the Gordian knot of oligarchy by means of a vertical confrontation. All of these popular leaders taught their followers to look *up* to find their meaningful target. They felt that the monopoly of power and wealth by the rich had to be broken so that the people at large could avail themselves of the national treasure, whatever it might be. They sought to focus the light of consciousness upon the political, diplomatic, and economic behavior of the oligarchies and to unmask the use that they made of horizontal antagonisms to distract and confuse the public as to the underlying reality of their lives.

The study of Gaitán and Gaitanismo confirms both the strength and weakness of the charismatic leader in Latin American populism. The chief strength is the concentric unity achieved with a clientele relatively unable to unify itself in a linear, specialized fashion because of its lack of education, its merely marginal socioeconomic function, and its disoriented subjectivity. The charismatic leader is the hub of an emotional wheel. The spiritual unity produced has a tendency to dissolve the horizontal antagonisms and to provide the people with a common goal.

The weakness is that if fate deprives the people of the charismatic leader the emotional wheel falls apart. Also, the device of charisma places an inordinate burden of virtue upon the leadership. There is, as well, a paradox inherent in the very nature of the *patrón-peón* relationship. The dependency involved in this relation is inevitable because of circumstances, but unfortunately it lies open to its defects. The most perceptive populist leaders, such as Gaitán and Fidel Castro, see the charismatic wheel as, at best, a temporary ideal.

Charisma, however, is not the major defect in populism. Although Latin American populism is effective in raising the political consciousness of the people and in mobilizing disaffected elites along with the dispossessed proletariat, it is not a long-term solution to the problems of nation-building, dependency, and underdevelopment. Populists have, it is true, shown a marked talent for gathering the vote, but they suffer from a major inadequacy. Populists cannot solve the problem of the army, which remains in the hands of the oligarchy or sets itself up as an independent power. As has been demonstrated time and again, the populists possess most of the feelings, thoughts, and votes; the oligarchy, however, possesses most of the bullets.

Perón achieved a partial success in Argentina in fostering self-reliance and organizational initiative among the working class, which has blunted the traditional plutocratic-militaristic thrust. Nevertheless, what has resulted is, at best, a standoff retarding progress of the Argentine people. The only populist leader who has succeeded in renovating the life of his people is Fidel Castro in Cuba. He seems to have solved the problem of the army once and for all. It would seem, therefore, that no populist leader could hope for success without a strong military organization. Indeed, it would seem from Castro's isolated success that any Latin American populism that does not ultimately combine the strategy of socialism with that of the destruction of the army is engaging in futile dreams.

The whole meaning of *la violencia* in Colombia points to that end. Gaitán was trying to turn capitalism into socialism by means of democracy. The latter, however, implies an appreciable measure of mutual regard and self-control. Gaitán was succeeding admirably in unifying these positive faculties of the people. The meaning of the march in silence and the "Oration for Peace" in February 1948 was that the people were not to fight each other. Gaitán was creating a popular morale that was transcending the oligarchic spirit of divide and conquer and was inoculating the people from the demoralization implicit in the very nature of *la violencia*. What would happen—one would ask—if the *campesinos*, like the urban masses, began to march in silence and fill their heads with thoughts of peace? What would happen, in that case, to the "sacred order"? At that point it appeared that demoralization and confusion are not always inconvenient to certain people.

Gaitanismo was not the only target of oligarchic violence and repression in the years after 1948. The forces of the old order struck to the very roots of modernization, Liberalism, which had become the seedbed of that forbidden thing—socialism. The "sacred order" had been maddened to fury; it thrust so deeply that it rent the very fabric of society and thus engaged the horizontal antagonisms of the past: Liberal versus Conservative, secular versus clerical, traditional versus modern, and oligarchic versus democratic. Fear and hatred held the minds of most Colombians. Gaitán's *pueblo* fell into the abyss of confusion, anarchy, and demoralization—*la violencia*.

Thus the story of Gaitán helps to teach us why, in modern Latin cultures, only Cuba has raised a successful challenge to plutocratic power.

Robert Dix described Gaitán as "part republican legalist, part populistic demagogue; at times verbally revolutionary, at heart a reformer and moralizer." Antonio García claimed that he was a "will put at the service of a socialist thought," and that he represented "a vehement desire for transformation on the part of the Colombian people."[7] Indeed, Gaitán was all of these. But most impressive of all were his consummate political skills and his intuitive grasp of the realities and requirements of the time. Gaitán was rooted in the common people and he had a profound understanding of their practical needs for decent livelihoods, respect, security, a nation that was truly their own. His adaptations to the varying conditions of his time caused him to use diverse tactics, but he remained loyal to his principles. From the time of *Ideas Socialistas en Colombia* until the Movement for the Moral and Democratic Restoration his goal was the same: a Colombia for all Colombians. His preaching of unity of country against the oligarchy fostered a new political consciousness; it awakened the people for the first time from the slumber of a pernicious past. And he did this despite great odds, against enormous obstacles that would have dismayed a less committed man. Not once, but several times he gave up fortune and honors and endured the scorn of the established power in order to fight for the vindication of *los de abajo*—those from below.

Notes
Bibliography
Index

Notes

Chapter 1: Introduction

1. For a fuller discussion of these points see Celso Furtado, *Economic Development of Latin America* (Cambridge: Cambridge University Press, 1970), pp. 250-52. On Latin American industrialization see Rawle Farley, *The Economics of Latin America* (New York: Harper and Row, 1972), pp. 205-11.

2. James Petras, *Politics and Social Structure in Latin America* (New York: Monthly Review Press, 1970), pp. 17-20.

3. Orlando Fals Borda, "Violence and the Break-Up of Tradition in Colombia," in *Obstacles to Change in Latin America,* ed. Claudio Veliz (New York: Oxford University Press, 1970), pp. 189-95.

4. Torcuato Di Tella, "Populism and Reform in Latin America," in *Obstacles to Change in Latin America,* p. 47.

5. Ibid., p. 53.

6. Petras, *Politics and Social Structure,* pp. 18-20.

Chapter 2: The Populist Seedbed

1. Various explanations have been provided for Colombia's nineteenth-century conflicts: regional competition; feuds and rivalry between aristocratic families; and ideological struggles between proclerical Conservatives who wanted a corporative social and economic structure and a centralized state, and Liberals who desired a secular society free of church influence, a federalized state, and a laissez-faire economy. Two convincing arguments that the country's political turmoil was the result of long-term economic stagnation are found in Luis Eduardo Nieto Arteta, *Economía y Cultura en la Historia de Colombia,* 2nd ed. (Bogotá: Ediciones Tercer Mundo, 1962); and William Paul McGreevey, *An Economic History of Colombia, 1845-1930* (Cambridge: Cambridge University Press, 1971), esp. chaps. 7 and 8.

2. Robert H. Dix, *Colombia: The Political Dimensions of Change* (New Haven: Yale University Press, 1967). This is an excellent study of the modernization process and its effects.

3. McGreevey, *Economic History,* p. 196.

4. Ibid., p. 198.

5. Ibid., p. 199.

6. American University (Washington, D.C.), Foreign Area Studies Division, *Special Warfare Area Handbook for Colombia* (Washington, D.C.: U.S. Department of the Army, 1961), p. 498.

7. McGreevey, *Economic History*, pp. 235, 255, and chap. 10, which discusses the development of transportation in Colombia.

8. J. Fred Rippy, *The Capitalists and Colombia* (New York: Vanguard Press, 1931), p. 152.

9. Miguel Urrutia, *The Development of the Colombian Labor Movement* (New Haven: Yale University Press, 1969), p. 84. Urrutia's figures are taken from Guillermo Torres García, *Historia de la Moneda en Colombia* (Bogotá: Imprenta del Banco de la República, 1945), pp. 369-85.

10. United Nations, Department of Economic and Social Affairs, Economic Commission for Latin America, *Analyses and Projections of Economic Development. III. The Economic Development of Colombia* (Geneva: United Nations Department of Economic and Social Affairs, 1957), p. 11. Hereafter cited as ECLA.

11. Urrutia, *Labor Movement,* p. 88.

12. ECLA, p. 12.

13. International Bank for Reconstruction and Development, *The Basis of a Development Program for Colombia, Report of a Mission Headed by Lauchlin Currie* (Washington, D.C.: International Bank for Reconstruction and Development, 1950), p. 87. Hereafter cited as Currie Mission Report.

14. ECLA, p. 12.

15. Ibid., pp. 16-17.

16. Dix, *Colombia,* p. 39.

17. ECLA, p. 18.

18. Urrutia, *Labor Movement,* p. 93.

19. Antonio García, *Gaitán y el Problema de la Revolución Colombiana* (Bogotá: M.S.C., 1955), p. 242.

20. Urrutia, *Labor Movement,* pp. 85-88.

21. Dix, *Colombia,* p. 34.

22. Urrutia, *Labor Movement,* pp. 232-33.

23. Vernon Lee Fluharty, *Dance of the Millions* (Pittsburgh: University of Pittsburgh Press, 1957), pp. 90-93.

24. Belisario Betancur, in *La Nación ante la Universidad,* Serie "Reforma Universitaria" (Bogotá: Editorial Antares, 1957), p. 20.

25. Fluharty, *Dance of the Millions*, pp. 18-19.

26. ECLA, p. 26; Camilo Torres Restrepo, *La Proletarizatión de Bogotá,* Monografías Sociológicas, no. 9 (Bogotá: Universidad Nacional, Facultad de Sociología, 1961).

27. García, *Gaitán,* p. 231 ff.

28. Urrutia, *Labor Movement,* pp. 55-58, 61, 73. The Liberal party polled only 15 percent in Medellín.

29. Ibid., pp. 93-99. In 1923 almost 40 percent of the work force was reported ill owing to poor health conditions in Barrancabermeja.

30. See chap. 5.

31. Urrutia, *Labor Movement,* pp. 53, 183.

32. Pierre Gilhodès, "Agrarian Struggles in Colombia," in *Agrarian Problems and Peasant Movements in Latin America,* ed. Rodolfo Stavenhagen (New York: Anchor Books, 1970), p. 412.

33. Ibid., pp. 413-17.

34. Dix, *Colombia,* p. 61. For a more complete discussion of Colombia's middle sectors, see pp. 55-63.

35. Ibid., p. 78.

36. Orlando Fals Borda, *Peasant Society in the Colombian Andes: A Sociological Study of Saucio* (Gainesville: University of Florida Press, 1955), chap. 5. Fals Borda placed the roots of party partisanship among *campesinos* in the authority of the *patrón*.

37. Dix, *Colombia*, p. 222.

38. Ibid., pp. 246–47. For more on the point, see pp. 232–48.

39. Ibid., pp. 246–47.

40. Fluharty, *Dance of the Millions*, p. 27.

41. "Socialismo de Estado," in Colombia, Ministerio del Trabajo, *El Pensamiento Social de Uribe Uribe* (Bogotá: Biblioteca del Ministerio del Trabajo, 1960), pp. 6–23.

42. Milton Puentes, *Historia del Partido Liberal Colombiano*, 2nd ed. (Bogotá: Editorial Prag, 1961), p. 588.

43. Urrutia, *Labor Movement*, p. 70.

44. For the Liberal platform, see Diego Montaña Cuéllar, *Colombia: País Formal y País Real* (Bogotá: Ediciones Suramerica, 1963), p. 130.

45. See García, *Gaitán*, pp. 27–97, for a discussion of this generation; see also *El Tiempo* of Bogotá, May 11, 1969, for a list of the prominent members and an analysis of their achievements and failures.

46. Robert J. Alexander, *Communism in Latin America* (New Brunswick: Rutgers University Press, 1957), pp. 243–45; Montaña Cuéllar, *Colombia*, p. 131. The party's founding grew out of events surrounding the labor congress that met in May 1924. Urrutia, *Labor Movement*, pp. 81–83.

47. See especially *Universidad* issues from June 1927 through September 1928, Biblioteca National, Bogotá.

48. *El Tiempo*, May 11, 1969.

49. Silvio Villegas, "La Verdad del Nacionalismo," *Universidad*, Sept. 17, 1927.

50. Quoted in García, *Gaitán*, pp. 80–81.

51. Fluharty, *Dance of the Millions*, pp. 43–44.

52. Dix, *Colombia*, pp. 83–84.

53. Fluharty, *Dance of the Millions*, p. 46.

54. See Dix, *Colombia*, pp. 82–91, for a discussion of the first López administration.

55. Fluharty, *Dance of the Millions*, p. 54. See pp. 51–55 for a discussion of the constitutional amendments.

56. Dix, *Colombia*, pp. 89–90; Fluharty, *Dance of the Millions*, pp. 55–57.

57. Dix, *Colombia*, p. 91.

Chapter 3: The Background of a Populist

1. Interview with Leopoldo Borda Roldán, October 4, 1969. The complete text of the interview is in the files of the author.

2. Luis David Peña, *Gaitán Intimo* (Bogotá: Editorial Iqueima, 1949), p. 88.

3. J. A. Osorio Lizarazo, *Gaitán: Vida, Muerte y Permanente Presencia* (Buenos Aires: Ediciones López Negri, 1952), p. 16.

4. Interview with Borda Roldán.

5. José María Córdoba, *Jorge Eliécer Gaitán, Tribuno Popular de Colombia* (Bogotá: Litografías "Cor-Val," 1952), p. 8.

6. Interview of B. Moreno Torralbo with Gaitán titled "Gaitán Ante Sí Mismo," in Alberto Figueredo Salcedo, ed., *Colección Jorge Eliécer Gaitán: Documentos para una Biografía* (Bogotá: Imprenta Municipal, 1949), I, 22.

7. Osorio, *Gaitán,* p. 12.

8. Ibid., p. 19, et passim; Córdoba, *Gaitán,* p. 9.

9. Interview by Moreno Torralbo, in Figueredo, p. 22.

10. "Simon Araújo," in Figueredo, pp. 45-46.

11. Osorio, *Gaitán,* pp. 28-29.

12. Peña, *Gaitán Intimo,* p. 90.

13. *Sábado,* August 28, 1943.

14. Osorio, *Gaitán,* p. 25; Córdoba, *Gaitán,* p. 9.

15. Peña, *Gaitán Intimo,* p. 88.

16. Osorio, *Gaitán,* p. 22, et passim.

17. Interview by Moreno Torralbo, in Figueredo, pp. 22-23.

18. Ibid., p. 32; interview with Borda Roldán.

19. Ricardo Jordán Jiménez, *Dos Viernes Trágicos,* (Bogotá: Editorial Horizontes, 1968), p. 30.

20. "Escuelas Dominicales," *El Tiempo,* July 8, 1918, reprinted in Figueredo, pp. 178-80.

21. Gaitán, "Los Universitarios Peruanos y Su Ejemplo," *El Tiempo,* Apr. 1920; and *El Comercio* of Lima, July 6, 1920, reprinted in Figueredo, pp. 181-83.

22. Gaitán, "Propaganda Cultural," in Figueredo, pp. 103-05.

23. *El Tiempo,* May 21, 1920, reprinted in Figueredo, p. 107.

24. Letter from Gaitán to *El Tiempo,* May 25, 1920, reprinted in Figueredo, p. 107.

25. Address, "El Centro de Propaganda Cultural y Los Fines Que Persique," *El Tiempo,* n.d., reprinted in Figueredo, pp. 110-13.

26. Articles from various newspapers reprinted in Figueredo, pp. 114-15.

27. Interview with Guillermo Hernández Rodríguez, March 5, 1970. The complete text of the interview is in the files of the author.

28. Osorio, *Gaitán,* p. 48.

29. Editorial by E. Rodríguez Triana in *Correo del Cauca,* Cali, December 1920, reprinted in Figueredo, pp. 117-19.

30. Letter from Gaitán to *El Espectador,* Jan. 20, 1921, reprinted in Figueredo, pp. 119-21.

31. Letter from Gaitán to *El Diario Nacional,* Jan. 28, 1921, reprinted in Figueredo, p. 122.

32. Kathleen Romoli, *Colombia: Gateway to South America* (New York: Doubleday, 1941), p. 281.

33. Merle Kling, "Toward a Theory of Power and Political Instability in Latin America," in *Latin America: Reform or Revolution?* ed. James Petras and Maurice Zeitlin (Greenwich, Conn.: Fawcett, 1968), pp. 90-92.

34. The platform of the coalition is in Figueredo, pp. 125-27.

35. Osorio, *Gaitán,* pp. 35-36.

36. *El Tiempo,* December 7, 1917, reprinted in Figueredo, pp. 134-35.

37. Figueredo, p. 133.

38. Casimiro de la Barra, "En La Plaza de Nariño," *El Tiempo,* Dec. 22, 1917, reprinted in Figueredo, pp. 135-38.

39. Figueredo, pp. 141-42.

40. Letter from Juan N. Escobar Navarro to *El Derecho* of Honda, Jan. 14, 1918, reprinted in Figueredo, pp. 143-44.

41. Figueredo, pp. 143-46.

42. *El Siglo,* Jan. 20, 1919, reprinted in Figueredo, pp. 153-54.

43. Letter from Gaitán to *El Siglo,* Nov. 1918, reprinted in Figueredo, pp. 151-53.

44. Letter from the Liberal Committee of Facatativá to *El Siglo,* Jan. 1919, reprinted in Figueredo, p. 155.

45. José Gutiérrez, *De la Pseudo-Aristocracia a la Autenticidad* (Bogotá: Ediciones Tercer Mundo, 1961), p. 32.

46. Alejandro Vallejo, *Políticos en la Intimidad* (Bogotá: Editorial "Antena," 1936), p. 14.

47. *El Tiempo,* Feb. 23, 1921.

48. Telegram from the Lenguazaque Liberal Committee, Jan. 1, 1922, reprinted in Figueredo, p. 158.

49. Various articles reprinted in Figuerdo, pp. 158-66.

50. Letter from the Ubaté Liberal Committee to *El Espectador,* Feb 3, 1922; see also a newspaper article on the same day, both reprinted in Figueredo, pp. 165-66.

51. Letter from Ubaté Liberals to *El Tiempo,* Jan. 12, 1923, *Diario Nacional,* Jan. 1923, reprinted in Figueredo, pp. 171-72.

52. *El Espectador,* Apr. 22, 1923.

Chapter 4: The University and Socialist Ideas

1. Osorio, *Gaitán,* pp. 44-45.

2. Ibid.

3. Interview by Moreno Torralbo, in Figueredo, p. 23; interview with Guillermo Barriga Casalini, May 11, 1971. The complete text of the interview is in the files of the author.

4. Osorio, *Gaitán,* pp. 83-84.

5. Gaitán always was extremely careful about his attire. Perhaps the memories of second-hand clothes in his youth were too strong. More likely he was following an inclination to appear prosperous and respectable in a society where the common dress still was the *ruana* (Colombian poncho) and sandals; the man in suit and tie clearly was in a class above. Good quality, fashionable dress always has been a distinguishing factor in Colombian society, especially for the middle and upper classes. As my wife, who is Colombian, once remarked: "Here the middle class prefers to dress well even if that means eating rice and beans and sleeping on a mattress on the floor."

6. Osorio, *Gaitán,* pp. 46-47.

7. Jordán, *Dos Viernes,* pp. 25-26

8. The library in Gaitán's former house, now the Casa Museo Gaitán, contains more than one thousand volumes, mostly literature, history, philosophy, and psychology.

9. Interview by Moreno Torralbo, in Figueredo, p. 24. Gaitán had varied opinions about his law school professors. In an article titled "Ferrotipos de Profesionales," Gaitán delivered a devastating attack on Dr. José María González Valencia, rector of the National University School of Law, in which he charged general incompetence. However, he highly praised a young Conservative priest, José Alejandro Bermúdez, who later was president of his thesis committee, with the words, "Dr. Bermúdez is the virtuous priest of truth." Figueredo, pp. 187-91.

10. Interview by Moreno Torralbo in Figueredo, pp. 23, 24.

11. Ibid., p. 25.

12. Gaitán's early literary and journalistic efforts are found in Figueredo, pp. 45-77 and pp. 177-205.

13. "Grecia y Homer," in Figueredo, pp. 57-60.

14. "Oraciones Funebres," in Figueredo, pp. 78-85.

15. Urrutia, *Labor Movement,* chap. 5.

16. García, *Gaitán,* pp. 81-82.

17. Luís Emiro Valencia, ed., *Gaitán: Antología de Su Pensamiento Social y Económico* (Bogotá: Ediciones Suramerica, 1968), p. 63. Subsequent citations of this edition of *Las Ideas Socialistas* will be given in the text.

18. García, *Gaitán,* p. 94.

19. Ibid.

20. Rafael Azula Barrera, *De la Revolución al Orden Nuevo: Proceso y Drama de un Pueblo* (Bogotá: Editorial Kelly, 1956), p. 63.

21. García, *Gaitán*, p. 97.

22. Córdoba, *Gaitán*, p. 13.

23. García, *Gaitán*, pp. 194–200.

24. Ibid., pp. 187–89.

25. Ibid., p. 188.

26. Córdoba, *Gaitán*, p. 10. Gaitán claimed that the published edition of the thesis was sold out. Interview by Moreno Torralbo, in Figueredo, p. 35.

27. Valencia, *Gaitán, Antología*, p. 55.

28. Jordán, *Dos Viernes*, p. 20. Gaitán provocatively selected a conservative thesis committee presided over, however, by a man he respected, the professor of canon law, Dr. José Alejandro Bermúdez. The committee at first did not want to accept the thesis because of its polemical tone and its lack of legal emphasis. Finally, it was accepted with modifications. Valencia, p. 38.

29. After graduation Gaitán rented a law office in the business district of Bogotá. He furnished it with a desk and several chairs rented for a few pesos a month. Since he had almost no clients, he spent most of his time reading. Interview by Moreno Torralbo, in Figueredo, p. 30.

30. Osorio, *Gaitán*, p. 92.

31. Córdoba, *Gaitán*, p. 10; Osorio, *Gaitán*, pp. 93–94.

32. Osorio, *Gaitán*, p. 100.

33. Ibid., pp. 106–07.

34. Gaitán had been attracted to Enrico Ferri's positivist criminology while he was still at law school in Bogotá. Once in Rome the two became friends. Gaitán was much impressed by Ferri's intellectual brilliance and eloquent speaking style. However, he also admired his early political activities as a socialist politician. Ferri obviously also was taken by his Colombian student. *Suplemento Literario Ilustrado*, Apr. 25, 1929.

35. Figueredo, pp. 386–87.

36. Osorio, *Gaitán*, p. 99.

37. Interview by *El Tiempo* (n.d.) with Gaitán in Barranquilla. From a collection of press clippings in the files of Gloria Gaitán de Valencia, Bogotá.

38. Gaitán, lecture on Fascism in Italy delivered in Bogotá's Municipal Theater, printed in *El Debate* (n.d.). Files of Gloria Gaitán de Valencia.

39. *El Espectador*, Feb. 14, 1928, files of Gloria Gaitán de Valencia.

Chapter 5: Early Politics

1. *El Espectador*, Feb. 14, 1928.

2. *El Espectador* clipping in the files of Gloria Gaitán de Valencia.

3. Montaña Cuéllar, *Colombia*, p. 127.

4. An excellent account of the United Fruit operations and the strike is found in Urrutia, *Labor Movement*, pp. 99–108; see also Allen Steele Vall-Spinosa, "Colombia's Semana Trágica: The Banana Strike of 1928" (MA thesis, University of Florida, 1969).

5. Urrutia, *Labor Movement*, p. 100.

6. Ibid.; Carlos Cortés Vargas, *Los Sucesos de las Bananeras* (Bogotá: Imprenta "La Luz," 1929), pp. 8–11.

7. Urrutia, *Labor Movement*, p. 101; Robert J. Alexander, *Organized Labor in Latin America* (New York: The Free Press, 1965), p. 134.

8. A running account of the strike and subsequent developments, including Gaitán's investiga-

tions, is found in *La Nación* of Barranquilla from November 14, 1928, through May 1929. Despite the Conservative affiliation of the paper the coverage is balanced. A journalist and friend of Gaitán, Clemente Manuel Zabala, wrote many of the articles. For the government's side of the story see Cortés Vargas, *Los Sucesos de las Bananeras;* the strikers' side is presented in Alberto Castrillón, *Ciento Veinte Días Bajo el Terror Militar: O La Huelga de las Bananeras* (Bogotá: Revista "Universidad," 1929).

9. Urrutia, *Labor Movement*, p. 102.

10. Ibid., p. 103.

11. *La Nación,* Dec. 13, 1928.

12. Osorio, *Gaitán*, p. 120.

13. Urrutia, *Labor Movement*, pp. 106-07.

14. *Universidad*, Jan. 12, 1929.

15. *El Espectador*, July 19, 1929; photographs taken in the banana zone are in the Gaitán Papers, Casa Museo Gaitán, Bogotá.

16. *El Espectador*, July 26, 1929.

17. Full accounts of the speeches are found in *El Espectador* and *El Tiempo;* the most important extracts are in Jorge Eliécer Gaitán, *Los Mejores Discursos de Jorge Eliécer Gaitán, 1919-1948* (Bogotá: Editorial Jorvi, 1958), pp. 29-59.

18. Gaitán, *Discursos*, pp. 30-33.

19. Ibid., pp. 46-48.

20. Ibid., p. 50.

21. Ibid., p. 58.

22. Letter from the "Madres de Santa Ana," Sept. 9, 1930, Gaitán Papers.

23. *El Tiempo*, June 8, 1929.

24. Ibid., Oct. 31, 1929.

25. Gaitán, *Discursos*, pp. 84-93.

26. Fluharty, *Dance of the Millions*, pp. 43-45.

27. Harry Bernstein, *Modern and Contemporary Latin America* (Philadelphia: J. B. Lippincott, 1952), p. 639.

28. Carlos Lleras Restrepo, *Diez Ensayos Sobra la Reforma Agraria en Colombia* (Bogotá: Ediciones Tercer Mundo, 1961), p. 18.

29. Osorio, *Gaitán*, p. 134.

30. *El Tiempo*, Feb. 2, 1930.

31. Ibid., July 31, Aug. 1, 1930.

32. Ibid., Aug. 22, 1930.

33. A. Eugene Havens and William L. Flinn, *Internal Colonialism and Structural Change in Colombia* (New York: Praeger, 1970), p. 130.

34. T. Lynn Smith, *Colombia: Social Structure and the Process of Development* (Gainsville: University of Florida Press, 1967), p. 237.

35. Ernest A. Duff, *Agrarian Reform in Colombia* (New York: Praeger, 1968), p. 6.

36. Albert O. Hirschman, *Journeys Toward Progress* (New York: Twentieth Century Fund, 1963), p. 99.

37. Havens, *Internal Colonialism*, p. 133.

38. Smith, *Colombia*, p. 103.

39. Hirschman, *Journeys*, p. 102.

40. Gilhodés, "Agrarian Struggles," p. 412.

41. Gloria Gaitán de Valencia, research notes for "Causas de la Presencia de los Movimientos Agrarios en el Occidente de Cundinamarca y el Oriente del Tolima y Su Incidencia en el Cambio de la Tenencia de la Tierra" (Doctorado en Economía thesis, Universidad de los Andes, Bogotá,

1970), p. 3; and extensive conversations of the author with Gloria Gaitán de Valencia, Oct.-Nov. 1969.

42. Gilhodés, "Agrarian Struggles," p. 413, 414-15.

43. *El Tiempo,* Aug. 1, 1930.

44. William Marion Gibson, *The Constitutions of Colombia* (Durham, N.C.: Duke University Press, 1948), p. 319.

45. Gaitán, *Discursos,* pp. 72-82; *El Tiempo,* Aug. 15, 1973.

46. Osorio, *Gaitán,* pp. 138-40.

47. *El Espectador,* June 6, 1931; clipping from *El Tiempo* in the files of Gloria Gaitán de Valencia.

48. *La Voz del Obrero,* Buga, May 7, 1932, in the files of Gloria Gaitán de Valencia.

49. Valencia, "Prólogo," in *Gaitán,* p. 32.

50. Ibid., p. 33.

51. *El Tiempo,* Oct. 14, 1931.

52. *La Casa Liberal,* Bucaramanga, July 2, 1932, in the files of Gloria Gaitán de Valencia.

53. *El Relator,* Cali, Jan. 29, 1932, in the files of Gloria Gaitán de Valencia.

54. Letter from Gaitán to Plinio Mendoza and Darío Samper, May 7, 1932, Gaitán Papers.

55. See editorials in *El Relator,* Cali, Jan. 30, 1932; *El Liberal,* Manizales, Feb. 6, 1932; *La Huila,* Neiva, July 16, 1932; in the files of Gloria Gaitán de Valencia.

56. *El Ideal,* Tumaco, Jan. 16, 1932, in the files of Gloria Gaitán de Valencia.

57. Letter to Gaitán from the Comité Liberal de Tequendama, Aug. 3, 1932. In reply to a letter of support from the chiefs of neighborhoods of Medellín, Gaitán wrote: "It is efforts like yours that overcome the silence with which the middle and working classes confront their problems, while a small group at the top makes noises in the name of public opinion. The people are admirable and only have to be organized in the defense of their interests." Copy of letter dated June 22, 1931, Gaitán Papers.

58. Letter from the Directorio Obrero del Departamento del Atlántico, July 4, 1932, Gaitán Papers.

59. *La Casa Liberal,* Bucaramanga, stated that the Liberal left consisted of Gaitán, Moisés Prieto, Félix Mejía, Eladio Cortés, Belisario Gómez, José Mar, Germán Arciniegas, Alejandro López, Carlos Lozano y Lozano, Alejandro Galvis Galvis, Darío Echandía, Alberto Lleras Camargo, Jaime Barrera Parra; clipping files of Gloria Gaitán de Valencia.

60. *El Tiempo,* June 29, 1932.

61. *El País,* June 30, 1932.

62. On June 30, 1932, *El Tiempo* headlined an interview with Gaitán in which he said that harmony existed between the Liberal leadership and the masses, and that he was absolutely satisfied with the state of Liberalism in the country. The editorial of the same day applauded Gaitán's harmonious leadership of the party, but added that he had brought into the open a latent ideological conflict. The writer noted that it was not the ideology of Gaitán that created an atmosphere of secession, but the manner in which he presented his speeches. However, this fastidious politeness covered serious differences. By August *El Tiempo* was again launching attacks on Gaitán, who had resigned from the Liberal directorate in July.

63. *El Tiempo,* Aug. 2, 1932. The massacre occurred in Viotá, a Communist party stronghold in western Cundinamarca.

64. Speech and editorial comment in *El Tiempo,* July 4, 1932.

65. Gilhodés, "Agrarian Struggles," p. 416.

66. Extensive newspaper clippings compiled by the Colombian Ministry of Foreign Relations attest to the favorable reception Gaitán received everywhere abroad. Clippings in the possession of the author.

67. *El Tiempo*, Jan. 19, 1933. Under the Colombian system it is possible for an individual to hold multiple offices simultaneously. For example, Gaitán was at one time a member of the Bogotá Municipal Council, the Cundinamarca assembly, and the House of Representatives. Candidates also may appear on electoral lists outside the district of their residence. This explains Gaitán's appearance on a list from Medellín, Antioquia.

68. Heliodoro Linares, *Yo Acuso: Biografía de Gaitán y Fajardo* (Bogoá: Editorial Iqueima, 1959), II, 62-63.

69. Peña, *Gaitán Intimo*, p. 108. However, the movement was closer in image to the Peruvian APRA. Gaitán had personal knowledge of the APRA through contact with exiled Peruvian Apristas he met during a secret diplomatic mission to Ecuador as an agent of the Olaya government, which was making soundings concerning the overthrow of the Peruvian regime. Antolín Díaz, *A la Sombra de Fouché; Pequeño Proceso de las Izquierdas en Colombia* (Bogotá: Editorial ABC, 1937), pp. 57-60.

Chapter 6: The Revolutionary Leftist National Union

1. In addition to Gaitán and Arango Vélez those taking part were Samuel Jaramillo, José Barbosa, Luis Alberto Galvis, Octavio Rodríguez, Julio Mendoza, Carlos Quiroga, and others. F. López Giraldo, *El Apóstol Desnudo: o Dos Años al Lado de un Mito* (Manizales: Editorial Arturo Zapata, 1936), p. 43.

2. *El Tiempo*, Apr. 29, 1933.

3. López Giraldo, *Apóstol*, p. 44.

4. Linares, *Yo Acuso*, p. 63; letter from Plinio Mendoza Neira to Gaitán, June 13, 1933, Gaitán Papers.

5. The founders and subsequent leaders of UNIR included: Roberto París Gaitán, Octavio Rodríguez, Jorges Villaveces, Bernardo Galvis Alvarez, Hernando Restrepo Botero, Vicente Saavedra, Luis Carlos Perilla, Jairo de Bedout, Fermín López Giraldo. The latter became inspector general and second-in-command. Peña, *Gaitán*, p. 111.

6. López Giraldo, *Apóstol*, pp. 45-46.

7. Osorio, *Gaitán*, p. 161; Mauricio Torres, *La Naturaleza de la Revolución Colombiana* (Bogotá: Editorial Iqueima, 1959), p. 57.

8. Peña, *Gaitán*, p. 112.

9. *Unirismo*, June 28, 1934; ibid., Nov. 1, 1934; ibid., June 21, 1934; ibid., July 12, 1934.

10. Ibid., Jan. 10, 1935; ibid., Apr. 4, 1934.

11. José María Nieto Rojas, *La Batalla contra el Comunismo en Colombia* (Bogotá: Empresa Nacional de Publicaciones, 1956), pp. 15-16.

12. Interview with Hernández Rodríguez; research notes of Gloria Gaitán de Valencia.

13. *Unirismo*, June 21, 1934.

14. Comité Central del Partido Comunista de Colombia, *Treinta Años del Partido Comunista de Colombia* (Bogotá: Ediciones Paz y Socialismo, 1960), p. 29. The Communists considered the left Liberals and Uniristas, instead of natural allies, the most dangerous adversaries because the Communists thought that they deliberately contributed to keeping the masses under the ideological influence of the bourgeoisie.

15. Osorio, *Gaitán*, p. 162.

16. López Giraldo, *Apóstol*, p. 48.

17. *Unirismo*, June 21, 1934.

18. López Giraldo, *Apóstol*, pp. 48, 52; *Unirismo*, June 21, 1934; ibid., July 12, 1934; ibid., August 2, 1934.

19. Díaz, *A la Sombra*, pp. 63-64.

20. *Unirismo,* Aug. 23, 1934; ibid., Oct. 4, 1934.

21. Díaz, *A la Sombra,* pp. 63–64.

22. *Unirismo,* Nov. 8, 1934.

23. Díaz, *A la Sombra,* p. 64.

24. López Giraldo, *Apóstol,* p. 60.

25. *El Crisol,* Cali, Mar. 18, 1934.

26. *El Manifesto del Unirismo,* in Valencia, *Gaitán,* p. 226. Hereafter cited in the text.

27. See, for example, *Unirismo,* Dec. 6, 1934, on tax reform, and Mar. 21, 1935, on education.

28. Accounts of the convention in *Unirismo,* Apr. 13, and 25, 1935. For most of the *campesino* and worker delegates, the convention was their first involvement in politics above the purely local level.

29. *Unirismo,* Apr. 13, 1935.

30. Ibid., Apr. 25, 1935.

31. Research notes of Gloria Gaitán de Valencia. Her information was based on interviews with *campesinos.*

32. Gilhodés, "Agrarian Struggles," p. 416. The support came from unions in Tolima, Valle, Boyacá, Magdalena, and Bolívar; see also the correspondence of this period in the Gaitán Papers. The successful land invasion was on the hacienda El Chocó, where Gaitán carried out political work among the farmers and organized them into a union. He took their case to court and won recognition of their rights to titles. Peña, *Gaitán,* p. 115.

33. According to the research notes of Gloria Gaitán de Valencia, 7.76 percent of the owners possessed almost 60 percent of the land in the region. See also Hirschman, *Journeys,* p. 102.

34. Gloria Gaitán de Valencia, research notes.

35. In 1933 the minister of industry, Francisco José Chaux, suggested that, for the peace of the coffee zone, the large plantations give way to coffee fincas of the type found in Caldas, with resident owner-growers. The minister's suggestion aroused a furious controversy, and the large landowners accused him of subverting the social order. During this period the Communists also were successful in seizing and breaking up plantations in the Viotá district. Hirschman, *Journeys,* pp. 103–04.

36. Ibid., p. 134.

37. Gloria Gaitán de Valencia, research notes.

38. *Unirismo,* Aug. 16, 1934; *El Tiempo,* Aug. 17, 1934.

39. *Unirismo,* Aug. 9, 1934.

40. Ibid., July 19, 1934; ibid., July 26, 1934.

41. *El Espectador,* June 25, 1934.

42. Letter of Dr. J. A. Concha y Venegas to Gaitán, Feb. 3, 1934, Gaitán Papers.

43. *El Espectador,* Feb. 5, 1934; *El Tiempo,* Feb. 5, 1934; Osorio, *Gaitán,* p. 166.

44. *El Espectador,* Feb. 5, 1934.

45. Ibid., Feb. 5, 1934; ibid., Feb. 6, 1934.

46. Osorio, *Gaitán,* p. 167. Numerous telegrams and letters in the Gaitán Papers support this.

47. *Unirismo,* July 14, 1934; interview May 31, 1968, with a former railroad worker, Cándido Giraldo, who participated in the events. The complete text of the interview is in the files of the author.

48. *Unirismo,* Sept. 6, 1934.

49. Ibid., Nov. 15, 1934.

50. Letter from Secretary Eliécer Padilla, Directiva Departamental, Sección de Bolívar, Oct. 11, 1934, Gaitán Papers; letter from F. Mantilla Gómez, general secretary, Directiva Departamental, Sección de Santander, Sept. 27, 1934, Gaitán Papers.

51. López Giraldo, *Apóstol,* p. 113; *Unirismo,* editorial, Nov. 21, 1934.

52. Copy of a message to Gaitán from the Directiva Central Nacional of UNIR, Oct. 9, 1933, Gaitán Papers.

53. *El Espectador,* Apr. 20, 1935; messages from Directivas Departamentales, Secciones de Barranquilla, Cartagena and Medellín during April, Gaitán Papers.

54. *Unirismo,* Apr. 25, 1935; ibid., May 4, 1935; *El Tiempo,* May 7, 1935.

55. *El Espectador,* May 16, 1935.

56. Letter to Gaitán from Fermín López Giraldo, inspector general of UNIR, May 14, 1935, Gaitán Papers. UNIR's third-in-command, Dr. Carlos Melguizo, also resigned at the same time with the accusation that Gaitán "had let fall the flag of revolution." López Giraldo, *Apóstol,* p. 136. Efe Restrepo, a columnist for *Unirismo* and prominent member from Manizales, Caldas, wrote to López Giraldo stating that he did not believe that Gaitán had betrayed UNIR, but that Gaitán, who had never ceased being a Liberal ideologically, wanted to be the planner and center of a Colombian revolution. Restrepo added that Gaitán now believed that the program of UNIR could be realized by a Liberal government. Letter dated May 14, 1936, Gaitán Papers. When President López was informed on May 11 of Gaitán's acceptance of a place on the Liberal list he remarked, "With this I consider that UNIR is finished." López Giraldo, *Apóstol,* p. 128.

57. *Unirismo,* May 23, 1935.

58. López Giraldo, *Apóstol,* pp. 117–23.

59. Interview by the author with Amparo Jaramillo de Gaitán, Oct. 9, 1969.

60. García, *Gaitán,* p. 269.

Chapter 7: The Professional

1. Interview with Amparo Jaramillo de Gaitán.

2. Osorio, *Gaitán,* p. 175.

3. Ibid., pp. 177, 179, 180, 183, 190.

4. Gaitán, *Mejores Discursos,* p. 194.

5. Osorio, *Gaitán,* p. 176.

6. *El Tiempo,* Oct. 7, 1935.

7. Osorio, *Gaitán,* pp. 183, 190.

8. Ibid., p. 174.

9. *Jornada,* May 17, 1947; Miguel Angel Gaitán, *El Porqué de un Asesinato y Sus Antecedentes* (Bogotá: Editorial Minerva, 1949), p. 128.

10. Osorio, *Gaitán,* p. 319.

11. Interview with Amparo Jaramillo de Gaitán.

12. Osorio, *Gaitán,* p. 181.

13. Conversations with Gloria Gaitán de Valencia.

14. On one occasion, which the author witnessed, she berated a Bogotá taxi driver for his and his union's lack of militancy. The reaction of the astonished man, confronted by a radical upper-class woman and a bemused gringo, is unprintable.

15. She told the author that on one occasion, when confronted with a particularly nasty crowd in Medellín, she encouraged her husband to face it down, which he did. Throughout, she remained at his side.

16. Osorio, *Gaitán,* p. 190.

17. Ibid., p. 191.

18. Jordán, *Dos Viernes,* p. 191.

19. Osorio, *Gaitán,* p. 192; see also *El Tiempo,* June 9, 1936.

20. *El Tiempo,* Feb. 23, 1930; ibid., Mar. 1, 1930; also various newspaper clippings (mostly undated) for this period in the files of Gloria Gaitán de Valencia.

21. Osorio, *Gaitán*, pp. 184–85.
22. *El Tiempo*, June 10, 1936.
23. Ibid., June 11, 1936.
24. Ibid.
25. The best source for Gaitán's mayoral activities is *El Tiempo* from mid-June 1936 through January 1937; see also Osorio, *Gaitán*, pp. 193–96.
26. *El Tiempo*, Sept. 19, 1936; ibid., Sept. 21, 1936.
27. Ibid., Sept. 26, 1936.
28. Ibid., Jan. 23, 1947.
29. The decree is in the Gaitán Papers.
30. Letter to Gaitán from ANDEC, Jan. 29, 1937, Gaitán Papers.
31. *El Tiempo*, Feb. 14, 1937.
32. Osorio, *Gaitán*, p. 197.
33. Interview with Amparo Jaramillo de Gaitán.
34. The two letters and the police report are in the Gaitán Papers.
35. Osorio, *Gaitán*, pp. 205–10.
36. Ibid., p. 216.
37. Ibid., p. 217.
38. Letter to Gaitán from Santos, Feb. 16, 1940, Gaitán Papers.
39. Interview with Amparo Jaramillo de Gaitán.
40. *El Espectador*, Jan. 3, 1934.
41. Peña, *Gaitán Intimo*, p. 129.
42. For Gaitán's activities as minister of education, see Colombia, Ministerio de Educación Nacional, *Memorias, 1939–40* (Bogotá: Imprenta Nacional, 1940), vol. 1, *La Obra Educativa del Gobierno en 1940*.
43. Ibid., pp. 111–12, 100–04.
44. Ibid., pp. 27–43, 87–90.
45. *El Tiempo*, Dec. 4, 1940.
46. Osorio, *Gaitán*, p. 235.
47. Orlando Fals Borda, *Subversion and Social Change in Colombia* (New York: Colombia University Press, 1969), pp. 139–41.
48. These groups were the National Association of Industrialists (ANDI), the National Federation of Businessmen (FENALCO), and the Society of Agriculturalists of Colombia (SAC). Their principal lobby organization was the National Employers' Economic Association (APEN), that openly worked for the repeal of Law 200 of 1936 concerning land tenure. Ibid., p. 141.
49. "Un Consejero de la Nación," *Semana*, Feb. 21, 1955.
50. Fals Borda, *Subversion and Social Change*, p. 141.
51. Quoted in Germán Arciniegas, *The State of Latin America*, trans. Harriet de Onis (New York: Knopf, 1952), p. 163.
52. García, *Gaitán*, p. 287.
53. Fals Borda, *Subversion and Social Change*, p. 141.
54. Colombia, Presidente, *Documentos Relacionados con la Renuncia del Presidente López y el Orden Público: Noviembre 16 de 1943 a Julio 26 de 1945* (Bogotá: Imprenta Nacional, 1945), p. 51.
55. Richard S. Weinert, "Violence in Pre-Modern Societies: Rural Colombia," in *Conflict and Violence in Latin American Politics*, ed. Francisco José Moreno and Barbara Mitrani (New York: Thomas Y. Crowell, 1971), p. 321.
56. Colombia, Presidente, 1945–1946 (Lleras Camargo), *Un Año de Gobierno, 1945–46* (Bogotá: Imprenta Nacional, 1946), pp. 131–34.

Chapter 8: Building the Populist Movement

1. Interview with Amparo Jaramillo de Gaitán.
2. Urrutia, *Labor Movement*, p. 186.
3. Letter to Gaitán and the Directorio Nacional Liberal from the Comando Nacional de Izquierdas, Mar. 11, 1944, Gaitán Papers.
4. Letter to Gaitán from J. A. Coquíes Pardo and others, Feb. 15, 1944, Gaitán Papers.
5. Letter to Gaitán from Edmundo Delgado, Tumaco, Mar. 18, 1944, Gaitán Papers.
6. Letter to Gaitán from Jorge Villaveces, Ibagué, Mar. 21, 1944, Gaitán Papers.
7. Interview with Jorge Padilla, Gaitanista lieutenant, in *Jornada,* Oct. 28, 1947.
8. Torres, *La Naturaleza,* p. 58.
9. Urrutia, *Labor Movement,* p. 187.
10. Gaitán, *Los Mejores Discursos,* p. 424.
11. Ibid., p. 425.
12. *El Siglo,* Mar. 1, 1945.
13. Francisco José Chaux, *Homenaje a Gaitán* (Bogotá: Editorial Minerva, 1949), p. 11.
14. Interview with Jorge Padilla, *Jornada,* Oct. 28, 1947.
15. Azula Barrera, *De la Revolución,* p. 159.
16. Interview with Amparo Jaramillo de Gaitán.
17. García, *Gaitán,* pp. 43–44.
18. Correspondence in Atlántico File, Gaitán Papers.
19. Peña, *Gaitán Intimo,* pp. 134–35. Those present at the picnic included: Luis Eduardo Garcharná, Julio Ortiz Márquez, Jorge Uribe Márquez, Alberto Uribe Ramírez, Milton Puentes, Hernando Restrepo Botero, Gabriel Muñoz Uribe, Agustín Alvarez Ruiz, Jorge Villaveces, Octavio Rodríguez, Roberto París Gaitán, Santiago Valderrama, Alvaro Rey Lara, and Alvaro Ayala. Others later incorporated as Gaitanista leaders were: Pedro Eliseo Cruz, Jorge Bejarano, Isaías Hernán Ibarra, Fernando Anzola, Alvaro Zea Hernández, David Luna Serrano, Bernardo Angel, Neftalí Henao Arismendi, José María Córdoba, Luis Cano, Jacobo and Carlos Barreto González.
20. *Jornada,* May 4, 1948.
21. *El Siglo,* Mar. 6, 1945.
22. Interview with Guillermo Hernández Rodríguez.
23. From various departmental files, Gaitán Papers.
24. Córdoba, *Gaitán,* p. 44.
25. Letter to Dr. Esaú Blanco Núñez, Gaitanista Directorate, Bolívar, from Gaitán, Dec. 17, 1945, Gaitán Papers.
26. Letter to Dr. José Blanco Núñez, Barranquilla, from Gaitán, Aug. 20, 1945, Gaitán Papers.
27. Telegram from National Liberal Directorate to Gustavo García, Andalucía, Sept. 18, 1945, Gaitán Papers.
28. Córdoba, *Gaitán,* pp. 58–59.
29. Departmental files for Tolima, Valle, Antioquia, Atlántico, Bolívar, and Magdalena, Gaitán Papers.
30. Departmental files for Boyacá, Santander, Nariño, and Cauca, Gaitán Papers.
31. Córdoba, *Gaitán,* pp. 41–43.
32. Letter-report to Gaitán from Dr. Guillermo Umaña Rocha, Villavicencio, Aug. 13, 1945, Gaitán Papers.
33. Ibid.
34. Minutes of the Bogotá Gaitanista committee, Circulars Nos. 002, July 11, 1945, and 004, July 15, 1945, Gaitán Papers. The circulars sent by Bogotá Secretary General Julio Eduardo

Macías provide instructions and running commentary on the state of the organization within the city of Bogotá.

35. Circulars Nos. 005, July 15, 1945, and 009, July 17, 1945, of the Bogotá committee, Gaitán Papers.

36. An explanation of the Gaitanista financial structure is found in a letter from Bernardo Angel, treasurer of the Gaitanista movement and member of the national directorate, to Margario Gómez, treasurer in Cúcuta, Nov. 12, 1945, Gaitán Papers. The author discovered in the Gaitán Papers numerous long overdue bills for such things as the repair of Gaitán's automobile.

37. Minutes of the Bogotá committee, Circular No. 025, Sept. 2, 1945, Gaitán Papers.

38. Peña, *Gaitán Intimo*, p. 38.

39. Reported in *Semana*, Dec. 20, 1947.

40. Peña, *Gaitán Intimo*, pp. 36–38, 42. The reportorial staff included Jorge Uribe Márquez, Joaquin Tiberio Galvis, Jorge Padilla (a former Unirismo staffer), and Victor Manuel García.

41. For example, *El Sesquiplano* in Santa Marta. Letter to Gaitán from the newspaper's director, Juan del Villar, Jan. 15, 1946, Gaitán Papers.

42. *La Razón* provided critical coverage of the Gaitanista movement, which it regarded as a major threat to the country.

43. Letter to Gaitán from Ramón Becerra, director of *Restauración*, Oct. 16, 1944, Gaitán Papers; there appeared to be between twenty and thirty mostly small newspapers founded to support the movement.

44. Córdoba, *Gaitán*, p. 42.

45. Letter to Gaitán from Director José A. Rivera. April 6, 1946, Gaitán Papers.

46. The pamphlet is in the files of the author.

47. Córdoba, *Gaitán*, p. 61.

48. The plans for the convention are in the Gaitán Papers. See especially the Córdoba file.

49. Córdoba, *Gaitán*, p. 61.

50. Photographs of the convention are found on the dust jacket of the phonograph record "Jorge Eliécer Gaitán: Tribuno del Pueblo," in the files of the author. Also, interview with Amparo Jaramillo de Gaitán.

51. Gaitán, *Los Mejores Discursos*, p. 394.

52. Ibid., pp. 395, 396–97.

53. Ibid., p. 396, 398–400.

54. Ibid., pp. 402, 403–04.

55. Córdoba, *Gaitán*, p. 14.

56. Interview with Guillermo Hernández Rodríguez.

57. Mario Fernández de Soto, *Una Revolución en Colombia: Jorge Eliécer Gaitán y Mariano Ospina Pérez* (Madrid: Ediciones Cultura Hispania, 1951), pp. 92–93.

58. Peña, *Gaitán Intimo*, pp. 13, 15.

59. Ibid., p. 14.

60. Milton Puentes, *Gaitán* (Bogotá: Editorial ABC, 1947), pp. 92–97; phonograph record, "Jorge Eliécer Gaitán."

61. Interview with Leopoldo Borda Roldán.

62. Peña, *Gaitán Intimo*, p. 50.

63. Ibid., p. 51.

64. The March 1946 schedule is in the Gaitán Papers.

65. Letter to Luis P. Hernández, Bucaramanga, from Córdoba, Dec. 6, 1946, Córdoba file, Gaitán Papers.

66. Letter to General Lázaro F. Soto, Bucamaranga, from Córdoba, Dec. 6, 1946, Córdoba file, Gaitán Papers.

67. *El Siglo,* Apr. 21, 1945.
68. Ibid., June 22, 1945.
69. Córdoba, *Gaitán,* p. 15.
70. *Jornada,* Feb. 20, 1947.
71. Peña, *Gaitán Intimo, p. 30.*

Chapter 9: Followers, Foes, and the Campaign of 1946

1. A letter describing Gaitanistas in Tolima placed the workers and *campesinos* in their party while merchants, big businessmen, and politicians supported the regular Liberals. Letter to J. M. Vesga Villamizar from Fidel Murillo Peláez, Ibagué, March 25, 1944, Gaitán Papers.
2. Resolution from the Directive Council of the Federation of Colombian Drivers, Dec. 1942, Gaitán Papers. Letters from other unions thanking Gaitán for his support and soliciting his help against the Liberals' antilabor legislation are also on file for this period.
3. Various "adhesions" from these groups are found in the Gaitán Papers.
4. Urrutia, *Labor Movement,* p. 188.
5. Córdoba, *Gaitán,* p. 43–44.
6. Letter to Gaitán from J. Guillermo Ortega L., executive vice-president of the Worker's Federation of Tolima, Ibagué, May 10, 1946, Gaitán Papers.
7. Letter to Gaitán from a municipal judge, Luis C. Lemus, Acandí, Chocó, May 18, 1945, Gaitán Papers.
8. Confidential report to Córdoba from José Leal Acuesta on Gaitanista activities in Norte de Santander, Durania, Dec. 11, 1945, Gaitán Papers.
9. Letter to Córdoba from Camilo Falla and J. A. Perdomo, Neiva, Huila, Dec. 20, 1945, Gaitán Papers.
10. Manifesto of the Gaitanista Liberal Directorate of Antioquia to Bernardo Angel, Medellín, Apr. 12, 1945, Gaitán Papers. Letter to Jorge Ospina Londoño from Bernardo Angel, Bogotá, May 12, 1945, Gaitán Papers.
11. Letter to Ospina Londoño from Córdoba, Bogotá, Dec. 9, 1946, Córdoba file, Gaitán Papers.
12. Circular No. 2 from the Junta Nacional de Amigos de Gabriel Turbay, Apr. 28, 1944, Gaitán Papers.
13. *La Razón,* Jan. 9, 1947.
14. *El Tiempo,* Mar. 15, 1944.
15. Ibid., Sept. 24, 1945.
16. Interview with Dr. Alberto Miramón, former director of the national library, Bogotá, June 19, 1969. Complete text of the interview is in the files of the author.
17. *El Tiempo,* Sept. 21, 1945.
18. Ibid., Apr. 11, 1945.
19. Letter to Gaitán from Marco A. Hormiga, Popayán, Jan. 6, 1945, Gaitán Papers.
20. *Semana* reported that Gaitanista "shock troops" had defeated the Communists in street battles in the working-class neighborhoods of the capital, and that, because of intimidation, many Communists voted for Gaitán. *Semana,* July 5, 1947.
21. Montaña Cuéllar, *Colombia,* p. 174.
22. Alexander, *Communism in Latin America,* p. 249.
23. Comité Central del Partido Comunista, *Treinta Años,* p. 76.
24. Letter to Gaitán from Juan Manuel Valderrama, Cartagena, Mar. 29, 1944, Gaitán Papers.
25. For a biography of Turbay see Agustín Rodríguez Garavito, *Gabriel Turbay, Un Solitario de la Grandeza,* 2nd ed. (Bogotá: Editorial Prócer, 1966).

26. Gabriel Turbay Ayala, *Las Ideas Políticas de Gabriel Turbay* (Bogotá: Editorial Minerva, 1945), pp. 20, 28, 29-30, 89, 182.

27. *El Siglo,* Mar. 31, 1946.

28. Peña, *Gaitán Intimo,* pp. 160-62.

29. Gaitán, *Los Mejores Discursos,* p. 431.

30. Peña, *Gaitán Intimo,* p. ·162.

31. Gaitán, *Los Mejores Discursos,* p. 431.

32. Peña, *Gaitán Intimo,* p. 162.

33. Letter to Gaitán from Jesús Amórtegui, Barranquilla, Mar. 29, 1946, Gaitán Papers.

34. Gaitán, *Los Mejores Discursos,* pp. 433, 435.

35. *El Tiempo,* May 6, 1946.

36. García, *Gaitán,* p. 43.

37. *El Tiempo,* May 6, 1946.

38. *La Razón,* May 6, 1946.

Chapter 10: The Gaitanista Program

1. Valencia, ed., *Gaitán: Antología,* p. 329. Subsequent citations of this edition of the *Plataforma* will be given in the text.

2. Recommendations for similar credit institutions were developed later by U.S. advisors under the Alliance for Progress.

3. *Jornada,* May 8, 1947.

4. Telegram concerning Liberalism's defense of national industry to Remos Mendoza in Bogotá from Gaitán, Barranquilla, Oct. 19, 1947, Gaitán Papers.

5. *El Espectador,* July 22, 1947.

6. Statement of Luis Gutiérrez Gómez printed in *Jornada,* Nov. 22, 1947.

Chapter 11: Gaitán and the Liberals

1. Osorio, *Gaitán,* pp. 280-81.

2. Telegram to Gaitán from Belén de Campo and other women, Manta, May 7, 1946, Gaitán Papers.

3. *El Tiempo,* May 8, 1946.

4. Letter to Elías Restrepo R., Cali, from Córdoba, June 17, 1946, Gaitán Papers.

5. Letter to Gaitanista organizations from Córdoba, Directorio Liberal Gaitanista, Bogotá, May 20, 1946, Gaitán Papers.

6. Letter to Geraldo Cuenca Doncel, Ortega, Tolima, from Córdoba, June 1, 1946, Gaitán Papers.

7. Letter to Gaitán from Fidel Murillo, Honda, Dec. 28, 1946, Gaitán Papers; "ACTA" of the Directorio Departamental Gaitanista, Ibagué, Oct. 25, 1946, Gaitán Papers.

8. *Semana,* Nov. 4, 1946.

9. *El Tiempo,* May 8, 1946; ibid., May 9, 1946; ibid., May 10, 1946.

10. Ibid., June 18, 1946.

11. Letter to Federaciones Departamentales de Comités Liberales from Córdoba, June 26, 1946, Gaitán Papers.

12. *Semana,* Nov. 4, 1946.

13. *La Razón,* Sept. 1946; ibid., Sept. 9, 1946; *Semana,* Nov. 4, 1946.

14. *El Tiempo,* Sept. 22, 1946.

15. *Semana,* Nov. 4, 1946.

16. *El Tiempo,* Dec. 13, 1946.

17. *Semana,* Jan. 4, 1947.

18. *Jornada,* Mar. 7, 1947.

19. Córdoba, *Gaitán,* pp. 85-86.

20. Peña, *Gaitán Intimo,* p. 17.

21. Fluharty, *Dance of the Millions,* pp. 86, 92-93.

22. Azula Barrera, *De la Revolución,* pp. 252-54. Azula provides the breakdown of the Liberal factions; vote totals (only by party, not faction) are found in Colombia, Departamento Administrativo Nacional de Estadistica, "Tendencias Electorales," *Boletín Mensual de Estadistica* 221 (Dec. 1969), p. 99.

23. *El Tiempo,* Mar. 18, 1947; Ibid., Mar. 28, 1947.

24. Alejandro Vallejo, *La Palabra Encadenada: Antes del 9 de Abril y Después* (Bogotá: Editorial Minerva, 1949), p. 37.

25. *Semana,* June 21, 1947.

26. *Sábado,* Apr. 12, 1947.

27. *La Razón,* Apr. 23, 1947.

28. Azula Barrera, *De la Revolución,* p. 265. A letter from Santos to Juan Lozano y Lozano setting forth this opinion is quoted by Azula Barrera.

29. *Jornada,* May 24, 1947; ibid., Dec. 10, 1947.

30. Ibid., Dec. 11, 1947.

31. Ibid., June 11, 1947.

32. *El Tiempo,* Dec. 10, 1947.

33. *Jornada,* Mar. 22, 1947.

34. Letter to Gaitán from Partido Liberal Izquierdista, Cartagena, Sept. 22, 1947, Gaitán Papers.

35. Letter to Gaitán from Juan Manual de la Mar, Cartagena, Dec. 2, 1947, Gaitán Papers.

36. Radiogram to Gaitán from E. Giraldo and others, Montería, Dec. 16, 1947, Gaitán Papers.

Chapter 12: Gaitán and the Gaitanistas

1. *Semana,* Mar. 1, 1947.

2. The complete resolution is in the Gaitán Papers.

3. *Semana,* Jan. 11, 1947; ibid., Jan. 18, 1947.

4. Ibid., Jan. 25, 1947.

5. *El Tiempo,* Jan. 22, 1947; ibid., Jan. 23, 1947.

6. *Semana,* Jan. 25, 1947.

7. Ibid.

8. *El Tiempo,* Jan. 22, 1947; ibid., Jan. 25, 1947; ibid., Jan. 18, 1947.

9. *Jornada,* Feb. 8, 1947; ibid., Feb. 17, 1947. *Jornada* contrasted this to the smaller crowds attracted to the Liberal campaigners. At one point the newspaper claimed that *El Tiempo* published a photograph of a crowd at a Liberal rally that was twenty years old. *Jornada,* Feb. 6, 1947.

10. *Jornada,* Feb. 27, 1947.

11. Ibid.

12. Ibid., Feb. 6, 1947.

13. *Semana,* Mar. 8, 1947.

14. *El Tiempo,* Feb. 23, 1947; ibid., Feb. 27, 1947. In the same issue *El Tiempo* charged that during a Conservative-provoked riot in Pasto the police deliberately used teargas on Darío Echandía who was attempting to deliver a campaign speech.

15. *Jornada,* Feb. 10, 1947.

16. Gaitán, *Mejores Discursos,* p. 478. Santos and Laureano Gómez also spoke the same night against violence.

17. *Jornada,* Apr. 19, 1947.

18. Ibid., June 9, 1947. Members of the commission were: Plinio Mendoza Neira, Carlos Lozano y Lozano, A. J. Lemos Guzmán, Francisco de Paula Vargas, and Pedro Alonso Jaimes. Lozano y Lozano refused to serve because of his opposition to Gaitán.

19. *Jornada,* June 17, 1947; *Semana,* Dec. 6, 1947.

20. *Jornada,* July 12, 1947.

21. Letter to Liberal directorates of Zipaquirá and Girardot from Gaitán, July 3, 1947, Gaitán Papers.

22. *Jornada,* July 12, 1947.

23. *Jornada,* Oct. 4, 1947.

24. *Jornada,* Oct. 6, 1947.

25. Ibid., Oct. 25, 1947; ibid., Oct. 26, 1947.

26. *Semana,* Nov. 10, 1947.

27. *El Tiempo,* Dec. 17, 1947. "Calibán" also noted that with Gaitán the party was headed for disaster. He added that 90 percent of upper-class Liberals were against him.

28. *Semana,* Feb. 1, 1947. Some of the new leaders included: in Atlántico, José Consuegra; in Boyacá, Armando Solano and Darío Samper; in Bolívar, Francisco de Paula Vargas and Efraín del Valle; in Cauca, Francisco José Cháux; in Cundinamarca, Parmenio Cárdenas; in Huila, Efraín Rojas Trujillo and Senator Godoy; in Magdalena, Juan B. Barrios; in Norte de Santander, José Gelvis; in Tolima, Senator Mauricio Jaramillo and Representative Alfonso Bonilla Gutiérrez; in Valle, Francisco Eladio Ramírez.

29. J. E. Navia Navia of Cali, in a letter to Francisco José Chaux, Oct. 8, 1946, complained bitterly that faithful workers for Gaitanismo were passed up as delegates in favor of "returnees" and petty politicians. Gaitán Papers.

30. Letter to Gaitán from twelve Gaitanistas in Campoalegre, Huila, Oct. 8, 1947, Gaitán Papers.

31. Letter to Gaitán from Julio Vélez, Cartagena, Oct. 25, 1947, Gaitán Papers.

32. Reply to Huila group from Gaitán, Oct. 18, 1947, Gaitán Papers; reply to Vélez from Gaitán, Nov. 3, 1947, Gaitán Papers.

33. Letter to Luís Ortega and others from Gaitán, Nov. 29, 1947, Gaitán Papers.

34. *Jornada,* July 3, 1947.

35. One of Gaitán's original associates, Jorge Uribe Márquez of the *Jornada* staff, resigned because of the former's decision to collaborate with the Ospina government after the March 1947 elections. *Semana,* May 10, 1947. The managing editor of *Jornada,* Luís David Peña, also resigned in January 1948 because Gaitán had placed on the paper's staff two journalists with whom he had "ideological differences." The journalists were not named. Letter to Gaitán from Peña, Jan. 12, 1948, Gaitán Papers.

36. *El Tiempo,* Dec. 10, 1947.

37. Statement of Jorge Villaveces, *Jornada,* Apr. 28, 1948.

38. Victor Julio Silva, president of the Colombian Confederation of Workers (CTC) was unofficially in the Gaitanista camp, although the confederation remained divided between Gaitanistas and regulars. However, the Gaitanistas clearly held the support of the majority of the rank and file. *Semana,* Feb. 22, 1947. The Communists, as stated previously, were allied with Gaitán. Their support in Bogotá, for example, resulted in the election of a leftist-dominated municipal council in October 1947.

39. Interview with Guillermo Barriga Casalini.

40. Interview with Dr. Alfonso Garcés Valencia, Cali, Aug. 15, 1974. The complete text of the interview is in the files of the author.

Chapter 13: Gaitán and the Ospina Government

1. Arciniegas, *State of Latin America,* p. 9.

2. Alberto Niño H., *Antecedentes y Secretos del 9 de Abril* (Bogotá: Editorial Pax, 1949), p. 9.

3. Azula Barrera, *De la Revolución,* p. 235. They included one Gaitanista, Dr. Rafael Herrera Anzoatequi, who was named minister of labor. The governors of Atlántico and Santander del Sur also were Gaitanistas.

4. *Jornada,* Feb. 6, 1947. López believed that the two parties were no longer ideologically incompatible and that they should work together to solve economic and social problems. Lleras Camargo and Santos both agreed. *El Tiempo,* July 24, 1946.

5. Niño H., *Antecedentes,* pp. 11–12.

6. Gaitán, *Los Mejores Discursos,* pp. 443–44; *Jornada,* Feb. 6, 1947.

7. *El Tiempo,* July 26, 1946.

8. Arciniegas, *State of Latin America,* p. 160.

9. Fluharty, *Dance of the Millions,* p. 91.

10. Colombia, Presidente, 1946–1950 (Ospina Pérez), *El Gobierno de Unión Nacional,* 4 vols. (Bogotá: Imprenta Nacional, 1950), I, p. 150. Hereafter cited as Ospina Pérez, *El Gobierno.* Donald Marquand Dozer, "The Roots of Revolution in Latin America," *Foreign Affairs* 27 (Jan. 1949), p. 283; Fluharty, *Dance of the Millions,* p. 92.

11. Ospina Pérez, *El Gobierno,* I, 153.

12. Urrutia, *Labor Movement,* p. 183.

13. *Semana,* Nov. 18, 1946.

14. Ospina Pérez, *El Gobierno,* I, 73, 79.

15. *Semana,* Dec. 30, 1946.

16. Ibid., Jan. 18, 1947.

17. Montaña Cuéllar, *Colombia,* p. 184.

18. *La violencia* has aroused widespread interest among social scientists and others, both Colombians and foreigners. As a result there is a considerable body of literature on the subject. For a critical review of the sources available, see Russell W. Ramsey, "Critical Bibliography on *La Violencia* in Colombia," *Latin American Research Review* 8 (Spring 1973), pp. 3–44. The single best Colombian source, despite defects, is Germán Guzmán, Orlando Fals Borda, and Eduardo Umaña Luna, *La Violencia en Colombia* (Bogotá: Ediciones Tercer Mundo, 1962). For excellent explorations of the causes of the violence, see Camilo Torres Restrepo, "Social Change and Rural Violence in Colombia," *Studies in Comparative International Development* 4 (1969); and John C. Pollock, "Violence, Politics and Elite Performance: The Political Sociology of *La Violencia* in Colombia," *Studies in Comparative International Development* 10 (Summer 1975), pp. 22–50. Gaitán's electoral support in 1946, rank-ordered by Colombian departments, can be compared with a rank-ordering of departments by levels of violence as elaborated in the Pollock article to determine whether Gaitanismo was associated with relatively high levels of protest during *la violencia.* The author is indebted to Professor Pollock for this observation.

19. *El Siglo,* Sept. 2, 1947; *Semana,* Sept. 6, 1947.

20. Arciniegas, *State of Latin America,* p. 158.

21. *Semana,* Dec. 30, 1946.

22. Ospina Pérez, *El Gobierno,* II, 59; *Semana,* Sept. 6, 1947.

23. Ospina Pérez, *El Gobierno,* II, 63–66.

24. "ACTA" sent to the governor of Nariño by the Departmental Liberal Directorate, Sept. 27, 1947, Gaitán Papers.

25. Fluharty, *Dance of the Millions,* p. 87.

26. *Jornada,* Jan. 18, 1948.

27. *Semana,* Nov. 18, 1946.

28. *Jornada,* Feb. 7, 1947, and the following editions. See also the editorials of Feb. 4, and Apr. 10.

29. *Semana,* May 3, 1947; *El Tiempo,* Apr. 27, 1947. Three Gaitanistas served in the cabinet: Delio Jaramillo Arbeláez, minister of labor; Pedro Eliseo Cruz, minister of health; and Moisés Prieto, minister of economy.

30. *Jornada,* May 17, 1947.

31. The newspapers articles are quoted in *Semana,* May 24, 1947.

32. *Jornada,* May 15, 1947.

33. Ibid., May 28, 1947.

34. *Semana,* Dec. 13, 1947.

35. *El Tiempo,* Sept. 7, 1947; ibid., Sept. 12, 1947; *Jornada,* Sept. 20, 1947.

36. Ibid., Sept. 13, 1947; *Semana,* Sept. 20, 1947.

37. *Semana,* Sept. 20, 1947.

38. *Semana,* Feb. 7, 1948.

39. *Jornada,* Oct. 11, 1947.

40. A photo on the front page of *Jornada,* Dec. 5, 1947, shows Conservative Representative Pablo A. Toro pointing a pistol at Liberal Representative César Ordóñez Quintero.

41. *Jornada,* Nov. 7, 1947; *Semana,* Nov. 15, 1947; ibid., Nov. 22, 1947.

42. *Jornada,* Feb. 12, 1947.

43. The memorandum is in the Gaitán Papers. See also *Jornada,* Apr. 12, 1947; and *Semana,* Apr. 19, 1947.

44. *Jornada,* June 4, 1947; ibid., June 6, 1947. The day before Gaitán's nationalization law was introduced, the Conservative governor allowed the free sale of arms and munitions.

45. The secretary of the governor of Caldas cited mutual hostility by local leaders of both parties as the cause of the violence. Telegram to Gaitán signed A. Jaramillo Concha, Manizales, July 8, 1947, Gaitán Papers.

46. John D. Martz, *Colombia: A Contemporary Political Survey* (Chapel Hill: University of North Carolina Press, 1962), pp. 51, 53; Fluharty, *Dance of the Millions,* p. 86.

47. *Jornada,* Aug. 23, 1947.

48. *Semana,* Aug. 30, 1947.

49. *Jornada,* Aug. 30, 1947; ibid., Sept 11, 1947.

50. Letter from Gaitán to the Conservative governor of Boyacá, José María Villareal, Nov. 27, 1947, Gaitán Papers; letter from Gaitán to the Liberal directorate of Caldas, Feb. 12, 1948, Gaitán Papers. In the letter to Villareal, who had asked Gaitán to intervene to stop the murdering of Conservatives by Liberals, Gaitán said he would do all in his power to end the violence. But he closed by saying "only those can claim justice who practice it," intended for the governor.

51. Peña, *Gaitán Intimo,* p. 20.

52. *Jornada,* May 26, 1947; *El Tiempo,* Feb. 7, 1948.

53. An untitled, undated article from a Venezuelan newspaper in the Gaitán Papers; and an expense account for Colombian police traveling in Venezuela from the *Caja* of the national police, dated Feb. 2, 1948, Gaitán Papers.

54. Peña, *Gaitán Intimo,* pp. 59-61; *El Deber* of Montería had a banner on its Dec. 21, 1947, front page: "The Gaitanistas of Santander are responsible for the assassination of 54 Conservatives

in the past sixty days. . . . Why doesn't Gaitán pay with his own life for so many Conservatives that have died because of him?"

55. Peña, *Gaitán Intimo,* p. 62.

56. Telegram to Gaitán from Bentancourt, Feb. 1, 1948, Gaitán Papers.

57. Letter to the Liberal directorate of Cucutá from Gaitán, Jan. 30, 1948, Gaitán Papers; resolution of the National Liberal Directorate, Feb. 26, 1948, Gaitán Papers.

58. Telegram to Gaitán from Governor Rafael Ortíz González, Bucaramanga, Santander del Sur, Feb. 6, 1948, Gaitán Papers. The telegram thanks Gaitán for his success in convincing Liberals to call off demonstrations and "other actions."

59. Letter to Gaitán from Ospina, Jan. 23, 1948, Gaitán Papers. In this moving letter Ospina declared that "the maximum preoccupation of my government and me personally has been nothing more than to secure an effective pacification of Santander del Norte." He asked for Gaitán's cooperation.

60. *Semana,* Jan. 31, 1948.

61. *El Tiempo,* Feb. 14, 1948.

62. See *El Tiempo,* for Feb. 14–28, esp. Feb. 14, 24, 25.

63. *El Tiempo,* Feb. 29, 1948; *Jornada,* Feb. 29, 1948; *Semana,* Feb. 28, 1948.

64. *Semana,* Feb. 14, 1948.

65. Peña, *Gaitán Intimo,* p. 19.

66. The entire text of the "Oración por la Paz" is found in Gaitán, *Mejores Discursos,* pp. 506–07.

67. *Semana,* Mar. 27, 1948.

68. Alfonso López Michelsen, *Cuestions Colombianas: Ensayos* (Mexico, D.F.: Impresiones Modernas, 1955), p. 73.

69. *Jornada,* Feb. 27, 1948.

70. Antolín Díaz, *Los Verdugos del Caudillo y de su Pueblo* (Bogotá; Editorial ABC, 1948), p. 66.

71. Azula Barrera, *De la Revolución,* p. 306.

72. One of them was a Cuban student named Fidel Castro. For a discussion of leftist activities in Colombia during this period, see Fluharty, *Dance of the Millions,* pp. 93–99; Niño H., *Antecedentes,* pp. 50–54; Nieto Rojas, *La Batalla,* pp. 171–75.

73. Fluharty, *Dance of the Millions,* p. 99.

74. Arciniegas, *State of Latin America,* pp. 161–62.

75. Osorio, *Gaitán,* p. 293.

76. Osorio, *Gaitán,* p. 294. Castro had an appointment with Gaitán scheduled for three o'clock on the afternoon of April 9 to discuss the latter's help in securing a meeting hall. See Gaitán's schedule calendar on display in the Casa Museo Gaitán; also interview with Amparo Jaramillo de Gaitán.

Chapter 14: The Aftermath

1. The best brief account of the *bogotazo* is in *Semana,* Apr. 24, 1948. It was reprinted with several other accounts of the events of April 9, in *El Espectador* (Magazine Dominical), Apr. 7, 1968. For other accounts and analyses, see Rául Andrade, *La Internacional Negra en Colombia y Otros Ensayos* (Bogotá: Editorial Quito, 1954), pp. 45–98; Azula Barrera, *De la Revolución,* pp. 303–465; Enrique Cuéllar Vargas, *13 Años de Violencia* (Bogotá: Editorial SIPA, 1960), pp. 15–79; Fluharty, *Dance of the Millions,* pp. 84–107; Carlos Lleras Restrepo, *De la República a la Dictadura* (Bogotá: Editorial ARGRA, 1955), pp. 241–49; Martz, *Colombia,* chap. 4; Nieto

Rojas, *La Batalla,* chaps. 7–8; Niño H., *Antecedentes,* pp. 60–78; Osorio Lizarazo, *Gaitán,* pp. 278–317.

2. Interview with Amparo Jaramillo de Gaitán.

3. Azula Barrera, *De la Revolución,* pp. 380–83.

4. Abelardo Forero Benavides, "El 9 de Abril de 1948," *El Espectador,* Apr. 7, 1968.

5. Azula Barrera, *De la Revolución,* pp. 398–99. Azula Barrera, then minister of education in the Ospina government, was present during these events.

6. Martz, *Colombia,* p. 61; Osorio Lizarazo, *Gaitán,* p. 305.

7. Joaquín Estrada Monsalve, *El 9 de Abril en Palacio* (Bogotá: Editorial ABC, 1948), pp. 85–95.

8. *Jornada,* May 16, 1948; ibid., May 19, 1948.

9. Peña, *Gaitán Intimo,* p. 169; Gutiérrez, *La Rebeldía Colombiana,* p. 71; García, *Gaitán,* p. 19. The quote is from García.

10. López Michelsen, *Cuestiones Colombianas,* p. 22.

11. Lleras Restrepo, *De la República,* p. 100. Gaitán's widow bitterly denounced Lleras Restrepo to the author as "the Liberal who had the most to gain from my husband's death."

12. Córdoba, *Gaitán,* p. 160.

13. Martz, *Colombia,* p. 76.

14. One of those was the author's father-in-law, Bernardo Benítez, a small businessman in Cali, who gave up any active involvement in politics.

15. Guzmán *et al.*, *La Violencia,* pp. 416–18.

16. Dix, *Colombia,* pp. 270–71.

17. The assassin of Gaitán was Juan Roa Sierra. He was a poor drifter from an obscure background who believed in the occult and had a history of mental instability. He nominally was a Conservative, and at least one author claimed that he at one time distributed propaganda for the embassy of the Third Reich and was supposedly close to Alvaro Gómez Hurtado, Laureano's son. See Cuéllar Vargas, *13 Años de Violencia,* pp. 63–64.

Every political group in Colombia, plus international Communist agents and Rómulo Betancourt of Venezuela, have been blamed for the killing of Gaitán. Shortly after the assassination the Ospina government called in an investigating team from Scotland Yard, and several other inquiries were made at later dates. None of the results of these investigations, however, has ever been made public; the mystery concerning the "intellectual authors" of the crime, if there were any, remains, and the question of responsibility still arouses considerable controversy.

Gaitán's widow and daughter are quick to implicate President Ospina and, secondarily, Laureano Gómez and his son Alvaro Gómez Hurtado. They argue, from their knowledge of the investigations and personal sources, that Ospina ordered Gaitán's death. Ospina allegedly had the assassination carried out by the Bogotá police commander, who supposedly admitted responsibility in a conversation overheard by a friend of the Gaitán family. The motive for the killing was the increasing danger Gaitán posed for the oligarchs. Both Amparo Jaramillo de Gaitán and Gaitán's son-in-law, Luis Emiro Valencia, believe that the "silent demonstration" in Bogotá on Feb. 7, 1948, was a decisive factor in the decision to eliminate Gaitán. The latter previously had been dismissed as a demagogue, but the silent march of one hundred thousand people totally obedient to Gaitán, convinced the government that the real power in the country was no longer in its hands, but in those of its principal adversary. His removal, therefore, became necessary.

When speaking of the events surrounding her husband's death, Señora Gaitán asks several cogent questions: Why are the results of the investigations not made public? Why were investigators removed when they began to reach the conclusion of their work? Why hasn't the mysterious death of the English translator for Scotland Yard been cleared up? And why was his Colombian wife soon afterward given a diplomatic assignment in Europe, unprecedented for a woman?

Conversations of the author with Amparo Jaramillo de Gaitán, Gloria Gaitán de Valencia, and Luis Emiro Valencia.

Chapter 15: The Legacy

1. Quoted in Valencia, *Gaitán*, p. 16.

2. For his understanding of populism the author is indebted to Di Tella, "Populism and Reform." Most of the characteristics of Gaitanismo fit within Di Tella's formulations.

3. *Semana*, Apr. 24, 1948.

4. From an interview with Fidel Castro by Luís Emiro Valencia published in the newspaper *Gaitán*, May 22, 1961. The newspaper was the organ of the movement that Gloria Gaitán de Valencia and her husband unsuccessfully attempted to build in the early 1960s. The interview with Castro took place in Havana (n.d.).

5. According to García, Gaitán's refusal to attempt an overthrow of the Ospina government by extralegal methods was a major error. García wrote that Gaitán was unwilling or unable to overcome "the superstition . . . of legalism, of the Santanderista idolatry for the law conceived as a *reality in itself* and not as a simple possibility of doing or not doing." García noted the "extraordinary" fact that in a country where dominant persons, parties, and classes "have substituted the 'order of law' for 'arbitrariness with laws,' a revolutionary mentality like Gaitán was seduced by republican myths and legalist prejudices." García, *Gaitán*, p. 10.

6. Martz, *Colombia*, p. 44.

7. Dix, *Colombia*, p. 44; García, *Gaitán*, p. 4.

Bibliography

Manuscript Collection

Bogotá. Casa Museo Gaitán. Gaitán Papers. These papers include a vast amount of correspondence, reports, documents, memoranda, pamphlets, telegrams, etc., relating to Gaitán's public career and located in the Casa Museo Gaitán, his former residence, and now an official museum. Also includes the correspondence of José María Córdoba while secretary-general of the Gaitanista Liberal Directorate. At the time of the author's research (1969-1970) this material was uncatalogued and unclassified.

Official Documents

Colombia. *La Opinión Nacional Ante la Reforma de la Constitución*. Bogotá: Imprenta Nacional, 1936.
_____. Consejo Nacional de Política Económica y Planeación. Departamento Administrativo de Planeación y Servicios Técnicos. *Colombia: Plan General de Desarrollo Económico y Social*. 2 vols. Bogotá, 1961-1962.
_____. Departamento Administrativo Nacional de Estadística. "Tendencias Electorales, 1935-1968." *Boletín Mensual de Estadística* 221 (December 1969).
_____. Ministerio de Educación Nacional. *Memorias, 1939-40*. 3 vols. Bogotá: Imprenta Nacional, 1940. Vol. 1: *La Obra Educativa del Gobierno en 1940*. Vol. 2: *Disposiciones sobre Educación en 1940*. Vol. 3: *La Extension Cultural en Colombia*.
_____. Ministerio de Educación Nacional. División de Normales Superiores y Educación Primaria. *Educación Colombiana*. Tomo I: 1903-1958. Bogotá: Imprenta Nacional, 1959.
_____. Ministerio de Trabajo. *El Pensamiento Social de Uribe Uribe*. Bogotá: Biblioteca del Ministerio del Trabajo, 1960.
_____. Presidente. *Documentos Relacionados con la Renuncia del Presidente López y el Orden Público: Noviembre 16 de 1943 a Julio 26 de 1945*. Bogotá: Imprenta Nacional, 1945.
_____. Presidente. *La Oposición y el Gobierno del 9 de Abril 1948 al 9 de Abril de 1950*. Bogotá: Imprenta Nacional, 1950.
_____. Presidente. 1930-1934 (Olaya Herrera). *Administración Olaya Herrera, 1930-1934*. Bogotá: Editorial Minerva, 1935.

———. Presidente. 1934–1938 (López Pumarejo). *Mensajes del Presidente López al Congreso Nacional, 1934–1938*. Bogotá: Imprenta Nacional, 1939.

———. Presidente. 1934–1938 (López Pumarejo). *Política Oficial: Mensajes, Cartas y Discursos del Presidente López*. 5 vols. in 4. Bogotá: Imprenta Nacional, 1935–1939.

———. Presidente. 1938–1942 (Santos). *Declaraciones Presidenciales*. 2 vols. Bogotá: Imprenta Nacional, 1942.

———. Presidente. 1945–1946 (Lleras Camargo). *Un Año de Gobierno, 1945–46*, Bogotá: Imprenta Nacional, 1946.

———. Presidente. 1946–1950 (Ospina Pérez). *El Gobierno de Unión Nacional*. 4 vols. Bogota: Imprenta Nacional, 1950.

———. Presidente. 1946–1950. (Ospina Pérez). *El Gobierno de Unión Nacional y los Acuerdos Patrióticos*. Bogotá: Publicaciones de la Oficina de Información y Prensa de la Presidencia de la República, 1948.

International Bank for Reconstruction and Development. *The Basis of a Development Program for Colombia, Report of a Mission Headed by Lauchlin Currie*. Washington, D.C.: International Bank for Reconstruction and Development, 1950.

United Nations. Department of Economic and Social Affairs. Economic Commission for Latin America. *Analyses and Projection of Economic Development. III. The Economic Development of Colombia*. Geneva: United Nations Department of Economic and Social Affairs, 1957.

Books and Dissertations

Alexander, Robert J. *Communism in Latin America*. New Brunswick: Rutgers University Press, 1957.

———. *Organized Labor in Latin America*. New York: The Free Press, 1965.

American University, Washington, D. C. Foreign Areas Studies Division. *Special Warfare Area Handbook for Colombia*. Washington, D.C.: U.S. Department of the Army, 1961.

Andrade, Raúl. *La Internacional Negra en Colombia y Otros Ensayos*. Quito: Editorial Quito, 1954.

Andrade de Pombo, Helena. *Tres Godos en Aprietos*. Bogotá: Editorial Santafé, 1956.

Arciniegas, Germán. *Entre la Libertad y el Miedo*. Santiago de Chile: Editorial del Pacífico, 1953.

———. *The State of Latin America*. Translated by Harriet de Onís. New York: Knopf, 1952.

Azula Barrera, Rafael. *De la Revolución al Orden Nuevo: Proceso y Drama de un Pueblo*. Bogotá: Editorial Kelly, 1956.

Beaulac, Willard L. *Career Ambassador*. New York: Macmillan, 1951.

Bernstein, Harry. *Modern and Contemporary Latin America*. Philadelphia: J. B. Lippincott, 1952.

Betancur, Belisario. *Colombia Cara a Cara*. Bogotá: Ediciones Tercer Mundo, 1961.

Blanco Núñez, José M. *Memorias de un Gobernador: El Nueve de Abril de 1948*. Barranquilla, 1968.

Burnett, Ben G. "The Recent Colombian Party System: Its Organization and Procedure." Ph.D. diss., University of California at Los Angeles, 1955.

Caballero Calderón, Eduardo. *Cartas Colombianas*. Bogotá: Editorial Kelly, 1949.

Caballero Calderón, Lucas. *Figuras Políticas de Colombia*. Bogotá: Editorial Kelly, 1945.

Cadavid, J. Iván. *Los Fueros de la Iglesia ante el Liberalismo y el Conservatismo en Colombia*. Medellín: Editorial Bedout, 1955.

Canal Ramírez, Gonzalo. *El Estado Cristiano y Bolivariano del 13 de Junio*. Bogotá: Editorial Antares, 1955.

Castrillón, Alberto. *Ciento Veinte Días Bajo el Terror Militar: O la Huelga de las Bananeras*. Bogotá: Revista "Universidad," 1929.

Centro de Investigaciones Sociales (CIS). *Estudios Sobre Desarrollo. Informe No. 1. Condiciones de Desarrollo y Reconstrución en el Municipio de Sonsón (Antioquia)*. Bogotá: CIS, 1963.

Chaux, Francisco José. *Homenaje a Gaitán*. Bogotá: Editorial Minerva, 1949.

Colombia. Directorio Nacional Conservador. *Manifesto Sobre Cuestiones Económicas y Fiscales*. Bogotá: Escuela Tipográfica Salesiana, 1934.

_____. Directorio Nacional Conservador. *Los Programas Conservadores de 1849 a 1949*. Bogotá: Editorial Tipográfica Voto Nacional, 1952.

_____. Dirección Nacional Liberal. *Quince Meses de Política Liberal: Abril 1848–Julio 1949*. Bogotá, 1949.

_____. Fondo Universitario Nacional. *La Nación ante la Universidad*. Reforma Universitaria. Bogotá: Editorial Antares, 1957.

Comité Central del Partido Comunista de Colombia. *Treinta Años del Partido Comunista de Colombia*. Bogotá: Ediciones Paz y Socialismo, 1960.

Córdoba, José María. *Jorge Eliécer Gaitán, Tribuno Popular de Colombia*. Bogotá: Litografías "Cor-Val," 1952.

Cortés Vargas, Carlos. *Los Sucesos de las Bananeras*. Bogotá: Imprenta "La Luz," 1929.

Cuéllar Vargas, Enrique. *13 Años de Violencia*. Bogotá: Editorial SIPA, 1960.

Currie, Lauchlin. *Ensayos sobre Planeación*. Bogotá: Ediciones Tercer Mundo, 1963.

Díaz, Antolín. *A la Sombra de Fouché: Pequeño Proceso de las Izquierdas en Colombia*. Bogotá: Editorial ABC, 1937.

_____. *Los Verdugos del Caudillo y de su Pueblo*. Bogotá: Editorial ABC, 1948.

Dix, Robert H. *Colombia: The Political Dimensions of Change*. New Haven: Yale University Press, 1967.

Dubois, Jules. *Freedom is My Beat*. New York: Bobbs-Merrill, 1959.

Duff, Ernest A. *Agrarian Reform in Colombia*. New York: Praeger, 1968.

Durán, Augusto. *Voceros del Pueblo en el Parlamento*. Bogotá: Ediciones Sociales, 1943.

Estrada Monsalve, Joaquín. *El 9 de Abril en Palacio*. Bogotá: Editorial ABC, 1948.

Fals Borda, Orlando. *El Hombre y la Tierra en Boyacá*. Bogotá: Editorial Antares, 1957.

_____. *Peasant Society in the Colombian Andes: A Sociological Study of Saucio*. Gainesville: University of Florida Press, 1955.

_____. *Subversion and Social Change in Colombia*. New York: Columbia University Press, 1969.

Fandiño Silva, Francisco. *La Penetración Soviética en América Latina y el 9 de Abril*. Bogotá: Editorial ABC, 1949.

Farley, Rawle. *The Economics of Latin America*. New York: Harper and Row, 1972.

Fernández de Soto, Mario. *Una Revolución en Colombia: Jorge Eliécer Gaitán y Mariano Ospina Pérez*. Madrid: Ediciones Cultura Hispania, 1951.

Figueredo Salcedo, Alberto, ed. *Colección Jorge Eliécer Gaitán: Documentos para una Biograffia*. Vol 1. Bogotá: Imprenta Municipal, 1949.

Fluharty, Vernon Lee. *Dance of the Millions*. Pittsburgh: University of Pittsburgh Press, 1957.

Forero Morales, Néstor. *Laureano Gómez: Un Hombre, un Partido, una Nación* Bogotá: Ediciones "Nuevo Mundo," 1950.

Friede, Juan. *El Indio en Lucha por la Tierra*. Bogotá: Ediciones Espiral Colombia, 1944.

Gaitán, Jorge Eliécer. *Las Ideas Socialistas en Colombia*. Bogotá: Editorial América Libre, 1963.

_____. *Los Mejores Discursos de Jorge Eliécer Gaitán, 1919–1948* Bogotá: Editorial Jorvi, 1958.

Gaitán, Miguel Angel. *El Porqué de un Asesinato y sus Antecedentes*. Bogotá: Editorial Minerva, 1949.

Gaitán de Valencia, Gloria. "Causas de la Presencia de los Movimientos Agrarios en el Occidente de Cundinamarca y el Oriente del Tolima y Su Incidencia en el Cambio de la Tenencia de la Tierra." Doctorado en Economía thesis, Universidad de los Andes, Facultad de Economia, Bogotá, 1970. (The author kindly allowed me to use her research materials, including interviews with *campesinos* in the region mentioned who were active in agrarian movements, including UNIR, in the early 1930s.)

Galbraith, W. O. *Colombia: A General Survey*. London: Royal Institute of International Affairs, 1953.

Galvis Gómez, Carlos. *Por Qué Cayó López*. Bogotá: Editorial ABC, 1946.

García, Antonio. *Gaitán y el Problema de la Revolución Colombiana* Bogotá:M.S.C., 1955.

García Cadena, Alfredo. *Unas Ideas Elementales sobre Problemas Colombianos*. Bogotá: Editorial Voluntad, 1943.

Gibson, William Marion. *The Constitutions of Colombia*. Durham, N.C.: Duke University Press, 1948.

Gómez, Eugenio J. *Problemas Colombianos*. 4 vols. Bogotá: "Mundo al Día," 1941–42, 1947.

Gómez, Laureano. *Comentarios a un Régimen*. Bogotá: Editorial Minerva, 1934.

_____. *Interrogantes sobre el Progreso de Colombia*. Bogotá: Editorial Minerva, 1928.

Guillén Martínez, Fernando. *Raíz y Futuro de la Revolución Colombiana*. Bogotá: Ediciones Tercer Mundo, 1963.

Gutiérrez, José. *La No-Violencia en la Transformación Colombiana*. Bogotá: Ediciones Tercer Mundo, 1964.

_____. *De la Pseudo-Aristocracia a la Autenticidad*. Bogotá: Ediciones Tercer Mundo, 1961.

_____. *La Rebeldía Colombiana*. Bogotá: Ediciones Tercer Mundo, 1962.

Guzmán, Germán; Fals Borda, Orlando; and Umaña Luna, Eduardo. *La Violencia en Colombia*. 2 vols. Bogotá: Ediciones Tercer Mundo, 1963–64.

Havens, A. Eugene, and Flinn, William L. *Internal Colonialism and Structural Change in Colombia*. New York: Praeger, 1970.

Havens, A. Eugene, and Romieux, Michel. *Barrancabermeja: Conflictos Sociales en Torno a un Centro Petrolero*. Bogotá: Facultad de Socilogía y Tercer Mundo, 1966.

Henao, Jesús María, and Arrubla, Gerardo. *History of Colombia*. Translated and edited by J. Fred Rippy. Chapel Hill: University of North Carolina Press, 1938.

Hirschman, Albert O. *Journeys Toward Progress*. New York: Twentieth Century Fund, 1963.

Holt, Pat M. *Colombia Today—And Tomorrow*. New York: Praeger, 1964.

Hunter, John M. *Emerging Colombia*. Washington, D.C.: Public Affairs Press, 1962.

Jaramillo Uribe, Jaime. *El Pensamiento Colombiano en el Siglo XIX*. Bogotá: Editorial Temis, 1964.

Jordán Jiménez, Ricardo. *Dos Viernes Trágicos*. Bogotá: Editorial Horizontes, 1968.

Lannoy, Juan Luis de, and Pérez, Gustavo. *Estructuras Demográficas y Sociales de Colombia*. Bogotá: Centro de Investigaciones Sociales, 1961.

Laserna, Mario. *Estado Fuerte o Caudillo*. Bogotá: Ediciones Mito, 1961.

Léndez, Emilio. *Por Qué Murió el Capitán?* Bogotá: Tipografico Escorial, 1948.

El Liberalismo en el Gobierno. Bogotá: Editoriales "Prag y Antena," 1947.

Liga de Acción Política. *Manifesto al País: La Izquierda ante el Presente y el Porvenir de Colombia*. Bogotá: Ediciones Políticas "El Común," 1943.

Linares, Heliodoro. *Yo Acuso: Biografía de Gaitán y Fajardo*. 2 vols. Bogotá: Editorial Iqueima, 1959.

Linke, Lilo. *Andean Adventure: A Social and Political Study of Colombia, Ecuador and Bolivia*. London: Hutchinson, 1945.

Lipman, Aaron. *The Colombian Entrepreneur in Bogotá*. Coral Gables: University of Miami Press, 1969.

Lleras Restrepo, Carlos. *De la República a la Dictadura*. Bogotá: Editorial ARGRA, 1955.

Londoño, Julio. *Nación en Crisis*. Bogotá: Ministerio de Educación Nacional, 1955.

Londoño Mejía, Carlos María. *Economía Social Colombiana*. Bogotá: Imprenta Nacional, 1953.

López, Alejandro. *Idearium Liberal*. París: Ediciones La Antorcha, 1931.

López de Mesa, Luis. *Escrutinio Sociológico de la Historia Colombiana*. Academia Colombiana de Historia, vol. 10. 2nd ed. Bogotá: Biblioteca Eduardo Santos, 1956.

López Giraldo, F. *El Apóstol Desnudo: o Dos Años al Lado de un Mito*. Manizales: Editorial Arturo Zapata, 1936.

López Michelsen, Alfonso. *Cuestiones Colombianas: Ensayos*. México, D. F.: Impresiones Modernas, 1955.

López Pumarejo, Alfonso. *La Re-Integración Liberal*. Bogotá: Editorial Cromos, 1941.

Lozano y Lozano, Carlos. *Ideario del Liberalismo Actual: Conferencia Pronunciada por el Doctor Carlos Lozano y Lozano el 14 de Febrero de 1939*. Bogotá: Imprenta Nacional, 1939.

MacDonald, Austin F. *Latin American Politics and Government*. New York: Thomas Crowell, 1949.

McGreevey, William Paul. *An Economic History of Colombia, 1845-1930*. Cambridge: Cambridge University Press, 1971.

Maffitt, Peter C. "Colombia, The Revolution on March 1934-1938." MS. New Haven: Scholars of the House Program, Yale University, 1963.

Manrique, Ramón. *Bajo el Signo de la Hoz*. Bogotá: Editorial ABC, 1937.

Martz, John D. *Colombia: A Contemporary Political Survey*. Chapel Hill: University of North Carolina Press, 1962.

Mendoza Neira, Plinio., ed. *El Liberalismo en el Gobierno, 1930-1946*. 3 vols. Bogotá: Editorial Antena, 1946.

Misión "Economía y Humanismo" (Louis J. Lebret, O.P., Director). *Estudio sobre las Condiciones del Desarrollo de Colombia*. Bogotá: Aedita, 1958.

Molina, Felipe Antonio. *Laureano Gómez: Historia de una Rebeldía*. Bogotá: Librería Voluntad, 1940.

Molina, Geraldo. *Proceso y Destino de la Libertad*. Bogotá: Biblioteca de la Universidad Libre, 1955.

Monsalve, Miguel. *Liberalismo*. Cali: Editorial Pacífico, 1953.

Montaña Cuéllar, Diego. *Colombia: País Formal y País Real*. Bogotá: Ediciones Suramérica, 1963.

———. *Sociología Americana*. Bogotá: Universidad Nacional, Sección de Extensión Cultural, 1950.

Morales Benítez, Otto. *Muchedumbres y Banderas*. Bogotá: Ediciones Tercer Mundo, 1962.

———. *El Pensamiento Social de Uribe Uribe*. Bogotá: Tercer Mundo, 1964.

———. *Revolución y Caudillos*. Medellín: Editorial Horizonte, 1957.

Moreno, Francisco José, and Mitrani, Barbara, eds. *Conflict and Violence in Latin American Politics*. New York: Thomas Y. Crowell, 1971.

Navia Varón, Hernando. *Caudillo y Gobernante*. Cali: Imprenta Departamental, 1964.

Nieto Arteta, Luis Eduardo. *Economía y Cultura en la Historia de Colombia*. 2nd ed. Bogotá: Ediciones Tercer Mundo, 1962.

Nieto Rojas, José María. *La Batalla contra el Comunismo en Colombia*. Bogotá: Empresa Nacional de Publicaciones, 1956.

Niño H., Alberto. *Antecedentes y Secretos del 9 de Abril*. Bogotá: Editorial Pax, 1949.

Orrego Duque, Gonzalo. *El 9 de Abril Fuera del Palacio*. Bogotá: Editorial Patria, 1949.

Osorio Lizarazo, J. A. *Gaitán: Vida, Muerte y Permanente Presencia*. Buenos Aires: Ediciones López Negri, 1952.

──. *Ideas de Izquierda: Liberalismo, Partido Revolucionario*. Bogotá, n.d.

Ospina Londoño, Jorge. *Los Partidos Políticos en Colombia*. Medellín: Imprenta Universidad, 1938.

Ospina Vásquez, Luís. *Industria y Protección en Colombia, 1810-1930*. Medellín: Editorial Santafé, 1955.

Parsons, James J. *Antioqueño Colonization in Western Colombia*. Berkeley: University of California Press, 1949.

Patiño B., Abelardo. "The Political Ideas of the Liberal and Conservative Parties in Colombia During the 1946-1953 Crisis." Ph.D. dissertation, American University, Washington, D.C., 1954.

Payne, James L. *Patterns of Conflict in Colombia*. New Haven: Yale University Press, 1968.

Peña, Luís David. *Gaitán Intimo*. Bogotá: Editorial Iqueima, 1949.

Pérez, Luis Carlos. *El Pensamiento Filosofico de Jorge Eliécer Gaitán*. Bogotá: Editorial Los Andes, 1954.

Pérez, Luís David. *Los Delitos Políticos: Interpretación Jurídica del 9 de Abril*. Bogotá: Distribudora Americana de Publicaciones, 1948.

Pérez Ramírez, Gustavo. *El Campesinado Colombiano*. 2nd ed. Bogotá: Centro de Investigaciones Sociales, 1962.

Petras, James, and Zeitlin, Maurice. *Latin America: Reform or Revolution?* New York: Fawcett Publications, 1968.

Petras, James. *Politics and Social Structure in Latin America*. New York: Monthly Review Press, 1970.

Plaza, Humberto. *La Noche Roja de Bogotá: Páginas de un Diario*. Buenos Aires: Imprenta López, 1949.

Puentes, Milton. *Gaitán*. Bogotá: Editorial ABC, 1947.

──. *Grandes Hombres de Colombia*. Bogotá: Tipografía Hispana, 1962.

──. *Historia del Partido Liberal Colombiana*. 1942, 2nd ed. Bogotá: Editorial Prag, 1961.

Ramírez Moreno, Augusto. *La Crisis del Partido Conservador en Colombia*. Bogotá: Tipografía Granada, 1937.

──. *Una Política Triumfante*. Bogotá: Libería Voluntad, 1941.

Reichel-Dolmatoff, Gerardo, and Reichel-Dolmatoff, Alicia. *The People of Aritama*. Chicago: University of Chicago Press, 1961.

Restrepo Jaramillo, Gonzalo. *El Pensamiento Conservador: Ensayos Políticos*. Medellín: Tipografía Bedout, 1936.

Rippy, J. Fred. *The Capitalists and Colombia*. New York: Vanguard Press, 1931.

Robinson, J. C. "Jorge Eliécer Gaitán and His Socio-Political Movement." Ph.D. dissertation, Indiana University, 1971.

Rodríguez Garavito, Agustin. *Gabriel Turbay, Un Solitario de la Grandeza*. 2nd. ed. Bogotá: Editorial Prócer, 1966.

Rogers, Everett M. *Modernization Among Peasants: The Impact of Communication*. New York: Holt, Rinehart and Winston, 1969.

Romero Aguirre, Alfonso. *Ayer, Hoy y Mañana del Liberalismo Colombiano*. 3rd ed. Bogotá: Editorial Iqueima, 1949.

Romoli, Kathleen. *Colombia: Gateway to South America*. New York: Doubleday, 1941.

Rueda Vargas, Tomás. *El Ejército Nacional*. Bogotá: Editorial Antena, 1944.

Salamanca, Guillermo. *Los Partidos en Colombia*. Bogotá: Editorial "El Voto Nacional," 1961.

──. *La République Liberal*. 2 vols. Bogotá: Editorial Centro, 1937.

Santa, Eduardo. *Sociología Política de Colombia*. Bogotá: Tercer Mundo, 1964.

Santos, Eduardo. *Análisis de la Política Colombiana que Hace el Director del Partido Liberal Dr. Eduardo Santos*. Cartagena: Imprenta Departamental, 1944.

———. *Una Política Liberal para Colombia*. Bogotá: Editorial Minerva, 1937.

Santos, Enrique. *Danza de las Horas*. Bogotá: Compañía Editorial Club de Lectores, 1969.

Santos Forero, Julio Enrique. *Yo Sí Ví Huir al Verdadero Asesino de Jorge Eliécer Gaitán*. Bogotá: Graficas Atenas, 1959.

Smith, T. Lynn. *Colombia: Social Structure and the Process of Development*. Gainesville: University of Florida Press, 1967.

Stavenhagen, Rodolfo, ed. *Agrarian Problems and Peasant Movements in Latin America*. Garden City, N.Y.: Anchor Books, 1970.

Tierra: 10 Ensayos sobre la Reforma Agraria en Colombia. Bogotá: Tercer Mundo, 1961.

Torres, Mauricio. *La Naturaleza de la Revolución Colombiana*. Bogotá: Editorial Iqueima, 1959.

Torres Restrepo, Camilo. *La Proletarización de Bogotá*. Monografías Sociológicas, no. 9. Bogotá: Universidad Nacional, Facultad de Sociología, 1961.

Turbay Ayala, Gabriel. *Las Ideas Políticas de Gabriel Turbay*. Bogotá: Editorial Minerva, 1945.

Urrutia, Miguel. *The Development of the Colombian Labor Movement*. New Haven: Yale University Press, 1969.

Valencia, Luís Emiro, ed. *Gaitán: Antología de su Pensamiento Social y Economico*. Bogotá: Ediciones Suramerica, 1968.

Vall-Spinoza, Allen Steele. "Colombia's Semana Trágica: The Banana Strike of 1928." MA thesis, University of Florida, Gainesville, Fla., 1969.

Vallejo, Alejandro. *Bogotá, 8 de Junio*. Bogotá: Publicaciones de la Revista "Universidad," 1929.

———. *Hombres de Colombia*. Caracas: Avila Gráfica, 1950.

———. *La Palabra Encadenada: Antes del 9 de Abril y Después*. Bogotá: Editorial Minerva, 1949.

———. *Políticos en la Intimidad*. Bogotá: Editorial "Antena," 1936.

Vélez, Jorge. *Veinticinco Años de Régimen Conservador*. Bogotá: Editorial Centro, 1935.

Veliz, Claudio, ed. *Obstacles to Change in Latin America*. New York: Oxford University Press, 1970.

Vidales, Luís. *La Insurrección Desplomada*. Bogotá: Editorial Iqueima, 1948.

Villaveces, Jorge. *La Derrota: 25 Años de Historia*. Bogotá: Editorial Jorvi, 1963.

Villegas, Silvio. *No Hay Enemigos a la Derecha*. Manizales: Editorial Arturo Zapata, 1937.

Weiss, Anita. *Tendencias de la Participación Electoral en Colombia, 1935-1966*. Bogotá: Universidad Nacional, Departamento de Sociología, 1968.

Whitaker, Arthur P. *The United States and South America: The Northern Republics*. Cambridge, Mass.: Harvard University Press, 1948.

Whiteford, Andrew H. *Two Cities of Latin America*. Beloit, Wis.: Beloit College, 1960.

Wiesner Durán, Eduardo. *Control Personal de la Economía Colombiana*. Monografía No. 6. Bogotá: Universidad de los Andes, Centro de Estudios sobre Desarrollo, 1960.

Zuleta Angel, Eduardo. *El Presidente López*. Medellín: Ediciones Albá, 1966.

Articles in Journals and Collections

Adams, Dale W. "Landownership Patterns in Colombia." *Inter-American Economic Affairs*, Winter 1964, pp. 77-86.

Aguirre de Jaramillo, Fabiola. "Por Qué en Colombia Son Dos los Partidos Políticos." *Cuadernos Americanos* (Mexico) 44 (Mar.-Apr. 1949), 24-30.

Arciniegas, Germán. "La Dictadura en Colombia." *Cuadernos Americanos* (Mexico), 49 (Jan.-Feb. 1950), 7-33.

Di Tella, Torcuato. "Populism and Reform in Latin America." In *Obstacles to Change in Latin America*, edited by Claudio Veliz, pp. 47-74. Oxford: Oxford University Press, 1969.

Dozer, Donald Marquand. "Roots of Revolution in Latin America." *Foreign Affairs* 27 (Jan. 1949), 274-88.

Duque Gómez, Luis. "Los Problemas del Minifundio en Colombia." *Economía Colombiana* 3 (Jan. 1955), 577-85.

Espinosa S., Justiniano. "Veinticinco Años de Sindicalismo." *Revista Javeriana* 51 (Apr. 1959), 112-19.

Fals Borda, Orlando. "Violence and the Break-Up of Tradition in Colombia." In *Obstacles to Change in Latin America*, edited by Claudio Veliz, pp. 188-205. Oxford: Oxford University Press, 1969.

Fitzgibbon, Russel H. "Colombian Gadfly." *The Inter-American* 4 (Feb. 1945), 15, 18, 35.

Gilhodès, Pierre. "Agrarian Struggles in Colombia." In *Agrarian Problems and Peasant Movements in Latin America*, edited by Rodolfo Stavenhagen, pp. 407-51. New York: Anchor Books, 1970.

Gilmore, Robert Louis. "Nueva Granada's Socialist Mirage," *Hispanic American Historical Review* 36 (May 1956), 190-210.

Goff, Fred. "Colombia: The Pre-Revolutionary Stage." Mimeographed. Stanford: Stanford University, Institute of Hispanic American and Luso-Brazilian Studies, 1963.

González, Miguel Angel, S.J. "La Violencia en Colombia: Análisis de un Libro." Bogotá: Centro de Estudios Colombianos, 1962.

Helguera, J. León. "The Changing Role of the Military in Colombia." *Journal of Inter-American Studies*, July 1961, pp. 351-57.

Holguín Holguín, Carlos. "Los Partidos Políticos." *Universidad Nacional de Colombia*, 2nd epoch, no. 17, 1953.

Holmes Trujillo, Carlos. "Gaitán y las Ideas Políticas en Colombia." *Revista Jurídica* 13-14 (October 1948), 513-19.

Humphrey, Norman David. "Race, Caste and Class in Colombia." *Phylon* 13 (June 1952, 161-66.

Kling, Merle. "Toward a Theory of Power and Political Instability in Latin America." In *Latin America: Reform or Revolution?*, edited by James Petras and Maurice Zeitlin, pp. 76-93. Greenwich, Conn.: Fawcett, 1968.

"Land Reform and Social Change in Colombia." Discussion Paper No. 4. Madison: University of Wisconsin, Land Tenure Center, November 1963.

Lipman, Aaron, and Havens, A. Eugene. "The Colombian Violencia: An Ex Post Facto Experiment." Mimeographed. Madison: University of Wisconsin, Land Tenure Center, 1965.

López de Mesa, Luis. "Notas sobre la Clase Media en Colombia." *Ciencias Sociales* 3 (December 1952), 122-28.

López Michelsen, Alfonso. "Economía y Sociedad en Colombia." In *La Nación ante la Universidad*. Curso Académico, Organizado por la Universidad Nacional de Colombia. Bogotá: Fondo Universitario Nacional, 1957.

_____. "Influencia del Capital Extranjero en la Economía Colombiana." *Revista Bolívar* 51 (March-April-May 1959), 491-95.

Madrid Malo, Néstor. "Génesis e Ineficacia de la Reforma sobre Tierras." *Universidad Nacional de Colombia* 1 (Oct. 1944), 399-420.

Pollock, John C. "Violence, Politics and Elite Performance: The Political Sociology of *La Violencia* in Colombia." *Studies in Comparative International Development* 10 (Summer 1975), 22–50.

Ramsey, Russell W. "Critical Bibliography on *La Violencia* in Colombia." *Latin American Research Review 8* (Spring 1973), 3–44.

Sarria, Eustorgio. "La Obra Científica de Gaitán." *Revista Jurídica* 13–14 (October 1948), 410–13.

Shaw, Carey, Jr. "Church and State in Colombia, as Observed by American Diplomats, 1834–1906." *Hispanic American Historical Review* 31 (Nov. 1941), 577–613.

Torres Restrepo, Camilo. "Social Change and Rural Violence in Colombia." *Studies in Comparative International Development* 4 (1969), 263–283.

Triffin, Robert. "La Moneda y las Instituciones Bancarias en Colombia." *Revista del Banco de la República* (1944).

Weinert, Richard S. "Violence in Pre-Modern Societies: Rural Colombia." In *Conflict and Violence in Latin American Politics,* edited by Francisco José Moreno and Barbara Mitrani, pp. 310–24. New York: Thomas Y. Crowell, 1971.

Williamson, Robert C. "Toward a Theory of Political Violence: The Case of Rural Colombia," *Western Political Quarterly* 18 (March 1965), 35–44.

Yepes, Horacio. "El Movimiento Sindical Colombiana." *Universidad de Antioquia* 18 (February-May 1959), 71–81.

Young, Allen. "Revolutionary Parties in Contemporary Colombia." Mimeographed. Stanford: Stanford University, Institute of Hispanic American and Luso-Brazilian Studies, 1963.

Newspapers

Batalla, Bogotá.
La Casa Liberal, Bucaramanga.
El Colombiano, Medellín.
El Crisol, Cali.
El Deber, Montería.
Diario Nacional, Bogotá.
El Espectador, Bogotá.
Gaitán, Bogotá.
La Huila, Huila.
El Ideal, Tumaco.
Jornada, Bogotá.
El Liberal, Bogotá.
El Liberal, Manizales.
La Nación, Barranquilla.
New York Times, New York.
El Nuevo Tiempo, Bogotá.
El País, Cali.
La Razón, Bogotá.
El Relator, Cali.
El Siglo, Bogotá.
El Tiempo, Bogotá.
Unirismo, Bogotá.
La Voz del Obrero, Buga.

Periodicals

La Nueva Prensa, Bogotá.
Sábado, Bogotá.
Semana, Bogotá.
Suplemento Literario Illustrado, Bogotá.
Universidad, Bogotá.

Interviews

Barriga Casalini, Guillermo. Former Colombian naval officer. Interview, Easton Pa., May 11, 1971.

Borda Roldán, Leopoldo. Childhood friend of Gaitán; former Colombian ambassador to India, Japan, and Sweden. Interview, Bogotá, October 4, 1969.

Gaitán, Amparo Jaramillo v. de. Widow of Gaitán. Interview, Bogotá, October 9, 1969, and subsequent conversations.

Garcés Valencia, Alfonso. Conservative politician and former senator from Valle. Interview, Cali, August 15, 1974.

Hernández Rodríguez, Guillermo. Liberal collaborator and adviser of Gaitán; former Colombian ambassador to United Nations, minister of justice, and other political posts. Interview, Bogotá, March 5, 1970, and subsequent conversations.

Miramón, Alberto. Author, intellectual, and former director of the National Library, Bogotá. Interview, Bogotá, June 19, 1969.

Valencia, Luís Emiro, and Valencia, Gloria Gaitán de. Son-in-law and daughter of Gaitán. Interview, Bogotá, October 6, 1969, and subsequent conversations.

Miscellaneous

Scrapbooks, containing newspaper and magazine articles about Gaitán in the possession of Amparo Jaramillo de Gaitán and Gloria Gaitán de Valencia.

Index

ANDI (Asociación Nacional de Industriales), 136
APRA (Alianza Popular Revolucionaria Americana), 77
Arango Vélez, Carlos, 71
Arango Vélez, Dionisio, 50
Araújo, Alfonso, 180
Araújo, Simón, 31, 34
Arciniegas, Germán, 24, 159, 172
Arriaga Andrade, Adán, 144, 145
Arteaga, Francisco, 34–35
Asociación Nacional de Choferes (ANDEC): strike against JEG, 93, 94

Betancourt, Rómulo, 169
Bogotá: JEG as mayor, 89–93; JEG campaigns in, 108, 109, 110, 111; and the *Bogotazo*, 177–80
Bogotazo, 177–80

Camacho Carreño, José, 25
Camacho Gamba, Eduardo, 181
Camacho Matiz, Luis, 90
Cano, Luis, 180
Cárdenas, Lázaro, 187
Cárdenas, Permenio, 142, 150
Castrillón, Alberto, 56
Castro, Fidel, 173, 186, 188, 189
Castro González, Ramón, 73
Catholic church: traditional role of, 22
Chaux, Francisco José, 106, 149, 181
Colegio Araújo, 31, 32
Colegio Martín Restrepo Mejía, 31
Colombia: and JEG's death, 3, 179–82; economic development, 11–16; mobiliza-
tion and social conflict, 16–21; political ferment, 21–28; agrarian unrest, 63, 64
Comando Nacional de Izquierdas, 104
Communist party, 150, 181; and organized labor, 19; and rural unrest, 20; origins in Colombia, 24, 44; and UNIR, 73; attitude toward JEG's movement, 125
Communists. *See* Communist party
Concha y Venegas, J. A., 80
Confederación de Trabajadores de Colombia (CTC), 19, 120, 121, 160, 164
Confederación Nacional de Trabajadores (CNT), 121
Confederación Sindical de Colombia, 93
Conservative party: and War of the Thousand Days, 11; attitude toward organized labor, 18; and Liberal reaction, 19; during 1920s, 19, 20, 23, 25; traditional role of, 21, 22, 23; and United Fruit, 56; reaction to JEG, 58; collapse of, 60, 61; on JEG as mayor, 92, 93; selects Ospina, 126; supports JEG, 157; pact with Liberals, 168
Córdoba, José María, 108, 109, 110, 121, 122, 140, 141, 142
Cortés Vargas, Carlos, 57, 59
Cruz, Pedro Eliseo, 173

Durán, Augusto, 150

Echandía, Darío, 94, 143, 144, 145, 146, 156, 169, 171, 178, 179, 180, 181
Esmeral, José, 107

Falange (Spanish), 25
Fascism, 51–52

Ferri, Enrico, 51
Ferri Prize, 51

Gacharná, Luis Eduardo, 108
Gaitán, Amparo Jaramillo de (wife), 88, 89
Gaitán, Eliécer (father), 29–30; break with
    JEG, 42
Gaitán, Jorge Eliécer, 11, 29–34; as populist,
    4, 6, 12, 17, 28, 34, 41, 52, 59, 70, 84,
    100, 136, 185, 187, 188, 189; program of,
    130–36; assessment of, 183–90
—early activities of: in University Center of
    Cultural Propaganda, 34–36; in 1917 presi-
    dential campaign, 36–39; in politics, 39–40;
    in 1922 presidential campaign, 40–41;
    elected to Cundinamarca Assembly, 41
—as university student: at National University
    School of Law, 42–44; thesis of, 44–50; in
    Rome, 50–52
—1928–1933: elected to House of Representa-
    tives, 57; banana strike debate, 56–60; in-
    vestigates Conservatives, 60; "Tribune of
    the People," 60; introduces social legisla-
    tion, 62–65; article, "Individualism and
    Socialism," 66; Liberal party role, 65–69;
    article, "Manifesto to the Leftists," 68;
    diplomatic mission, 68
—1933–1935: decision to organize UNIR,
    71–72; role of, in UNIR, 74, 81; elected to
    House of Representatives, 82–83
—1935–1944: return to Liberal party, 87–89;
    as mayor of Bogotá, 89–93; elected to
    Municipal Council, 94; in opposition,
    94–95; as minister of education, 95–97; as
    rector of Universidad Libre, 96; as minister
    of labor, 97; elected to Senate, 100
—1944–1946: Movement for the Moral and
    Democratic Restoration, 104–12; the popu-
    lar convention, 112–15; technique of per-
    sonalism, 115–19; 1946 presidential cam-
    paign, 120–29
—1946–1948: postelection strategy, 139–43;
    1947 campaigns, 144–47; elected Jefe
    Unico, 146; consolidating the movement,
    148–57; and Ospina administration, 158–
    66; la violencia, 167; break with Ospina,
    168–70; the silent demonstration and "Ora-
    tion for Peace," 170–71; Inter-American
    Conference, 171–72; assassination, 173
Gaitán, Manuela Ayala de (mother), 30, 33
Gaitanismo, 179, 181, 182. See also Gaitán,
    Jorge Eliécer, 1944–1946 and 1946–1948
Gaitanista National Liberal Directorate, 108
Galvis, Enrique, 93
Garcés, Enrique, 90

García, Antonio, 108, 134, 179, 181
García Peña, Roberto, 24, 44
Generation of the Centenario, 24, 94
Gómez, Laureano, 28, 37, 69, 98, 99, 111,
    126, 168, 171, 172, 180
González, Ernesto, 35
González Londoño, César, 74

Haya de la Torre, Victor Raúl, 187
Hernández Rodríguez, Guillermo, 35, 74,
    108, 134
Herrera, Benjamín: "socialization" of
    Liberalism, 24; and JEG, 37, 39, 40; over-
    tures to socialists, 44

Ideas Socialistas en Colombia, 43–50
Inter-American Conference, Ninth, 171, 177

JEGA, 107, 113, 149

Lemus Guzmán, J., 145
Leopards, 25
Liberal party: and War of the Thousand Days,
    11; in 1920s, 18, 19, 20, 25, 38–40; and
    violence, 19, 139; traditional role of, 21,
    22, 23; "socialization" of, 23, 24; and
    "Revolution on the March," 26–28; break
    with JEG, 68, 69, 87, 94, 95; and UNIR,
    80, 81, 82; López-Santos split, 95; in disar-
    ray, 104, 122; reaction to JEG's movement,
    123–25; internal condition, 142, 143; anti-
    JEG campaigns, 144, 145, 146, 147; and
    Ospina, 158, 168, 170, 179, 180
Lleras Camargo, Alberto, 99, 121, 143
Lleras Camargo, Felipe, 38
Lleras Restrepo, Carlos, 80, 89, 99, 142, 145,
    180
López de Mesa, Luís, 144, 145
López Giraldo, Fermín, 74, 82
López Pumarejo, Alfonso, 127, 143, 158,
    170; and the "Revolution on the March,"
    19; 1934–1938 administration of, 20,
    26–28, 84, 85, 89, 97, 98; 1922 campaign
    of, 40; and UNIR, 83; and JEG, 86, 87, 94,
    95, 99; fires JEG as mayor, 93; 1942–1945
    administration of, 98, 99, 103
Lozano y Lozano, Carlos, 95, 143, 145, 170
Lozano y Lozano, Juan, 123, 145, 146, 183

Manifesto of Unirismo, 75–78
Manrique, Julio, 35
Mantilla Gómez, Trino, 74
Mar, José, 24, 44
Maurras, Charles, 25
Mejía, Diego, 44

Mejía, Luis Emiro, 72
Mendoza Neira, Plinio, 67, 71, 145, 173, 180
Mendoza Pérez, Diego, 34
Molina, Gerardo, 108, 179
Montalvo, José Antonio, 166, 180
Movement for the Moral and Democratic Restoration, 104-15. *See also* Gaitán, Jorge Eliécer, 1944-1946
Mussolini, Benito, 51, 52

National Union, Government of. *See* Ospina Pérez, Mariano
National University, 42, 96
Nieto Caballero, L. E., 37
Nuevos, Los (the "New Ones"), 24, 25

Ocampo, Germán, 180
Olaya Herrera, Enrique, 89, 94; 1930-1934 administration of, 18, 25, 61, 68, 69; assures JEG's reelection, 65
Ordóñez, Antonio, 134
Osorio Lizarazo, J. A., 139, 186
Ospina Londoño, Jorge, 108, 123
Ospina Pérez, Mariano, 89; 1946-1950 administration of (Government of National Union), 126, 139, 158, 159, 160, 161, 162, 165, 166, 169, 171, 178, 179, 180, 181

Padilla, Jorge, 106, 173
Pareja, Carlos, 179
París Gaitán, Roberto, 74
Partido Nacional Revolucionario de México, 69
Partido Popular Socialista Colombiano, 181-82
Partido Socialista Revolucionario, 56, 64
Peña, Luis David, 111
Pérez, Luis Carlos, 108
Perón, Juan, 7, 187
Plan Gaitán, 130-36
Plataforma del Colón, 130-36
Prieto, Moisés, 24

Quintero Calderón, Guillermo, 43

Ramírez Moreno, Augusto, 25
Rengifo, Ignacio, 59, 60
Revolución en Marcha, 19, 26-28
Reyes, Rafael, 61
Roble, Luis Rafael, 134
Rojas Pinilla, Gustavo, 179, 182
Ruiz Camacho, Mario, 142
Russian Revolution, 24, 43

Salazar Ferro, J. R., 90, 143
Samper, Darío, 67, 181

Santos, Eduardo, 89, 94, 123, 126, 127, 129, 143, 144, 145; 1938-1942 administration of, 19, 28, 98; 1917 campaign of, 37; 1922 campaign of, 40; JEG opposes, 94; appoints JEG minister of education, 95
Santos, Enrique ("Calibán"), 129, 146, 155
Silva, Victor Julio, 164
Sindicato Central Nacional de Choferes, 93
Socialist Ideas in Colombia, 43-50
Socialist party, 18, 23, 24
Soto del Corral, Jorge, 145
Suárez, Marcó Fidel, 33
Supreme Court: JEG nominated to, 95

Tejada, Luis, 24, 44
Turbay, Gabriel, 120, 143; as *Nuevo*, 24; as Marxist, 44; as presidential candidate, 123, 124, 126, 127, 129
Tropical Oil Company, 18

Unión Nacional Izquierdista Revolucionaria (UNIR): membership and organization of, 72-74; program of, 75-78; political activity of, 78-81; dissolution of, 81-83; impact of, 83-85
Union of Colombian Workers (UTC), 164
United Fruit Company, 18, 19, 56-60, 87
United States of America: Latin American dependence upon, 4, 5; investment in Colombia, 13; sends tear gas, 165; Inter-American Conference, 172
Universidad, 24, 57
Universidad Libre, 96
University Center of Cultural Propaganda, 34-36
Urdaneta Arbeláez, Roberto, 168, 171
Uribe Márquez, Jorge, 139, 150, 180, 181
Uribe Prada, Carlos, 90
Uribe Uribe, Rafael, 23, 43, 77, 106

Valencia, Guillermo: JEG campaigns for, 37, 38, 39
Vallejo, Alejandro, 24
Vanegas, Carlos, 162
Vargas, Getulio, 7, 187
Vieira, Gilberto, 92
Villaveces, Jorge, 104
Villegas, Silvio, 25, 97
Violencia, La, 160, 161, 162, 167, 168, 169, 170, 181, 189

War of the Thousand Days, 11, 21, 22
Week of the Reconquest, 149, 153

Zalamea Borda, Jorge, 179

PITT LATIN AMERICAN SERIES
Cole Blasier, Editor

Argentina in the Twentieth Century
David Rock, Editor

Army Politics in Cuba, 1898–1958
Louis A. Pérez, Jr.

Authoritarianism and Corporatism in Latin America
James M. Malloy, Editor

Barrios in Arms: Revolution in Santo Domingo
José A. Moreno

Beyond the Revolution: Bolivia Since 1952
James M. Malloy and Richard S. Thorn, Editors

Bolivia: The Uncompleted Revolution
James M. Malloy

Constructive Change in Latin America
Cole Blasier, Editor

Cuba, Castro, and the United States
Philip W. Bonsal

Cuban Sugar Policy from 1963 to 1970
Heinrich Brunner

Essays on Mexican Kinship
Hugo G. Nutini, Pedro Carrasco, and James M. Taggart, Editors

Female and Male in Latin America: Essays
Ann Pescatello, Editor

Gaitán of Colombia: A Political Biography
Richard E. Sharpless

The Hovering Giant: U.S. Responses to Revolutionary Change in Latin America
Cole Blasier

My Missions for Revolutionary Bolivia, 1944–1962
Víctor Andrade

The Overthrow of Allende and the Politics of Chile, 1964–1976
Paul E. Sigmund

Panajachel: A Guatemalan Town in Thirty-Year Perspective
Robert E. Hinshaw

Puerto Rico and the United States, 1917–1933
Truman R. Clark

Revolutionary Change in Cuba
Carmelo Mesa-Lago, Editor

Selected Latin American One-Act Plays
Francesca Colecchia and Julio Matas, Editors and Translators

Society and Education in Brazil
Robert J. Havighurst and J. Roberto Moreira

The United States and Cuba: Hegemony and Dependent Development, 1880-1934
Jules Robert Benjamin